JERUSALEM AND ROME

JERUSALEM AND ROME

The Writings of Josephus

Selected and introduced by
NAHUM N. GLATZER

MERIDIAN BOOKS, INC.   NEW YORK

JOSEPHUS

Flavius Josephus, one of the great historians of classical antiquity, was born in A.D. 37 or 38 in Jerusalem and died in Rome between the years 110 and 120. In his JEWISH WAR he gave an account of the war of 66 to 73 between Judaea and Rome; in his ANTIQUITIES OF THE JEWS he told the history of his people from its biblical beginnings to the outbreak of the rebellion against Rome. His minor works are his LIFE and a treatise AGAINST APION.

NAHUM N. GLATZER

Mr. Glatzer is Professor of Jewish History and Chairman of the Department of Near Eastern and Judaic Studies at Brandeis University. Among his books are PHILOSOPHY OF HISTORY OF THE TANNAITES, HISTORY OF THE TALMUDIC PERIOD, HILLEL THE ELDER, FRANZ ROSENZWEIG: LIFE AND THOUGHT.

AN ORIGINAL MERIDIAN BOOK
Published by Meridian Books, Inc. November 1960
First printing October 1960

TO DANIEL AND JUDITH
with love

CONTENTS

PREFACE

This volume is an attempt to tell in the words of Josephus the story of Judaea from 134 B.C. to A.D. 73, i.e., from the rule of the Hasmonaean House to the fall of Jerusalem and the last fortresses, a narrative that is here preceded by a chapter using Josephus' words dealing with the Jewish "sects" of the period and especially with the Essene brotherhood. The book, therefore, is not a selection of individual passages from the entire work of Josephus. Rather, it is a consecutive account compiled from the accounts in the *Jewish War* and in the *Antiquities* and co-ordinated in a manner designed to present a most decisive period in Jewish history.

The sources are clearly indicated ("War" and "Antt.," respectively) to allow the reader ready identification of the citation in the original. Certain passages were omitted "for the sake of the connection of matters and that my history may not be incoherent," in the words of our historian (*War* IV, 9:2). Such passages, or chapters, are, in most cases, briefly summarized in italicized paragraphs. These paragraphs also give essential information on historical background and literary parallels, and references to relevant talmudic and midrashic sources. Notes on dates and on personal and place names appear bracketed in the text. Brief sketches of Josephus' *Life* and his treatise *Against Apion* are given in the Introduction.

The present English translation constitutes a newly revised and, at times, a free version of Robert Traill's translation of the *Jewish War* and of Whiston-Shilleto's translation of the *Antiquities*. The reader should be informed of one decisive deviation from the Josephan text: the terms "robbers," "brigands," etc., as applied to the Zealots, are rendered through most of the book as "rebels," or "revolutionaries." The ancient historian's personal animosity should be well realized; it should, however, not be made to interfere with the impression of the drama he, at times unwillingly, unfolds before our eyes.

The volume is not intended for the specialist, who will of course turn to the original Greek text or to a complete translation, but for the intelligent reader and the college student interested in early post-biblical Judaism, in the origins of Christianity, in the Qumran or Dead Sea Sect, in late Roman antiquity, in the human drama of the Judaeo-Roman war, and in the drama of Josephus, a man torn between two worlds, Jerusalem and Rome.

The editor wishes to express his gratitude to Professors Paul Alexander and Arnold Band for their help in interpreting difficult passages in the Greek text; to Miss Sonia Volochova for her keen sense of style, which aided in the preparation of the English rendition; to Mrs. Ruth Alexander for her able technical assistance; and finally to my friends, Alfred and Hanna Fromm, for their gracious hospitality.

Nahum N. Glatzer

Brandeis University

Waltham, Massachusetts

INTRODUCTION

THE EMERGENCE OF ROME

Rome and Jerusalem: what strange antagonists on the plane of world history, of what unequal strength and disparate motivation! Yet, the factual end of the armed conflict between the two—the fall of Jerusalem—did not terminate vanquished Judaea's aspirations, or its will to live. Neither did Rome emerge victorious in the usual sense of the term. The fall of Jerusalem provided a mighty impetus to nascent Christianity—a Jewish sect in the age of the Romans—adding strength to its progress toward the transformation of the world, the Roman world, in the name of "the son of man" who was believed to have come to fulfill the Messianic hopes of biblical prophecy. Ultimately, *victi victoribus leges dederunt*, the vanquished have imposed their laws upon the victors.

The ascent of Rome to world supremacy was not the result of a preconceived plan of conquest and expansion, nor was it the consequence of any inherited belief in Rome's destiny to establish a universal dominion. Originally, certain concrete political situations presented themselves and Rome acted when it saw its position periled; Rome intervened in the political fate of others when intervention was appealed for. However, the lust for brutal aggression and exercise of destructive power soon took hold of the Roman mind, "a matter not without offense to the gods," as Cicero said.

At the battle at Zama in 202 B.C. Rome defeated

Semitic Carthage and its general, Hannibal; Carthage surrendered its Spanish possessions and the Mediterranean islands under its control. From the western Mediterranean Rome's attention was drawn east, ostensibly with the aim of safeguarding the freedom of the Greeks. In the beginning of the second pre-Christian century, Rome defeated Antiochus III of Syria, who had interfered in the affairs of Greece and disturbed Roman interests in Asia Minor; the Roman victory eliminated the Seleucids, Hellenist rulers of the Syrian realm, from the ranks of major powers. In the mid-second century, Egypt recognized the suzerainty of Rome, Carthage ceased to exist, Macedonia became a Roman province, and Corinth, central city of the Achaean league of Greek city-states, was destroyed. About the same time, the last king of Pergamum made Rome heir to his possession of Asia Minor. Spain, which attempted to resist Roman pressure, was brought under Roman rule. Rome's position in Gaul was later, in the mid-first century B.C., expanded by Julius Caesar to include what is now France and Belgium; the conquest of Britain was to follow. In 31 B.C. Octavian Augustus made Egypt a Roman province and completed Rome's dominion in the Mediterranean world. Only the Parthians in the East remained to make Rome conscious of the limitation of its universal power.

Augustus, who succeeded as well in bringing peace and stability into the sorry state of internal affairs of Rome, is spoken of in Greek inscriptions as "God the son of God, the Benefactor," as "a savior through whom have come good tidings [*euangelia*]," and as "the savior sent to make wars cease and to order all things." But it was the poet Virgil who gave voice not only to the glory of the Augustan age but also to Rome's universal power. In Virgil's interpretation, it was Rome's destiny to complete and fulfill the humanizing efforts of the Greeks, to unify the world in order "to shut fast the dreadful steel-clenched gates of war," "to ordain the law of peace, to be merciful to the conquered and beat the haughty down." Now, sang Virgil, liberated mankind is united in one civilized body to protect which is the sacred office of Rome. This Rome has "neither period nor boundary of empire," but "dominion without end." From henceforward, the idea of Rome as the eternal City of Man is to endure, however transformed, in the historical and religious consciousness of Western humanity.

It is against this background of the rise of Rome both as a political power and as a historical idea that Flavius Josephus' presentation of contemporaneous Jewish history must be viewed, if for no other reason than that Josephus himself was constantly conscious of the implication of Rome's position in the world. That Jerusalem and the small state of which it was the center should rise in determined opposition to a Rome that had reached the acme of its power and, to concur with Virgil, had assumed its historic mission, called for an interpretation, and Josephus was prepared to offer it. An exposition of the issues involved was more opposite still, since Josephus the historian did not believe that the fall of Jerusalem had brought to an end the faith of Israel, a faith that many considered irrevocably joined to the national existence of the Jew, the soil of Judaea, and the functioning of the central sanctuary in Jerusalem. What constituted a problem to the Jews, was an enigma and a mystery to the Romans. Josephus addressed himself to both, yet chiefly to the Romans.

THE SECOND JEWISH COMMONWEALTH

The Jewish state that, at the time Josephus' dramatic story reached its tragic culmination, declared war on Rome, rose from insignificant beginnings. When, in 538 B.C., some fifty thousand persons returned from the Babylonian Exile and started to rebuild Jerusalem, the district of Judaea, part of the vast Persian satrapy "Across the River," measured some thirty-five miles in length and not more than thirty miles in breadth. But the modest, priest-ruled community from which the so-called Second Commonwealth grew (the First Commonwealth being identical with the biblical period) was animated by prophetic affirmations that "the Lord will dwell in the midst of Jerusalem and Jerusalem shall be called The city of truth" (Zechariah 8:3), that Israel shall live "not by might, nor by power, but by My spirit" (ibid., 4:6), and that in the final battle between Israel and "all the nations" Israel will emerge victorious and "the Lord shall be King over all the earth." Those "remaining of all the nations that have come against Jerusalem shall go up . . . to worship the King" in Jerusalem (ibid., 14:9 and 16). Thus in the case of Rome the sense of mission and of universal destiny came as the result of a long and arduous series of conquests; in the case of the commonwealth of Jerusalem an original awareness of a divine purpose drove the "community of the Lord" toward a future day in which promise was to be fulfilled.

Very little is known about events in Judaea in the second century of Persian rule, which ended in 331 B.C. when Alexander the Great became master of the East and created the basis for an empire in which East and West would meet and Hellenic civilization would unite peacefully with the cultures of the East. This short-lived empire—young Alexander died in 323 —fell into the hands of ambitious, power-minded "Successors," among them Ptolemy, who received Egypt and southern Syria (Coele-Syria), which included Palestine, and Seleucus, who received Syria, Babylonia, and the territory to the Indus. Cheapened, all-too-popular forms of Greek civilization became the vogue throughout the Near East, while genuine Hellenism inspired the small groups of serious minds. In

Judaea, worldly "wisdom" was fostered by a new class of masters whose schools were independent of the priestly organization and its sacral traditions.[1] Ancient Jewish dedication to the instruction of young and old could only be enriched by the Greek ideal of *paideia,* defined by Werner Jaeger as an education that aims at molding human character in accordance with an ideal and at fashioning each individual in the image of the community.[2]

In 198 B.C., Antiochus III the Great, king of Syria, conquered Coele-Syria, and with it Judaea. When, in 168, one of his successors, Antiochus IV Epiphanes ("the illustrious"), encouraged by the class of prosperous, worldly, pro-Hellenist Jews, introduced practices of crude heathen rites and enacted prohibitions of Jewish laws, Judaea rose in rebellion against this first major religious persecution in Western history.

The story of Mattathias and his five sons, called the Maccabees, or Hasmonaeans, leaders of the war against Seleucid Syria, is well known. The revolt, which started for the sake of securing religious freedom, culminated in complete political independence; in 140, Simon, the youngest of the Maccabean brothers, was recognized as "leader and High Priest for ever." In an attempt to strengthen their position in the struggle for independence, the Maccabean brothers turned to Rome, whose power they well realized, and concluded with the Roman Senate "a league of amity and confederacy" and a treaty of mutual aid in time of war. Little could the Maccabees foresee that soon their spiritual descendants—the rebels of Galilee and Jerusalem—would have to turn the spirit of revolt against that same Rome. Neither could they know that the hard-won independence of Judaea would be used to pursue a policy of cruel conquest, that the spirit that battled for liberty would later turn to court intrigue and to violent power politics, offering an all-too-easy justification for the intervention of Rome.

The heroic tale of the Maccabees is told in the Books of the Maccabees, the first of which is Josephus' source for his version of the story. What followed— the rise of the Hasmonaean kingdom, the expansion of its state, the entry of Rome into Judaean affairs, the rule of king Herod, the function of the three religious "sects," the rise of the fourth, religio-nationalist, party, the revolt against Rome, the fight for Jerusalem and the Temple, the fall of the Jewish state—we learn from Flavius Josephus' historical work. It is as if this crucial period in the life story of the Jewish people, destined, as time progressed, to relative silence on the world-historical scene, could not have come to a close without rendering to posterity an account of itself.

JOSEPHUS' LIFE

In his autobiographical essay (*Life*), Josephus gives us some information on his early life, details which help us to understand his later position as historian. Like Thucydides, who took a leading part in the events he described in his *History of the Peloponnesian War,* Josephus was personally involved in the drama he presented, in his *Jewish War*. Both the Athenian and the Jerusalemite wrote their histories in exile, after the fall of their native cities.

Joseph, or Josephus, later surnamed Flavius in honor of his Roman patrons, Vespasian, the founder of the Flavian dynasty, and his son Titus, was born in Jerusalem in A.D. 37 or 38. On his father's, Matthias', side he belonged to a noble priestly family; his mother descended from the royal family of the Hasmonaeans.

Josephus speaks with a measure of pride of his progress in education and his love of letters. As a young man of sixteen he decided to study the various schools of Jewish thought in order to be able to form his own opinion. Very little is known to us about the schools of the Sadducees. The leading sage of the

Pharisees at the time was Gamaliel I, son, or grandson, of Hillel the Elder. Josephus does not mention the names of his teachers.

Josephus received formal training in the several doctrines; in addition he was for three years a disciple of an Essene hermit, a certain Banus, "who lived in the desert, wore clothing made out of what grows on trees, ate only what grew wild, and bathed frequently in cold water, both by night and by day, for the sake of ritual purity" (*Life* 2). The Essenes, whose sect was identical with, or closely related to, that of the Dead Sea Covenanters, were the particular exponents of ascetic life at the time, and the ascetic life of the Essenes influenced Josephus to the end. He left the wilderness, however, and began to conduct himself according to the tenets of the Pharisees, in which, by the way, he says he found parallels to the teachings of the Stoics (ibid.). Some knowledge of Greek he apparently acquired as a young man.

In 64, the year of the burning of Rome, Josephus, then a man of twenty-six or twenty-seven, was sent on a diplomatic mission to Rome, where he had occasion to be introduced to Poppaea, the emperor Nero's consort and a woman of great influence (*Life* 3). When he returned to Judaea, he found the country ready to revolt against the Romans. The oppressive measures of the Roman procurators had become intolerable, especially to the patriotic revolutionaries. Having gained a personal impression of the grandeur of Rome, Josephus endeavored to impress upon the instigators of the rebellion the powerful position of Rome, and their own military inferiority. However, his "impassioned exhortation" failed to persuade the desperate patriots (*Life* 4).

The various groups of rebels, though in agreement on the principle of liberation from Rome, lacked unanimity in matters of both external and internal policy. A moderate group, led by Eleazar, son of Ananias, was strongly opposed by adherents of the so-called Fourth Philosophy, advocates of extreme action, headed by Menahem, son of Judah of Galilee. Fear that he might be considered friendly to the enemy forced Josephus to go into hiding. Only the victory—temporary as it was—of the moderate group and the fall of Menahem (*War* II, 17:9) enabled him to "steal out" again; it was impossible, however, to quench the spirit of rebellion that had engulfed the populace. Josephus and the peaceable among the Pharisees had to pretend to share the anti-Roman sentiment, trying merely to avoid taking up arms except in self-defense. Secretly Josephus hoped that the Romans would take speedy action and crush the rebellion in its initial stage. But Cestius Gallus, the Roman governor of Syria, met with defeat when he and the Twelfth Legion marched into Judaea (*War* II, 19), a turn that, because it raised Judaean hopes for an ultimate victory over the Romans, was considered "disastrous" by Josephus (*Life* 5-6). Rebellion won the day.

The aristocratic and conciliatory provisional government in Jerusalem, headed by the former high priest Ananus, met to plan the defense of the country. This body sent Josephus to Galilee. About the nature of his mission Josephus left two accounts; these accounts are contradictory, and they have not ceased vexing historians. In *Life*, Josephus relates that he and two other priests were sent to Galilee "in order to persuade the disaffected there to lay down their arms," to wait and see what the Romans would do, and to keep the arms in reserve against any emergency (*Life* 7). But in *Jewish War* he claims that the government, in appointing military leaders for the various sections of the country, entrusted him with the supreme command of the district of Galilee and assigned him to fortify the towns, train an army, and organize the district's defense (*War* II, 20:3-7).

Josephus' conflicting reports point to the complexity

of the position of a man who, pro-Roman at heart, had to preserve himself in a country of rebels ready to defend their country to the last and ready, if need be, to die for the sake of liberty. In Galilee, Josephus, not yet thirty years of age when he arrived, was faced by his most outspoken antagonist, John of Gischala, a valiant revolutionary who later headed the defense of the Temple. Josephus states that he considered John a treacherous character unequaled in wicked practices (*War* II, 21,1); John considered Josephus a power-hungry egoist and plotted his assassination (*Life* 18). Behind the personal conflict between the two men was a decisive clash of opinion on the issue of Rome; Josephus, even though he seemed at times to concur in the sentiment of the population, was pro-peace, while the Galilean olive grower John led the resistance to tyranny.

The emperor Nero sent his trusted general, Vespasian, who had fought in Germany and Britain, to "chastise the Jewish rebels" (*War* III, 1). In the spring of 67, Vespasian overran the flat regions of Galilee and attacked the stronghold Jotapata, defended by Josephus. In July 67, after a brave stand of forty-seven days, the fortress fell and Josephus surrendered to Vespasian. Facing the Roman, the Jew turned prophet and predicted Vespasian's future elevation to the throne. By the end of the year 67 the Romans completed the conquest of Galilee. John of Gischala escaped and made his way into Jerusalem, where the pro-war group had gained the upper hand.

Josephus, first held in bonds, was freed when his prediction that Vespasian would be proclaimed emperor was fulfilled in July 69. The former defender of Galilee accompanied Vespasian to Alexandria and later, in spring 70, joined the camp of Titus, who was about to lay siege to Jerusalem. Josephus served as Titus' adviser and as his spokesman, exhorting the defenders of Jerusalem to surrender and save the Holy City. His

life was frequently in danger. The Jewish rebels
wanted to capture and punish him; the Romans
blamed him for every reverse of their armies. Both
sides considered him a traitor. Titus, however, had
full confidence in Josephus (*Life* 75).

After the fall of Jerusalem, in summer 70, Titus
permitted Josephus to take whatever he wished from
the ruins. He asked for the freedom of his family and
his friends and for permission to take some sacred
books. "When my country was destroyed, I thought
nothing else that I could take and keep as comfort in
my misfortunes to be of any worth." Entering the
Temple, he freed captive women and children. He also
tried to rescue three old friends from crucifixion; one
survived (ibid.). Then he accompanied Titus to Rome.

Josephus' parents and his first wife apparently
perished during the siege of Jerusalem. "At the command of Vespasian," he married a woman taken captive
at Caesarea. This marriage did not last long. At
Alexandria Josephus took another wife, who bore him
two children who died early and another child, a son,
Hyrcanus, who survived. But Josephus was "not
pleased" with his wife's behavior and divorced her to
marry a Jewess of a noble Cretan family. By her he
had two sons, Justus and Simonides Agrippa (*Life*
75-76).

Vespasian conferred Roman citizenship upon Josephus and gave him an apartment in his own former
palace, and an annual pension. After Vespasian's death,
in 79, Titus continued his father's generous attitude
toward Josephus. The favorite of the Roman court
was frequently subjected to accusations from Jews who
envied his good fortune. Among other things, he was
accused of having rendered aid to the Jews who rose
in revolt in Cyrene, North Africa; by "God's providence," and with the help of his imperial patrons, he
emerged unharmed (*Life* 76). After the death of
Titus, in 81, a history of the Judaeo-Roman war, by

Justus of Tiberias, appeared. This history, designed to undermine Josephus' reputation, compelled him to defend himself and his role in the war. Little else is known about Josephus' personal life during his thirty or more years in Rome.

His activity during this time is, however, of great importance. Here the historian Josephus wrote the works that present the entire history of the Jews and that, more than any others, provide a source for the understanding of the decisive period from the reign of the Hasmonaean kings to the fall of Jerusalem. For the Jew, this is the final period of an independent, or semi-independent, state and of the Jerusalem Temple; for the Christian, it is the historic, social, and religious background of Early Christianity.

THE JEWISH WAR

Josephus' first work was the history of the *Jewish War,* often quoted by the Latin title *De bello Judaico;* the original title is assumed to have been *About the Capture* (of Jerusalem). The first draft—no longer extant—the historian wrote in his native Hebrew or Aramaic and had copies sent to his "countrymen beyond the Euphrates" (*War,* Preface 2). Then, for the benefit of the Hellenist reading public, Josephus reworked his script in the Greek language. Its seven books cover the period from the attack upon Jerusalem by the Syrian king Antiochus IV Epiphanes to the fall of the last fortress in Judaea, in A.D. 73, and the aftermath of the Judaeo-Roman war.

For the description of the war, Josephus used, besides his own memory and notes, the official reports, or "commentaries," of Vespasian and Titus (see *Life* 65) and other, no longer identifiable, Roman sources. For the preceding period, he used the *Universal History*—no longer extant—of Nicolas of Damascus, the Greek counsellor and court historian of Herod the Great, and friend of both Herod and Augustus. The style of the *Jewish War* (and, to a lesser degree, of Josephus' later writings) shows acquaintance with Herodotus, Thucydides, Xenophon, and Polybius, and with Homer, Greek tragedy, and Virgil. It is known that Josephus did not rely on his knowledge of the Greek idiom but employed assistants (*Against Apion* I, 9) trained in classical Greek literature. Later in life Josephus stated that he had "taken great pains to acquire the learning of the Greeks and to comprehend the elements of the Greek language," although he "cannot pronounce Greek with sufficient exactitude" (*Antiquities* XX, 11:2).

The *Jewish War* appeared between 75 and 79. Josephus presented copies first to Vespasian and Titus, "and after them to many Romans who had participated in the war." The work reached a large number "of our own men who understood Greek learning, among whom . . . was the admirable king Agrippa," Agrippa II, the last ruler from the House of Herod and the last descendant of Herod's wife, the Hasmonaean princess Mariamne (*Against Apion* I, 9).

Josephus tells us of his *Jewish War:* "I have written my work for those who love truth, not for those who read merely for pleasure" (*War,* Preface 12). The first and foremost requirement of a historian, Josephus postulates, is accuracy in recording the facts. With reference to his *War* he asserts that since he was "in person present at all its transactions," nothing escaped his knowledge. "For what happened in the Roman camp I saw and wrote down carefully, and I alone took cognizance of the news that the [Jewish] deserters brought." So confident was he of the truthfulness of his account of the war that upon completion of the work, he appealed to Vespasian and Titus to attest his accuracy; both these war leaders, as well as king Agrippa II, bore testimony to his "strictest regard for the truth" (ibid.).

But on the factual level Josephus cannot be said to

have been faithful to the principle of truth. Throughout the work certain biases become clearly discernible, biases responsible for what may be termed distortions of fact. Josephus wished to defend the honor of Rome and the humaneness of Titus, and he wished also to localize and to limit the anti-Roman spirit in Judaea.

Thus Josephus fails to mention the ruthless treatment of Jewish war prisoners by the Romans, a fact known to us from the *History of Rome* of Dio Cassius (LXVI, 5). The same historian informs us of the Roman army's growing belief in the invincibility of Jerusalem, a belief that led some Roman soldiers to desert to the Jewish side (ibid.); this interesting detail, which would detract from the image of the Roman man our historian wished to convey, is omitted in Josephus' story. Titus appears in Josephus' account to be concerned about the preservation of the Jerusalem Temple (*War* VI, 4:3); yet the *Chronica* of the fourth-century writer Sulpicius Severus contains a more authentic reference to Titus as advocating its destruction (II, 30). Josephus places the responsibility for the catastrophe upon the numerically circumscribed groups of revolutionary activists. From his presentation we would not suspect the fact, recorded by Dio Cassius (LXVI, 4), that the coreligionists in the Roman provinces, and even those in Mesopotamia, were in favor of the war against Rome. The Messianic tendency underlying the rebellion against Rome is grossly underplayed by Josephus.

The people of Jerusalem appear in Josephus' account as heroic defenders of their city, yet disunited to the very end. But Dio Cassius tells us that they, their leaders, and their priests all took the positions assigned to them and—as one—opposed the superior might of the Romans, that the Jews considered it good fortune to fall while fighting for their Temple, and that to be buried in the ruins of their Temple they deemed not death but victory and salvation (LXVI,

6). This spirit of complete dedication occurs in Josephus' account of the defense and fall of the last fortress, Masada, but his account of the last days of Jerusalem is marred by persistent deprecation of the rebels.

Josephus' magnificent chapter on the organization and military discipline of the Roman army (*War* III, 5) concludes with a note on Josephus' dual purpose: besides wishing to impart "information to those of my readers who are unacquainted with the subject," the historian states that he intended "not so much to extol the Romans as to console those whom they have vanquished and to deter the disaffected [from revolt]." In its political as well as its psychological implications, Josephus' conciliatory tendency gained the upper hand over dispassionate presentation of facts and figures. Later this tendency will be discussed more fully.

THE JEWISH ANTIQUITIES

The period following the writing of the *Jewish War*, a period of some eighteen years, Josephus devoted to a major project, a work that was to begin with the creation of the world and present the entire history of the Jewish nation from the biblical period to the outbreak of the rebellion against Rome in 66. This work, twenty books written in Greek, was completed in the year 93; it bears the title *Jewish Archaeology,* or *Antiquities of the Jews.* Domitian, who succeeded his older brother Titus in 81, was a prominent general but a cruel, suspicious man and averse to literature; he had no interest in Josephus, whose patron became a certain Epaphroditus, "a lover of all kinds of learning who especially delighted in the knowledge of history" (Preface to *Antt.*). Epaphroditus published the *Antiquities* and the shorter treatises that followed it. Stylistic assistants were employed, but they are less evident in the *Antiquities* than in the *War.* The title of the work, its division into twenty books, its em-

phasis on the high merit of the ancient institutions
find their parallels in the *Roman Archaeology,* or
Antiquities, of Dionysius of Halicarnassus, completed
in 7 B.C. It has been suggested that Dionysius' work
served as a model for Josephus, who intended to show
that "his race had a history comparable, nay, in antiquity far superior, to that of the proud Roman." [3]

The first half of Josephus' *Antiquities* retells the
biblical story, weaving the account in the biblical book
of Kings and in that in the Chronicles into one co-
herent whole and enriching this material by the traditions cultivated in the Pharisaic schools, by some biblical Apocrypha, and by data culled from the writings of
the religious philosopher Philo of Alexandria. According to Josephus the history of the biblical period can
teach man that "those who follow the will of God and
do not venture to break His excellent laws are offered
felicity for their reward" (Preface to *Antt.*). The
events of the last decades, which shook and stirred the
world outlook of Messianic visionaries and apocalyp-
tics, confirmed Josephus in his simple biblical faith.

The second, post-biblical, half of the work starts
with the period between Nehemiah and Antiochus IV
Epiphanes, a period about which very little is known;
Josephus described it mostly in terms of legendary
traditions. For the following, better documented period, Josephus made use of the *First Book of Maccabees,* Nicolas of Damascus' *History,* the no longer
extant *Historical Sketches* of Strabo, various Roman
edicts and official documents, and other, no longer
identifiable sources, both Hellenist and Jewish. In
rewriting the story of king Herod, Josephus introduced
an element of moral censure, thus deviating from the
wholly friendly attitude he followed in the *War.*

The *Antiquities* failed to achieve a strict harmony of
all parts; from a literary viewpoint it is less carefully
prepared than the *War.* The presentation as a whole
reveals the historian's desire to defend politically de-

feated Israel before the victorious world and to stress
its ancient origin, religious constitution, high ethical
standards, and place among the nations of the world.
He states his intention "to reconcile other people to
us and to remove any reasons for that hatred which
unreasonable men bear towards us." Religious rites
and institutions differ from nation to nation but
"natural justice is for the advantage of all men equally,
both Greeks and barbarians" and for this "our laws
have the greatest regard and thereby render us . . .
benevolent and friendly to all men." Josephus expected
the nations to show a similar liberal attitude towards
the Jewish people, since "the difference of institutions
is not a sufficient cause of alienation"; he felt the
nations should "join with us in the pursuit of virtue
and probity for this belongs to all men in common"
(*Antt.* XVI, 6:8). His advocacy of universal humanism
must be called a failure, but Josephus' influence on the
historical knowledge of the coming centuries was considerable.

With the authors of the biblical writings Josephus
firmly believed that God reveals Himself in history and
that in the workings of history His ways may be
apprehended. To Josephus the Jew, the history of his
nation is *one* story, though the first, biblical, part of
that story is more authoritative than the subsequent
one, in which "there was no precise succession of
prophets" (*Against Apion* I, 8). In *Antiquities,* therefore, he starts at the very beginning of the biblical
account and ends with the period of Nero.

In the *Antiquities* and the *Jewish War* together,
Josephus narrates the events that befell his people as
a consecutive story, a drama constructed upon *one* set
of premises. How different is this approach from that
of the post-Josephan period in Jewish history writing,
a period in which it was no longer believed that a
meaning can be construed from historical events or

that occurrences in the world of men can be used as "proof" of anything concerning the fate of the Jewish community or its position in the world of nations. It was this critical attitude that caused Jewish thought to cease to concern itself with what was going on in the world and caused Jewish scholars to lose the ability to write history.

At the conclusion of the *Antiquities*, Josephus states that he intended to follow this work with a brief review of the Judaeo-Roman war and an account of "what befell us up to date." He also planned to write "four books concerning our Jewish beliefs about God and His being and concerning our laws . . ." (*Antt.* XX, 11:3). These plans, however, did not materialize.

Shortly after the year 100 a history of the Judaeo-Roman war by Justus of Tiberias appeared; Justus criticized Josephus' political actions in Galilee and, in fact, presented Josephus as the instigator of the Galilean uprising. Justus' work is lost, but his charges are referred to by Josephus, who answered in a frantic attempt at self-defense by writing an autobiographical essay, *Life* (*Vita*), which he appended to a second edition of the *Antiquities*. This essay, written in inelegant Greek, deals only briefly with Josephus' private life; it concentrates on his political mission to Galilee and his strategy in the early phase of the war.

Another, and far more important, short book of Josephus, written, as was his *Life*, after the *Antiquities*, is *Against Apion* (*Contra Apionem*); the title refers to a first-century grammarian and anti-Jewish writer of Alexandria. In refuting various attacks on Judaism, Josephus discusses ancient anti-Semitic writers whose works are now lost and whose views survive only in Josephus' copious quotations.

Josephus died between the years 110 and 120. According to Eusebius, his memory was honored in Rome by a statue (*Church History* III, 9).

ROME AND JERUSALEM

We return to the central issue of the *Jewish War* and to its author's part in the action described. Josephus' half-hearted defense of Galilee, the clever manipulation by which he became the last survivor at the fall of the fortress Jotapata, his surrender to Vespasian, and finally, his acceptance of comfortable security in Rome while his people preferred death to the loss of liberty—all this has led some modern historians to consider him an egotist, a shameless opportunist who sold his soul to the Romans, and a traitor to the cause of Israel. Johanan ben Zakkai, leading rabbi, heir to the tradition of the sage Hillel the Elder, also left Jerusalem during the siege; he left, however, not to find asylum in the Roman camp, but to establish in Jabneh a new school to take the place of the religious center in Jerusalem. Only a few interpreters ventured to rise to Josephus' defense and tried to explain the actions of the last Jewish historian of antiquity as stemming from a disposition not evil, but weak, and from a character lacking the inner strength needed to hold its own against the fierce, militant stand of the patriotic rebels.

We do not intend to defend Josephus. Some of his decisive actions were guided by vanity and personal ambition. These characteristics, however, do not exhaust the complex and many-faceted personality of the historian. The key to the understanding of Josephus is to be found in the attitude to the problem presented by Rome, when seriously approached by a Jew who was, simultaneously, both rooted in his tradition and open to the world around him.

The Zealots, Sicarii, and followers of John of Gischala, whom their antagonist Josephus describes as bandits, robbers, brigands, opposed Rome so bitterly not because it was impossible to live peacefully within the vast boundaries of its empire; indeed, such a possibility existed for all nations subjected to Rome. Their zealous stand was motivated by the view that a Jew cannot acknowledge the Lord and at the same time give Caesar what is Caesar's. God is king of the universe; Roman emperorship, therefore, must be considered a violation of the kingdom of God. At the time of the Maccabean rebellion against the Syrian rule, Daniel prophesied of the stone, "cut out by no human hand," that smote the mighty "image"—symbol of the four heathen kingdoms—and shattered it, "but the stone . . . became a great mountain and filled the whole earth," and indeed, the heathen kingdoms will be replaced by "a kingdom which shall never be destroyed, nor shall its sovereignty be left to another people" (ch. 2). Daniel's parallel vision (ch. 7) saw the kingdoms as "four great beasts" whose dominion was to come to an end; a new, human kingdom was to rise, receive the acclaim of "all peoples, nations, and languages," and last forever.

This Messianic faith, itself rooted in earlier prophesies of the historic mission of Israel, motivated the Hasidim, the "pious men" who joined in the Maccabean uprising; the same faith lived in the rebels, the followers of the "Fourth Philosophy" of religious patriotism, and the Zealots, who were determined to fight mighty Rome. For Rome was understood to be the "fourth kingdom." Jerusalem's resistance to Rome, sheer madness from the viewpoint of political realities, was a necessity if viewed within the context of a Messianic philosophy of history. The outcome was not in doubt. Even death was no proof of failure; the martyr was a witness for the approaching kingdom of God.

Josephus presents the rebel leader Judah the Galilean, founder of the "Fourth Philosophy," as saying that "God alone must be their ruler and their lord" and "fear cannot force them to call any man lord" (*Antt.* XVIII, 1:6). Even after the fall of Judaea, the extremist Sicarii endured torture and pain, but not one of them complied "to acknowledge Caesar as their lord," neither could their children be compelled "to call Caesar lord" (*War* VII, 10:1).

It is in this belief that Josephus most radically differed from the rebels of Galilee and Jerusalem. He, a priest, scion of the Hasmonaean rulers, knew of the Messianic covenant between God and Israel. But at a point that cannot be determined, he arrived at the realization—tragic indeed—that in its precise sense, this covenant no longer held. Thus he faced Vespasian, the Roman general, and—in the name of God—predicted his rise to kingship.

It may be assumed that young Josephus' journey to Rome, where he was confronted by the might and majesty of the empire, initiated, or contributed to, his realization that Rome was there to stay. Upon his return to Jerusalem he tried to impress those planning the rebellion not only with the military skill but also with the "good fortune" of Rome (*Life* 4). The victory of the Jews in the first battle with the Romans under Cestius Gallus, a victory that elated the revolutionaries, appeared to Josephus as a sign that "God had already turned away from His sanctuary"; a Roman victory, Josephus reasoned, would have ended the uprising and prevented a war that had to end in catastrophe (*War* II, 19:6).

His passionate appeal for peace with Rome and for recognition of Roman sovereignty Josephus puts into the mouth of king Agrippa II, who addresses the Jerusalem rebels before the outbreak of hostilities (*War* II, 16), conveying the bitter dictum: It is too late now to venture a struggle for freedom. The crucial time which separates a meaningful resistance from a meaningless outburst Josephus fixes at Pompey's intervention in the political fate of Judaea, 63 B.C. Invited by the quarreling Hasmonaean brothers, Hyrcanus II and Aristobulus II, Pompey put an end to independent Judaea and established Rome's authority in Jerusalem.

At that time "our forefathers and their kings . . . could not withstand" the power of Rome. God himself "reduced those unworthy of liberty to subjection to the Romans" (*War* V, 9:4). That was the turning point not only in the political state of affairs but, what is far more significant, in Israel's position in history. Now Rome ruled the world—Agrippa's speech paints a stirring picture of a world of strong, freedom-loving, peoples bowing to Rome—not merely through superior strategy but by the will of God. Only if one keeps in mind the biblical, Messianic idea of the kingdom of God that is to supplant the four heathen kingdoms, can the full impact of Josephus' radical statement be realized. "Without God's aid it would not have been possible to consolidate so great an empire." Later, when asked by the Romans to urge the Jews to surrender to them, Josephus declares: "Fortune has everywhere been transferred to them . . . and God, who had given all the nations power in turn, has now settled in Italy." Now it appears to Josephus "that warfare has never been allowed our nation; our fighting is always followed by defeat" (*War* V, 9:3-4).

An ambiguous oracle that was current in Judaea at the time, mentioned also by Tacitus and Suetonius, to the effect that "a man from their [the Jews'] country would become ruler of the world" was interpreted by the rebels of Judaea in the context of Jewish Messianism "and incited them to the war." But Josephus, in keeping with his belief in the high calling and destiny of Rome, interpreted the oracle as "certainly denoting the rule of Vespasian, who was declared emperor [while] in Judaea" (*War* VI, 5:4).

In this spirit Josephus wrote his history of the Judaeo-Roman war. It is clear that he did not penetrate the mind of the various revolutionary groups and had to denounce them as misguided patriots, even though he could approve of their apparent prototypes, the Maccabean rebels. The pro-Roman attitude is less in evidence in his magnum opus, the *Antiquities,* a fact that has puzzled some interpreters of Josephus. It may well be that this change in attitude was caused not only by the deterioration in Josephus' personal relationships to Roman leaders but also, as time went on, by his closer observation of Roman life and his more intimate knowledge of Roman thought. A sensitive resident of Rome noticed what the impressionable young visitor to the metropolis may have failed to realize: that the expansion of Roman power had caused a breakdown of ancient *virtus,* had caused the display of utter heartlessness towards the classes of the poor, the spread of violence and vulgarity, the addiction of the populace to the bloody gladiatorial sports. Not a few critical minds relinquished the lofty Virgilian faith in heaven on earth to be established by the Empire. Among them was the historian Tacitus, contemporary of Josephus, who revolted against the demoralization of the Rome of the Caesars—and looked for an escape in the presumably more perfect virtues of the Teutons.[4] Josephus, who lost his trust in the historic destiny of the Empire, turned to the history of his own people. Under the impact of what he witnessed in Rome, his concept of the Jewish people gained in depth.

JOSEPHUS' VIEW OF JUDAISM

In his treatise *Against Apion,* written in exquisite Greek, we encounter Josephus as a defender of the Jewish name against the prejudices and calumnies of anti-Semites of whom Apion of Alexandria was but one. Beyond this defense, given with passionate eloquence, Josephus offers an exposition of his concept of Judaism. The apologetic implication of this part of the treatise does not exhaust its importance.

The teachings and practices of Judaism, he postulates, are contained in the ancient Torah, in the laws of Moses. It was a world without law and order into which the Torah introduced the love of order, and one law for all (II, 16). As lawgiver, Moses precedes Lycurgus and Solon; the very term law, *nomos,* is unknown to Homer (ibid.). To his constitution Moses gave a form of theocracy; Josephus is the first to coin this term, and he realizes that it may easily be misunderstood. To Josephus it means that "all sovereignty and authority is in the hands of God." This God is unbegotten, immutable through all eternity, surpassing all mortal conception of beauty. Though He is known to us by His power, His essence is beyond our comprehension; He knows the actions and the thoughts of man, and He is the author of all blessings (II, 17).

Can there be, Josephus asks, a more just constitution than one which places God at the head of the universe? God is "perfect and happy, self-sufficing and sufficient for all other beings, the beginning, the middle, and the end of all things." His "form" cannot be conceived or depicted, but He is manifest in His works. In dealing with Creation, Josephus excludes all anthropomorphic concepts, as well as the Platonic idea of divine assistants. It was God's will alone that "determined that the works should be created and be good also," and thus they came into being (II, 22-3).

One paramount difference between the Greek thinkers, who held similar ideas about God, and the Hebrew lawgiver, Josephus sees in this: the former disclosed their philosophy only to a few chosen disciples, leaving the masses to their preconceived views, whereas Moses "made actions square with the laws" and took care not only of his contemporaries but of their descendants as well. "The faith concerning God" is an issue for all people in all generations. It is also characteristic of the Torah that religion is not turned into a subdivision of general virtue, but the various virtues—such as justice, fortitude, self-control, and communal harmony—become components of religion. "All our actions, studies, and words are linked with piety towards God."

There can be no ignorance of the law among the Jews. The Torah is read regularly every week, and leaving their work, people assemble to listen to the reading "and to gain perfect knowledge of the laws." Instruction in the laws starts in early youth, so that they become "engraven on our souls." Whereas most men hardly know their own laws, "any one of our people can more easily recite the laws than he can tell his own name." Living under the law is "like living under both a father and a master" (II, 17-19). Children are being taught the laws and the deeds of their forefathers in order that they should be prepared to emulate them (II, 26). Among the ideal biblical institutions and statutes, Josephus singles out the Jerusalem Temple, which is "common to all men because God is common to all men." Sacrifices call for prayer, first "for the common welfare of all, for we are made for fellowship with one another," then for ourselves (II, 24).

Josephus continues with a description of the laws that regulate sex relations and safeguard the lives of offspring; abortion or destruction of the fetus by any other method is regarded as infanticide (II, 25). Parents are to be honored next to God Himself; elders are to be respected and friends accorded absolute confidence. The neighbor is to be aided and justice rendered in litigation. Such rules "unite us in bonds of fellowship with one another" (II, 28).

Acceptance of these norms, and not blood kinship alone, establishes relationship; therefore those who "wish to come and live under our laws" are given a friendly welcome. "Willingly we admit those who desire to share our ways" (II, 29 and 37). However, all men, even foes, are to be treated "gently and humanely" (II, 30); the gods avowed by other people may not be blasphemed, "out of respect for the very name of God" (II, 34). Nor do the laws neglect the care of animals; "ill-treatment even of a brute beast is with us a capital crime" (II, 30 and 38). Thus theocracy, which means recognition of the rule of God, comprises the totality of life, public and private, the totality of thought and action; and the basic principle of all the laws is—mercy (II, 30).

The laws teach true piety, contentment with one's possession, and dedication to one's calling. They are designed to banish idleness and extravagant living and to encourage people freely to share what they have with others; they establish justice among men, forbid men to wage war for the sake of conquest, but inspire them with valor in the defense of the laws. Sophistry is shunned; right action is stressed.

"What is more beneficial than mutual love and concord, neither to be divided by adversity nor to be arrogant and seditious in prosperity, in war to despise death and in peace to cultivate crafts and farming, realizing that God surveys and directs the whole world?" (II, 42). It is well known, Josephus says, "that many of our people have on many occasions bravely resolved to endure any suffering" rather than forsake the Torah. But each one of them, "having his own conscience as witness," believes that life lived according to the Torah—even if that life is to be surrendered in martyrdom—holds within it the divine promise of a "renewed existence in the revolution of time" (II, 31).

Thus Josephus offers a picture, somewhat idealized, not of the Jewish state the fall of which he had dramatically presented in his historical works, but of a religious society. The king, the instruments of national authority, international relations, play no role in his doctrine. God is king. Life according to His law is freedom. The Zealots, Josephus' antagonists, also acknowledged the kingship of God, but in their view that kingship had to be translated into immediate political reality. Freedom was not possible as long as Caesar could claim recognition as lord. Josephus, on the other hand, recognized the rule of Rome, and made his peace with Caesar, while adhering to the non-political concepts of what he termed theocracy and of a fellowship of men perfecting their lives according to the laws. Such life could well be maintained under a foreign political ruler, as long as he did not interfere with the internal aspects of the fellowship. No wonder that Josephus was attracted by the brotherhood of the Essenes.

Josephus did not believe that this nonpolitical existence of Judaism would lead to a gradual withdrawal from the world at large. He notes that the simple life and fellowship have been advocated not alone by Greek philosophers following Moses, and that people everywhere are attracted by the Jewish religious life. The seventh day of rest is universally observed; many of the dietary regulations are emulated, and so are "our mutual concord with one another, the charitable distribution of our goods, our diligence in the crafts, and our fortitude in persecution on behalf of our laws." It is the attempt to create a perfect community of men that leads Josephus to consider the Jewish law universally valid. "As God Himself pervades the cosmos, so has our law found its way among all men" (II, 40).

A man so deeply imbued with the spirit of an extra-national Judaism could not but see in the patriotic rebels of Judaea men who betrayed the ancestral Covenant, and in Jerusalem's war against Rome, a loss of nerve and a confusion of issues. These convictions underlie Josephus' views as the historian of the *Jewish War.*

In his *Antiquities,* Josephus freely paraphrases the biblical passage on Balaam's prophecy (Numbers 23-4) to read: "You shall retain that land to which He hath sent you, and it shall ever be the possession of your children; but both all the earth, as well as the sea, shall be filled with your glory; and you shall be sufficiently numerous to supply all the world, and every region of

it in particular, with inhabitants out of your stock.
. . . Truly, the land of Canaan can now hold you, as
being yet comparatively few; but know ye that the
whole world is proposed to be your place of habitation
for ever" (*Antt.* IV, 6:4). Here we read the basic
text for the life of a people that is no longer tied to
its ancestral soil but lives in dispersion among the nations of the world. In the time of Josephus there was
indeed a vast diaspora of Jewish communities between
the Euphrates and the Nile, and in Rome. With the
fall of Jerusalem this diaspora claimed more serious
attention than it had until then been given. Josephus
conceives Israel as a people with a political and a historical past, but devoid of the Messianic aspirations
of that past, and totally dedicated to religious life—an
extraterritorial society of a universally applicable
faith.

THE STORY OF JOSEPHUS' WORKS

The works of Josephus, like those of Philo of Alexandria, were early forgotten by the Jewish community
but eagerly preserved by the Church. Josephus, the
non-Christian who—in the commonly available texts—
testified to the events in the earliest period of Christianity (the so-called *testimonium Flavianum*), deserved close attention; his works offered important
background material for the history of the early
Church. Eusebius speaks of the high esteem in which
Josephus was held by both Jews and Romans, and he
mentions that the Romans placed Josephus' books in
the public library (*Church History* III, 9). Jerome
calls Josephus, Graecus Livius, "the Greek Livy"
(Epist. XXII ad Eustochium). Pagan writers, too,
showed interest in our historian. The neo-Platonist
and student of religions, Porphyry, in his treatise on
abstinence, quotes Josephus' statements on the Essenes.

Early translations into Latin spread the knowledge

of Josephus in the West. One, known as the *Hegesippus*
(a corruption of the name Josephus; *ca.* 4th century),
is a free, abridged rendition of the *Jewish War* con-
taining inserted passages from Josephus' *Antiquities*
and from the works of other Roman writers. It is a
Josephus for Christian readers, with references not
only to Jesus, but also to Peter and Paul. In addition,
another, more accurate, Latin translation of the *War*
existed.

Cassiodorus, the sixth-century Christian statesman
and author, initiated Latin translations of the *Antiquities* and *Against Apion.* An early Syriac translation of
the sixth book of the *War* became a part of the
Peshitta, the Syriac Old Testament. A Greek epitome
of Josephus' works was in use in the tenth century.

In a roundabout way, Josephus' work found its way
into Hebrew literature. Using as his source a Latin
manuscript of the major part of the *Antiquities* and
the *Hegesippus,* a tenth-century, south Italian author
produced a free Hebrew paraphrase known as *Yosippon;* Christian interpolations found in the Latin texts
were, of course, omitted; an attitude friendly to Rome
prevails throughout the story. *Yosippon,* whose author
is unknown, proved very popular throughout the Middle Ages; readers believed they had a work written
by Josephus himself. The book was rendered into
Arabic in the eleventh century; the Arabic translation
seems to have served as the basis for a translation into
Ethiopic. An English and a French translation of an
extract from the *Yosippon* date from the sixteenth
century.

In the beginning of this century, a long-forgotten,
medieval Old North Russian (the so-called Slavonic)
version of Josephus became known. Here John the
Baptist is spoken of as the "wild man," and Jesus, as
the "wonder worker." The "wild man" appears as the
head of a political freedom movement, and the "wonder
worker," as being pressed by his followers to lead a

rebellion against Rome. Some scholars hastily assumed that the "slavonic" version, in differing from the Greek text of Josephus, ultimately represented the original Aramaic text of the *War* that preceded Josephus' own Greek version. On this theory, ingeniously elaborated by Robert Eisler, a suggested daring revision of the early Christian story was based. However, Solomon Zeitlin challenged Eisler's theory and maintained that the "Slavonic" Josephus was translated in the twelfth or thirteenth century from a seventh- or eighth-century Greek version that freely paraphrased Josephus' *War* and that contained many Christian interpolations.

The earliest extant Latin manuscript dates from the sixth, the earliest Greek manuscript from the tenth, century. Many European libraries treasure manuscripts of Josephus' writings from various periods. The most famous illustrated manuscript is the fifteenth-century work *Antiquités Judaïques,* with the miniatures of Jean Fouquet (Paris National Library). The first printed edition, in Latin, appeared in 1470 in Augsburg, Germany; the first printed Greek edition appeared in 1544 in Basel, Switzerland.

For centuries the Western world read Josephus both for his "testimony" and for the story he had to tell. It was hard to escape the dramatic impact of Jewish history in the Roman period. Early modern England and America in particular took Josephus to heart. In Kipling's *Captains Courageous* a seaman on board the schooner *We're Here* recites on Sunday from a Josephus volume, which "was an old leather bound volume, very solid and very like a Bible, but enlivened with accounts of battles and sieges." In Schiller's celebrated drama *Die Räuber,* Spiegelberg says to Moor: "Josephus—that's what you ought to read!"

In the seventeenth century the first English translation was made from the Greek text (Thomas Lodge, London, 1640). A later translation (Dublin, 1738-41) by the Cambridge, England, Unitarian scholar William

Whiston became the standard English rendition and
was frequently reprinted; a revision by A. R. Shilleto,
also of Cambridge, appeared in London in 1889-90,
and one by D. S. Margoliouth, in London, 1909. A
translation of the *War* by Robert Traill, London, 1862,
was edited by Isaac Taylor. The scholarly edition of
the Greek text (Berlin, 1885-95), with full *apparatus
criticus,* is the work of Benedictus Niese. The most
reliable English translation today is by H. St. J.
Thackeray and Ralph Marcus (Loeb Classical Library,
London and Cambridge, Mass., 1926-43); the final
volume (*Antiquities* XV-XX) is still to appear. A
translation into French (Paris, 1900) was started under the editorship of Théodore Reinach and completed
by Solomon Reinach. A modern Hebrew translation of
the *War* was produced by Y. N. Simhoni (reprinted,
Tel Aviv, 1957), and one, still incomplete, of the
Antiquities (Jerusalem, 1944), by Abraham Shalit.

JERUSALEM AND ROME

THE JEWISH
COMMUNITY

The social, political, and religious views of the Phari-
sees and the Sadducees have a long history; as parties
the two groups enter the scene after the Maccabean
rebellion. The community of the Essenes, too, was
rooted in older pietist doctrines before it emerged as a
sect. In presenting these three "philosophical sects,"
Josephus had the Roman reader primarily in mind.

Josephus had personal contact with the Essenes. As
a young man he dwelt three years with the Essene
hermit Banus (Life 2). His account of the Essenes
gained special importance when the writings of the
Dead Sea Sect became known and their identity (or,
at least, kinship) with the Essenes was established.

THE PHARISEES AND THE SADDUCEES

The Pharisees, who are reputed to be the most accurate
interpreters of the laws and who constitute the leading
sect, ascribe all events to fate and to God; they admit,
however, that to act rightly or otherwise is, in the
main, in man's own power, though in both cases fate
co-operates. They hold all souls to be imperishable, but
contend that only the souls of the good migrate into
other bodies and that the souls of the wicked suffer
eternal punishment.

The Pharisees live simply, despise delicacies, and
are guided by their tradition; what that prescribes as
good, they do. They think they ought earnestly to
strive to observe the school's dictates, respect those

advanced in years; and are not so bold as to oppose anything these have initiated. They love one another and foster harmony and esteem for the community.

They valued themselves highly upon the strict observance of the law of their fathers and made men believe they were highly favored by God. They had great influence over women. They . . . ventured even to oppose kings. Through these doctrines the Pharisees wield great influence over the people; divine worship, prayers, and sacrifices are performed according to their directions. And their steadfast practice of virtue, in deeds as well as discourse, has earned them the people's high esteem.

Comp., "Our nation does not encourage those who learn many languages and thereby adorn their discourses with the smoothness of their periods, because this accomplishment is considered common not only to free men but to as many of the servants as please to learn such languages. Only he is called wise who is learned in our laws and able to interpret the meaning of the holy writings." (Antt. *XX, 11:2.*)

The Sadducees . . . disregard fate entirely and place God beyond the commission or the very sight of evil. Good and evil, they contend, are man's choice, and everyone is free to embrace one or the other according to his will. The soul's permanence after death and the punishments and rewards of Hades, they reject.

The Sadducees hold that souls die with the bodies. They observe only what the [written] law enjoins and consider disputations with the teachers of their school a virtue. Their views are received by only a few, but these few are of the highest rank. They wield no influence over practical life; when they do become magistrates, as unwillingly and by compulsion they are sometimes obliged to, they apply the teachings of the Pharisees, for otherwise the people would not put up with them.

The Sadducees are rather rude to each other; in dealing with their peers they are wanting in urbanity as if they were strangers to them. (War II, 8:14; Antt. XVII, 2:4, and XVIII, 1:2-4.)

THE ESSENE COMMUNITY

The Essenes are reputed to cultivate peculiar sanctity. Jews by birth, they love each other more than do the other sects. Pleasures they reject as evil; continence and control of the passions they deem a special virtue.

They disdain marriage, but adopting the children of others, while yet pliant to instruction, they treat them as kin and mold them in accordance with their own principles. Wedlock, indeed, and the progeny arising from it, they do not on principle condemn; but they guard against the levity of women and are convinced that none of them stay faithful to but one man.

They hold riches in contempt; the community of goods among them is to be admired. No one among them has more than another. It is their law that whoever joins the sect relinquishes his fortune to the order; there is therefore neither poverty nor excess of wealth among them. Everyone's possessions are commingled, so that all as brothers enjoy one patrimony. They regard oil as defiling; if one of them accidentally comes in contact with it, he wipes his body, for they consider a dry skin to be good, and clothe it always in white. The trustees of the common property are elected; every member is eligible for this office, and all have the right to vote.

They are concentrated in no single city; there are many of them in every town. The property of the brethren is at the disposal of any member coming from another place as though it were his own; they enter the homes of people they have never seen as though they were the most intimate of friends. They therefore carry nothing with them on a journey save arms for protection against brigands. In every city of the order a member is appointed to attend to strangers and to provide them with clothing and other necessities. In their dress and general deportment they resemble children reared in awe of their masters. They renew neither clothing nor shoes until these are in shreds or worn out from long use. Nor do they buy or sell among themselves, one another; but each gives whatever he possesses to those in need of such objects, taking from them in turn what he may need. Even without making any return, each may take from the others what he needs.

Towards the Deity they are singularly pious. Before the sun is up they speak no word of worldly matters, but offer certain prayers handed down from their fathers, as though imploring the sun to rise. They are then dismissed by their superiors to their labors in which each is skilled, and work diligently until the fifth hour of the day, when they again assemble in one place and, girding themselves with linen cloths, wash their bodies with cold water.

After this cleansing, they meet in a special building, which none of the uninitiated is permitted to enter. Then, purified, they proceed to the refectory as though it were a holy shrine. When they have taken their seats in silence, the baker serves them loaves in order, while the cook sets a single plate of one kind of food in front of each. Prior to the meal the priest says grace, and none may taste the food before the prayer. Dinner over, he prays again. Thus at both beginning and conclusion of the meal they give homage to God as the provider of their sustenance. Then, laying aside their garments as sacred, they resume their labors until evening.

On their return they sup in a similar manner; strangers who may happen to be present sit down with them. No clamor or disturbance ever contaminates the dwelling, each being granted liberty to speak in turn. To those outside, the silence within seems like some awesome mystery; but the cause of this silence is but perpetual temperance and making the demands of nature the measure of food and drink.

In other matters they do nothing without directions from their superiors; only two things are left to their own discretion—rendering help, and compassion. They may of their own volition help the deserving, when in need, and give food to those in distress. But they are not permitted to give presents to relatives without leave from their superiors.

They give vent to anger in a just manner and restrain their passions, are eminently faithful, and are the very servants of peace. A simple affirmation is more valid among them than an oath; they avoid swearing, regarding it as worse than perjury. He who cannot be believed without an appeal to God is, they say, already condemned.

They diligently study the writings of the ancients, concentrating on matters that tend to the welfare of soul and body. They thus learn medicinal roots and the properties of minerals useful in the treatment of disease.

A man anxious to join the sect is not immediately admitted. For one year they impose upon him their own rule of life, while he remains excluded from the fraternity. They present him with a small hatchet, the aforementioned vestment, and a white robe. Having given proof of continence during that period, he advances a step nearer to their discipline; he is allowed to participate in the waters of purification but is not yet admitted to the meetings of the community, for after this proof of his fortitude, his principles are tested for two more years. Only then, if found worthy, is he accepted into the society.

But before he may touch their common food he is bound by fearful oaths, first to exercise piety toward God; then to observe justice toward men; to hurt no one, either of his own volition or at another's command; always to hate the wicked and fight the battle of the righteous; ever to show good faith to all men and especially to those in authority, for none holds office except by divine appointment; and should he himself be in authority, never to abuse his office nor excel those subject to him either in dress or adornment; always to be a lover of truth and reprove those guilty of falsehood; to keep his hands pure of theft and his soul pure of unlawful gain; neither to secrete anything from the brotherhood nor to reveal their doctrines to outsiders, not even if tortured to death. He must further swear to communicate their tenets exactly as he himself reecived them, to abstain from robbery, and to preserve alike the books of the sect and the names of the angels. Through such oaths do they secure their proselytes.

Those found guilty of grave crimes are expelled from the order; a man so expelled often comes to a most miserable end. Bound by his oaths and the sect's usages, he cannot partake of the food of others; subsisting on herbs, his body is wasted by hunger and he perishes. Out of compassion, therefore, the Essenes readmit many when they reach the last extremity, accepting the torments that had brought them to the point of death as sufficient atonement for their misdeeds.

They are just and most careful in their judgments, never pronouncing sentence in a court of less than a hundred members. A sentence so pronounced is irrevocable. Next to God, they revere most highly the name of their lawgiver [Moses]. Whoever blasphemes him is punished with death. They honor obedience to age and the majority; should ten be sitting together, one will not speak if nine desire silence. They are also careful not to spit into the midst of the company or to the right side.

They are more scrupulous than all other Jews in abstaining from work on the seventh day. They therefore not only prepare their food the day before in order not to light a fire on the seventh, but move no vessel, nor obey the calls of nature. On other days they dig a small, foot-deep pit with a mattock, a kind of hatchet given to them on their admission, and spread a cloak about them in order not to offend the divine rays of light. They then cover up the pit with the earth they had removed. On these occasions they are careful to seek out the more lonely spots. And though these functions are but a natural discharge of bodily impurity, it is their rule to wash afterwards, as if defiled.

They are divided, according to the duration of their discipline, into four grades; and so greatly inferior are the junior members to the senior that the latter if but touched by the former, wash as if they had come into contact with an alien. They are long-lived, many attaining a hundred years and more. This longevity is, I think, a consequence of their simple life and regular habits.

They treat misfortune with contempt, and through their resolute will, are superior to pain, thinking death if it come with honor, better than immortality. Their strength of mind under all circumstances was fully evinced during our war with the Romans. Racked and maimed, burned and broken, tried by every implement of torture to make them blaspheme their lawgiver or eat forbidden food, they endured all torment rather than yield in either instance. They asked no mercy from their tormentors, nor did they shed a tear. Smiling in their agonies and mocking their persecutors, they joyfully surrendered their souls, certain of receiving them back again.

For they believe that bodies are corruptible and the matter they are composed of impermanent, but that souls are immortal and imperishable. Emanating from the subtlest ether, they are confined in bodies as if in prisons into which they are drawn by some natural spell. When set free from the bonds of the flesh they rejoice as if released from a long captivity, and are borne upward. Concurring in this opinion with the sons of Greece, they hold that good souls inhabit a region beyond the ocean, a region not oppressed by rain or snow or heat but refreshed by ever-gentle winds from the ocean. To the wicked souls they allot a gloomy, tempest-filled cavern, replete with never-ending punishments.

Similarly, the Greeks, it seems to me, allot to the brave, whom they call heroes and demigods, the isles of the blessed; but the souls of the wicked they consign to the site of the ungodly in Hades, where, so tell their legends, such men as Sisyphus, Tantalus, Ixion, and Tityus are punished. The Greeks postulate first that souls are immortal; from this tenet they derive their exhortations to virtue and abstention from vice. For the good become better still in life through hope of reward after death, while the wicked check the violence of their passions for fear that, though they may escape detection in life, they will after death be subjected to eternal punishment. Such are the theological views of the Essenes concerning the soul, an irresistible attraction to those who have once savored their philosophy.

There are some among them who, versed from childhood in sacred books and having recourse to several forms of purification and to the discourses of the prophets, profess to foretell the future. They seldom, if ever, err in their predictions.

There is still another order of Essenes. This order, while agreeing with the other on mode of life, customs, and regulations, differs from it on the question of marriage. They think that by not marrying they cut off life's greatest privilege, that of transmitting it; and furthermore, that were everybody to adopt this point of view, the whole race of mankind would perish. However, their wives undergo three years' probation; only after they have been thrice purified—[these purifications serving] as tests of their fruitfulness—is their union consummated. They do not consort with them during the period of pregnancy, as proof that they marry for love of offspring and not for any baser motive. When bathing, the women are partially clad, the men wear loincloths. Such are the usages of this order.

It is the doctrine of the Essenes that all things are left to the will of God. They . . . think that man ought to strive to draw near to righteousness.[1] When they send offerings to the Temple, they do not offer sacrifices, because they have purer lustrations of their own; and for this reason they are excluded from the common court of the Temple, and offer their sacrifices by themselves. Their conduct excels that of other men; and they devote themselves solely to husbandry.

They deserve our admiration for so greatly exceeding in justice all other men that addict themselves to virtue. Their mode of life has never existed, not even for a short span, among other men, whether Greek or barbarian; but it has long endured among them. They hold all things in common; the rich man enjoys no more of his wealth than he who has nothing. Some four thousand men live in this manner; they neither marry nor keep servants, holding that wives promote household discord and servants tempt men to be unjust. As they live alone, they minister to one another. They also appoint good men to be the receivers of their revenues and their agricultural produce and set priests over the preparation of their corn and food. . . . (War II, 8:2-13; Antt. XVIII, 1:5.)

THE HASMONAEAN RULERS—
THE INTERVENTION OF ROME

JOHN HYRCANUS (135-104 B.C.)

The thirty years' struggle of the Hasmonaean brothers, sons of Mattathias of Modin, for independence from the Seleucid rule was over in 142 B.C. Then "was the yoke of the heathen taken away from Israel" (I Macc. 13:41). In 140 B.C. the liberated Jewish nation honored Simon, last of the brothers, with the hereditary office of ruling high priest and prince (ibid., 14:25-49). The Roman Senate confirmed the confederacy with the Jewish people and recognized Simon as an independent ruler (ibid., 15:15-21). Simon, assassinated in 135 B.C., was succeeded by his son John Hyrcanus, the former governor of Gazara.

It was the task of John Hyrcanus, and of his successors, to strengthen the young state and to expand its limited territory. First, however, John Hyrcanus had to defeat the treacherous designs of the pretender Ptolemy, governor of Jericho, who had assassinated his own father-in-law, Simon, and John's two brothers. He besieged Ptolemy in the fortress Dagon, near Jericho, but because the storming of Dagon would have meant the death of his mother held as hostage by Ptolemy, he withdrew the siege. Ptolemy murdered John Hyrcanus' mother nevertheless (Antt. XIII, 8:1).

Antiochus VII Sidetes, of Syria, who did much to restore the power of the Seleucids, invaded Judaea and besieged Jerusalem. To secure the withdrawal of the

Syrians, Hyrcanus accepted terms involving the payment of tribute and the breaching of the walls of Jerusalem (Antt. XIII, 8:2-3). Later, Hyrcanus rebuilt the walls (I Macc. 16:23).

CONQUESTS IN THE EAST, NORTH, AND SOUTH OF JUDAEA

When Hyrcanus heard of the death of Antiochus [VII Sidetes], he at once made an expedition against the cities of Syria, hoping to find them destitute of fighting men, or of any able to defend them. However, it was only after six months that he took Medaba [east of the Jordan], and that not without great distress to his army. Then he took Samega and the neighboring sites; also Shechem, Gerizim, and the Cuthaean nation, which dwelt near the temple that Alexander [the Great] permitted . . . to be built. . . . This temple was now laid waste, two hundred years after it was built.

Hyrcanus also took the Idumaean cities Adora and Marisa, and after subduing all the Idumaeans, granted them permission to remain in their country if they accepted circumcision and conformed to the laws of the Jews. The Idumaeans so longed to live in the country of their forefathers that they submitted to circumcision and the rest of the Jewish modes of life. Ever since they have been adjudged no other than Jews. (Antt. XIII, 9:1.)

RENEWAL OF THE TREATY WITH ROME

Hyrcanus . . . also wished to renew the friendship with the Romans. Accordingly, he sent an embassy to them. The Senate received his epistle and made a pact of friendship with him as follows:

"Fannius, the son of Marcus the praetor, assembled the Senate . . . to discuss what the ambassadors of the people of the Jews . . . came to treat about, namely, the pact of friendship and mutual assistance that existed between them and the Romans, and other public affairs. They request that Jaffa and its harbors, Gazara and the springs [of the Jordan], and the several other cities and sites that Antiochus [VII] had taken from them in the war [against John Hyrcanus] contrary to the decree of the Senate be restored to them; that it be declared unlawful for the king's troops to pass through their country or the countries subject to them; that whatever had without the consent of the Senate been decreed by Antiochus during that same war, be voided; that the Romans send ambassadors to take care that restitution be made of what Antiochus had taken from them and to evaluate the worth of the country that had been laid waste in the war; and that they [the Jewish ambassadors] be granted letters of protection to the kings and free cities to safeguard their peaceful return home. It was decreed then to renew the pact of friendship and mutual assistance with these good men sent by a good and friendly people."

As for the letters, the Senate promised to take up the subject when their own affairs would let them, and that they would endeavor in the meantime to take care that no harm befell them [the Jewish ambassadors]. They also said that the praetor Fannius would give them money out of the public treasury to cover their expenses home. Thus did Fannius dismiss the Jewish ambassadors, giving them money out of the public treasury and the Senate decree to those assigned to conduct them on their way and guard their safe return home. (Antt. XIII, 9:2.)

After the death of Antiochus VII Sidetes in 128 B.C., Hyrcanus "no longer paid the Syrians the slightest deference either as subject or friend." (10:1.)

THE CONQUEST OF SAMARIA

Advancing to Samaria, on the site of which now stands Sebaste, a city built by King Herod, Hyrcanus encircled it, entrusting the direction of the siege to his sons Aristobulus and Antigonus. So closely did they press the operations that the besieged were compelled by famine to eat what had never before been used for food. They [the Samarians] sought the aid of Antiochus [VIII Grypus, of Syria] who, readily complying, was defeated by the forces of Aristobulus. Pursued by the brothers, he fled to the very gates of Scythopolis. The former, on their return to Samaria, re-enclosed its people within the walls, captured the town, razed it to its foundations, and enslaved the inhabitants. Their enterprises thus succeeding, they did not let their ardor cool, but marched, in force, as far as Scythopolis, ravaged it, and laid waste the entire country south of Mount Carmel. (War I, 2:7.)

HYRCANUS' BREAK WITH THE PHARISEES

However, this prosperous state of affairs moved the Jews to envy Hyrcanus; the Pharisees especially were ill-disposed towards him. . . . These men wield so great a power over the people that when they malign a king, or high priest, they are at once believed. Hyrcanus was a much-beloved disciple of theirs. He once invited them to a feast, entertained them well, and when he saw them in good humor, said to them that they knew he longed to be a righteous man and to do all things whereby he might please God, which was the very profession of the Pharisees; if, however, they had observed him offending in any manner and straying from righteous ways, they should lead him back and correct him.

But they affirmed to his being wholly virtuous and he was pleased with their commendation. However, one of the guests, whose name was Eleazar, an evil man who delighted in faction, said: "Since you desire to know the truth, if you wish to be righteous in earnest, lay down the high priesthood and be content with the government of the people." When Hyrcanus asked why he should lay down the high priesthood, Eleazar replied: "We have heard it from old men that your mother had been a captive under the reign of Antiochus Epiphanes." [2] But there was no truth in this tale. Hyrcanus was provoked with Eleazar, and all the Pharisees most indignant.

There lived at the time a certain Jonathan, a great friend of Hyrcanus, but of the sect of the Sadducees, whose beliefs are quite contrary to those of the Pharisees. He told Hyrcanus that all the Pharisees concurred in Eleazar's rebuke and that this fact would be made manifest if he but asked them what punishment, in their opinion, Eleazar merited. For only if they favored punishing him as his crime deserved, could he be certain that the rebuke was not made with their approbation. Hyrcanus asked the question. The Pharisees replied that Eleazar merited stripes and bonds, but that death seemed too harsh a punishment for a rebuke. As a matter of fact, the Pharisees, even on other occasions, do not as a rule mete out severe punishment.

This mild sentence enraged Hyrcanus, and he believed that Eleazar had rebuked him with the approval of the Pharisees. It was Jonathan who chiefly incited him against the latter and who influenced him to join the Sadducees, leave the Pharisees, abolish the decrees the latter had promulgated for the people, and penalize those who observed them. From this source sprang the people's hatred for Hyrcanus and his sons; but of these matters we shall speak hereafter.

What I would now state is this: the Pharisees imparted to the people many regulations handed down from their fathers that are not written in the laws of Moses. That is why the Sadducees reject them. They claim that we are to honor as obligatory only those regulations that are in the written word, but need not observe what is derived from the tradition of our forefathers. These views have occasioned great disputes and differences, as the Sadducees influence none but the rich and have not the populace on their side, but the Pharisees have the people to back them. . . . (Antt. XIII, 10:5-6.)

"Jealousy of the successes of Hyrcanus and his sons provoked a sedition among their [Pharisee] countrymen; great numbers assembled to oppose them and continued to agitate until bursting out in open war, they were defeated." (War *I, 2:8.*)

HYRCANUS' END

When Hyrcanus had put an end to this opposition he lived happily after. When he died after administering the government in the best manner for thirty-one years, he left five sons. He was esteemed by God worthy of the three greatest privileges: the government of his nation, the dignity of the high priesthood, and the power of prophecy. For God was with him and enabled him to know and to foretell the future. . . . (Antt. XIII, 10:7.)

The Talmud, too, records the Pharisees' criticism of Hyrcanus ("Let the crown of kingdom suffice you, and leave the crown of priesthood to the seed of Aaron") and Hyrcanus' turning away from the Pharisees (Kiddushin 66a). However, the names of those involved in the incident vary from those recorded by Josephus. Some of Hyrcanus' legal enactments are mentioned in Mishnah Sotah IX, 10. His coins bear the inscription: "Johanan the high priest and the congregation of the Jews," or "Johanan the high priest, head of the congregation of the Jews."

ARISTOBULUS I (104-103 B.C.)

After the death of Hyrcanus, his eldest son, **Aristobulus**, resolved to transform the government into a kingdom. He was the first to put a diadem on his head, four hundred eighty and one years and three months after the people had been delivered from the Babylonian exile and returned to their own country.[3] Aristobulus loved only the brother next to him, Antigonus, and treated him as his equal. The others he held in chains. His mother, too, he cast into prison, for she disputed the government with him, Hyrcanus having left her mistress of all the realm. He progressed to such a degree of barbarity as to starve her in prison. Worse still, he was even alienated from his brother Antigonus by calumnies, and added him to the rest of the victims he slew. . . . (Antt. XIII, 11:1.)

Here follows the report of the court intrigue in which Antigonus was denounced as trying to replace his brother. The suspicious king had him slain. One Judah, an Essene, is said to have foretold this tragic event. (11:1-2.)

But Aristobulus instantly repented this slaughter of his brother. Guilt aggravated a disease [that afflicted him] and so disturbed his mind that his entrails were wracked by intolerable pain and he vomited blood. Once, a servant carrying away this blood slipped and shed some of it—by divine providence, as I cannot but think—at the very spot where stains of Antigonus' blood still remained. When the spectators cried out, as if the servant had purposely shed the blood at that particular spot, Aristobulus heard the cry and inquired what was wrong. Receiving no answer, he became all the more anxious, for in such contingencies it is natural for men to suspect that whatever is being concealed is evil. His threats forced the terrorized spectators to speak, and they at length told him the truth. Whereupon, in the mental agony of his guilty conscience, he shed many tears and gave a deep groan: "I am not, I see, to escape God's detection of the impious and hideous crimes I have been guilty of. Unforeseen punishment threatens me for shedding the blood of my kin. And now, most impudent body of mine, how long will you retain a soul that, to appease the ghosts of my brother and my mother, ought to die? Why do I not resign everything at once? And why do I deliver my blood drop by drop to those whom I have so wickedly murdered?" With these words he died, having reigned one year.

He was called Philhellene, lover of the Greeks; had conferred many benefits on his country, and warred against Ituraea [in the Lebanon district], annexing a large portion of it to Judaea and compelling the inhabitants, if they would remain in that country, to be circumcised and to follow the Jewish laws. He was naturally a kind man and of great modesty, as Strabo bears witness in the name of [the historian] Timagenes [1st century B.C.], who says thus: "This man was a man of equity and very serviceable to the Jews, for he annexed another country to theirs, won part of the Ituraean nation for them, and secured the Ituraeans to them by the bond of circumcision." (Antt. XIII, 11:3.)

Emil Schürer assumes that northern Galilee was included in Aristobulus' conquests. Aristobulus' coins bear the inscription, "Judah the high priest and the congregation of the Jews."

ALEXANDER JANNAEUS (103-76 B.C.)

SALOME ALEXANDRA

At Aristobulus' death, his wife Salome, called Alexandra by the Greeks, freed his brothers from prison (Aristobulus having held them there, as I have already stated) and made Alexander Jannaeus, a man superior in age and moderation, king. He had been hated by his father [John Hyrcanus] from the moment of his birth, and was never permitted to come into his sight till he died. . . . (Antt. XIII, 12:1.)

THE SIEGE OF PTOLEMAIS—EGYPTIAN AID

On settling the government in the manner he judged best, Alexander Jannaeus made an expedition against Ptolemais [Acco]. After overcoming the men in battle, he enclosed them within the city, and encircling it, besieged them. For of the maritime cities only Ptolemais and Gaza remained to be conquered, besides Strato's Tower [the later Caesarea] and Dora, both held by the tyrant Zoilus. [The moment was propitious], for while Antiochus [VIII Grypus] Philometor [of Syria] and his brother Antiochus, called Cyzicenus, were warring against each other and destroying each other's armies, the people of Ptolemais could obtain no aid from them. . . .

Their only hope was help from the kings of Egypt and from Ptolemy Lathyrus, who now held Cyprus, whither he had fled when driven from the throne of Egypt by his mother Cleopatra [III]. They therefore sent envoys to the latter, pressing him to come as ally to deliver them from Alexander, since they now faced that danger. The envoys instilled the hope in Ptolemy that if he entered Syria, he would have the people of Gaza on the side of Ptolemais and that Zoilus, the Sidonians, and many others would assist him. Elated at this prospect, Ptolemy readied his fleet as quickly as possible. (Antt. XIII, 12:2.)

Alexander Jannaeus pretended to desire peace and a pact of friendship with Ptolemy, but secretly asked Cleopatra to march against the latter. Ptolemy, in taking revenge, invaded Judaea and massacred its inhabitants. (12:3-6.)

On seeing that her son had grown great, had laid Judaea waste with impunity, and held sway over Gaza, Cleopatra resolved to disregard his actions no longer; he was at her gates, and being much stronger than before, would probably want to rule Egypt. She therefore instantly marched against him with both naval and land forces, appointing Chelkias [Hilkiah] and Ananias [Hananiah],[4] the Jews, generals of her entire army, and sent her grandchildren, her testament, and the greater part of her riches to the people of Cos. She also ordered her son Alexander [Ptolemy IX] to sail with a great fleet to Phoenicia when that country revolted; she herself went to Ptolemais, which because the people of Ptolemais would not receive her, she besieged. But Ptolemy [VIII Soter (Lathyrus)] left Syria and hastened into Egypt, assuming that he would find it destitute of an army and would quickly take it. In this hope he failed. At this time Chelkias, one of Cleopatra's two generals, died in Coele-Syria while in pursuit of Ptolemy.

When Cleopatra heard of her son's attempt to capture Egypt and of the failure of his expedition, she sent part of her army there and drove him out. Returning from Egypt, Ptolemy spent the winter at Gaza. In the meantime, Cleopatra took both garrison and city of Ptolemais by siege. When, therefore, Alexander [Jannaeus] came to her, he gave her presents and accorded her the honors she deserved, since in the miseries he had endured from Ptolemy, she had been his only refuge.

At this time some of Cleopatra's friends urged her not to stay idle while so great a multitude of brave Jews were subject to one man, but to seize Alexander, overrun and take possession of his country. Ananias, however, counseled otherwise. She would commit an unjust deed, he said, if she deprived a man who was her ally of the authority that was his by right, and he a man related to them [the Jews]. "For," he continued, "I would not have you ignorant of this, that any injustice you inflict on him will make all us Jews your enemies." Cleopatra accepted Ananias' advice and did not harm Alexander, but entered into a pact of mutual assistance with him at Scythopolis in Coele-Syria. (Antt. XIII, 13:1-2.)

THE CONQUEST OF GAZA (CA. 100 B.C.)

Delivered from the fear of Ptolemy, Alexander at once made an expedition against Coele-Syria. He also took Gadara [east of the Jordan] after a siege of ten months, and Amathus, a very strong fortress of the people beyond the Jordan. . . . When Ptolemy withdrew from Gaza to Cyprus and his mother Cleopatra returned to Egypt, Alexander in his anger at the people of Gaza for having invited Ptolemy's aid, besieged their city and ravaged their country. But when Apollodotus, the general of Gaza's army, fell at night upon the camp of the Jews with two thousand mercenaries and ten thousand of his own forces, the men of Gaza prevailed as long as the night lasted, because their foes were tricked to believing that it was Ptolemy who attacked them. However, when day dawned and that mistake was corrected, the Jews, aware now of the truth, rallied, fell upon the men of Gaza, and slew some one thousand of them. Since, preferring any hardship to submission to the enemy, these men still stoutly resisted and could be made to yield neither by scarcity of provisions nor by the number of their slain, Aretas [II], king of the [Nabataean] Arabs, a most illustrious man, encouraged them by promising to come to their aid.

It happened, however, that before he came, Apollodotus was slain, murdered by his brother Lysimachus, who envied him his fame. Lysimachus then won over the army and delivered the city to Alexander. On first entering Gaza, Alexander was peaceful, but afterwards set his army upon the inhabitants and gave the city up to sack. So some of the soldiers went one way, some another, slaying the people of Gaza. These, however, did not behave cowardly, but fought those who came to slay them and slew as many Jews. Some, when they saw themselves deserted, burned their homes that the enemy might get none of their spoils; others with their own hands slew their children and wives, there being no other way of avoiding their enslavement. The five hundred councilmen took refuge in Apollo's temple, the attack having occured as they were in council;

still Alexander slew them. When he had completely razed the city, he returned to Jerusalem, having spent a year in the siege.[5] (Antt. XIII, 13:3.)

THE NATION AGAINST THE KING

As for Alexander, his own people were in revolt against him. When, at the festival then being celebrated, he stood at the altar and was going to sacrifice, they rose against him and pelted him with citrons, which were in their hands at the time, for at the feast of the Tabernacles the Jewish law requires everyone to carry palm branches and citrons. They also reviled him as being descended from captives, and therefore, unworthy of his dignity [as high priest] and of sacrificing.[6] At this he flew into a rage and slew some six thousand. . . .

He maintained mercenaries from Pisidia and Cilicia, since, being at war with them, he could not use the Syrians. He overcame the Arabs of Moab and Gilead, from whom he exacted tribute, and demolished Amathus. . . . But as he gave battle to Obadas [I], king of the [Nabataean] Arabs, he fell into ambush in a rugged and difficult region, was thrown by the hordes of camels into a deep valley . . . and barely escaped with his life.

From there he fled to Jerusalem, where because of his ill success, the people attacked him; he fought them for six years, slaying no less than fifty thousand men. When he begged the people to desist from their ill-will towards him, they hated him all the more because of this slaughter. When, therefore, he asked them what he ought to do, they cried in unison: "Die." Furthermore, they sent [envoys] to Demetrius [III] Akairos [a Syrian ruler] asking him to be their ally. (Antt. XIII, 13:5.)

It is assumed that the incident at the altar at Tabernacles is referred to in Mishnah Sukkah IV, 9 and

*Sukkah 48b, where "a certain Sadducee" priest is said
to have acted in contempt of the ritual, whereupon "all
the people pelted him with their citrons."*

*Demetrius and his army came, and together with the
forces of the Jewish national party, defeated Alexander Jannaeus, who was forced to flee to the mountains. (Antt. XIII, 14:1.)*

When Alexander fled to the mountains, six thousand
Jews mustered to him, moved by pity at the change of
his fortune. Alarmed, Demetrius withdrew. Later, the
Jews fought Alexander and were beaten and slain in
great numbers in several battles. The most powerful
of them . . . he brought to Jerusalem, inflicting a
most cruel punishment on them. As he feasted with
his concubines in sight of the entire city, he commanded some eight hundred of them to be crucified;
and while they were still alive had the throats of their
children and wives cut before their eyes. The deed, it
is true, was but reprisal for the injuries these men
had inflicted on him. Still, such punishment was in-
human, though he had undoubtedly suffered great distress from his wars with them, with both his life and
kingdom imperiled. For they had not been content to
fight alone, but had invited aliens too; had even, at
the end, reduced him to the necessity of restoring to
the king of the Arabs the lands of Moab and Gilead
he had subdued, and the cities in them, that they might
not join in the war against him. Ten thousand other
acts they committed that tended to affront and rebuke
him. Nonetheless, there was no need for such barbarity; and he was called Thrakidas [barbarian] by the
Jews for this extreme savagery. And the soldiers who
had fought against him, some eight thousand men, ran
away by night and stayed in exile until he died. While
he, freed from any further disturbance from them,
reigned thereafter in utmost tranquility. (Antt. XIII,
14:2.)

This tranquility did not extend to foreign relations.

Aretas III, king of the Nabataean Arabs, defeated the Syrian Antiochus XII and gained possession of Damascus. The victorious Arab then attacked Alexander Jannaeus who, to effect his withdrawal, was forced to come to terms with him. However, Alexander succeeded in extending his realm east of the Jordan; his conquests included the strong fortress of Gamala. When he returned home after three years in the field, he was joyfully received. (15:1-3.)

THE KING AT THE HEIGHT OF HIS POWER
AND HIS DECLINE

At this time the Jews held the following cities of Syria, Idumaea, and Phoenicia: at the seaside, Strato's Tower [the later Caesarea], Apollonia, Jaffa, Jamnia [Jabneh], Ashdod, Gaza, Anthedon, Raphia, and Rhinocorura; in the interior towards Idumaea, Adora, Marisa, the whole of Idumaea and Samaria, Mount Carmel, Mount Tabor, Scythopolis, and Gadara; in Gaulanitis, Seleucia and Gabala; in Moab, Heshbon, Medaba, Lemba, Oronas, Gelithon, Zoar, the Valley of the Cilicians, and Pella (the last they had demolished, because its inhabitants would not accept the religious rites of the Jews); and other large cities of Syria, which were destroyed.

Alexander, though now ill from hard drinking, and for three years troubled by a quartan fever, would not refrain from going out with his army, until, worn out from the rigors of his life, he died on the borders of the Gerasenes while besieging Ragaba, a fortress beyond the Jordan.

When his queen [Salome Alexandra] saw that he was ready to die and no longer had any hope of surviving, she came to him weeping and lamenting, and bewailed the desolate state she and her sons would be left in. "To whom," she said, "do you leave me and my children, who are destitute of all other support, especially when you know how great is the nation's ill-will towards you!" He then counseled her as follows, in order for her to retain the kingdom securely with her children: to conceal his death from the soldiers until she took the fortress Ragaba; then to go in triumph, as befits a victory, to Jerusalem and put some of her authority into the hands of the Pharisees, for they would commend her for the honor she did them and would reconcile the nation to her, for they wielded great power among the Jews, both to hurt those they hated and to help those to whom they were friendly, since they were most often believed when they spoke ill of others, even when they spoke thus only out of envy. He also said that he had incurred the displeasure of the nation because he had indeed injured those men [the Pharisees]. "When therefore," he continued, "you come to Jerusalem, send for the leading men among them, show them my dead body, and with appearance of sincerity, grant them leave to use it as they please, whether in retaliation for having suffered greatly at my hands, they dishonor the body by refusing it burial, or whether in their anger they inflict some other indignity on that body. Promise them also that you will administer nothing in the affairs of the kingdom without them. If you so address them, I shall have the honor of a more glorious funeral from them than you could give me; for if it is in their power to abuse my dead body, they will inflict no injury on it whatsoever, and you will rule in safety." Then he died, having reigned twenty-seven years, at the age of forty-nine. (Antt. XIII, 15:4-5.)

On the king's advice to his wife regarding the Pharisees, comp. the talmudic note: "King Yannai [Jannaeus] said to his wife, 'Fear neither the Pharisees nor the non-Pharisees but the hypocrites who pretend to be Pharisees.' (Sotah 22b). Of his coins, those bearing the bilingual inscription "Jonathan the King" (in Hebrew), "King Alexander" (in Greek) are of particular interest.

SALOME ALEXANDRA (76-67 B.C.)

A NEW ERA

Alexandra, after taking the fortress [Ragaba], did as her husband had counseled. She spoke to the Pharisees and put everything into their hands, in regard to both the dead body and the affairs of the kingdom. By so doing she appeased their anger against Alexander and gained their good will and friendship towards him. They in turn went among the people and made speeches, extolling Alexander's deeds and proclaiming that they had lost a just king. Their commendation moved the people to grieve and mourn, so that he had a funeral more splendid than had any king before him.

Alexander left two sons, Hyrcanus and Aristobulus, but committed the kingdom to [Salome] Alexandra. As for the two sons, Hyrcanus was indeed unfit to manage public affairs and preferred a quiet life; but the younger, Aristobulus, was active and bold. Alexandra herself was loved by the people, because she seemed displeased with the offenses her husband had been guilty of.

She made Hyrcanus high priest because he was the elder, but mainly because of his unwillingness to participate in affairs of state. She let the Pharisees do whatever they wanted, ordered the people to be obedient to them, and restored the ancestral practices that the Pharisees had introduced and that her father-in-law, [John] Hyrcanus, had abrogated. She had, it is true, the name of queen, but the Pharisees had the authority. They recalled exiles and set prisoners at liberty; in a word, they differed in nothing from lords of the realm. Nevertheless, the queen also attended to the affairs of the realm. She recruited a large body of mercenaries and so greatly increased her own army that she struck terror into the neighboring tyrants and received hostages from them. And the country was wholly at peace, except for the Pharisees. . . . (Antt. XIII, 16:1-2.)

"While she governed others, the Pharisees governed her" (War I, 5:2). They brought about the execution of the men who had urged Alexander Jannaeus to put the eight hundred rebels to death (Antt. XIII, 14:2). The Jerusalem aristocracy, led by Salome Alexandra's son Aristobulus, felt imperiled by the favor shown the Pharisees, and indicating that the Nabataean king Aretas III would welcome their services, appealed to the queen for protection. She was obliged to grant it. Toward the end of her reign, Tigranes, king of Armenia, invaded Syria and prepared to attack Judaea. Valuable gifts from the queen (and the intervention of Rome) averted the invasion (16:2-4).

ARISTOBULUS' ATTEMPT TO SEIZE POWER

Alexandra being taken ill, Aristobulus, her younger son, seized the opportunity. With the aid of his numerous servants, who, because of his spirited nature, were all warmly attached to him, he seized all the fortresses. Assembling an army of mercenaries with the money he found there, he then proclaimed himself king. His mother, moved by Hyrcanus' complaints about this state of affairs, imprisoned Aristobulus' wife and sons in the [fortress] Antonia. . . . But before she could chastise Aristobulus for the seizure of his brother's inheritance, she died, having administered the government nine years. (War I, 5:4.)

THE CHARACTER OF ALEXANDRA

Alexandra was a woman who showed none of the weakness of her sex. Most sagacious in her ambition to rule, she demonstrated by her actions her practical genius. . . . She preferred the present to the future and ranked power above everything. When that was at stake she had no regard for what was good or right. Because of her bent for interfering in spheres not appropriate to a woman, and by concurring in the opinions of those who bore ill will to her family and leaving the administration devoid of proper support, she in the end brought the affairs of her house to such an unfortunate state that she was the cause of its losing, at no distant date, the power that she had won for it by so much toil and danger. Indeed, her administration while she was still alive filled the palace after her death with calamities and confusion. Nevertheless, though such had been her way of reigning, she had preserved the nation at peace. . . . (Antt. XIII, 16:6.)

The Talmud tells that in the time of Salome Alexandra and her brother Simeon, son of Shetah, a leading Pharisee, "rain fell on the eve of Wednesdays and the Sabbaths so that the corns of wheat were as large as kidneys, the barley corns as large as the stones of olives, and lentils like golden denarii; they gathered such corns and stored them in order to show future generations the ill effects of sin" (Taanith 23a).

THE BROTHERS HYRCANUS II AND ARISTOBULUS II (67-63 B.C.)

Hyrcanus, although heir to the throne and although his mother even in her lifetime had committed the kingdom to him, was, in vigor and intelligence, surpassed by Aristobulus. A battle for the supreme power took place near Jericho. There a large body of troops deserted Hyrcanus for Aristobulus. Hyrcanus, with those who still adhered to him, retreated, took refuge in the [fortress] Antonia, and held the wife and children of Aristobulus as hostages for his safety. However before any irreparable mischief had occurred, the brothers agreed that Aristobulus was to be king and Hyrcanus, abdicating the throne, was to retain all his other dignities as brother of the king. The reconciliation on these terms took place in the Temple. Cordially embracing each other in the presence of the surrounding multitude, the brothers exchanged residences, Aristobulus proceeding to the palace, Hyrcanus to the house of Aristobulus. (War I, 6:1.)

During his mother's reign, Hyrcanus held the office of high priest.

ANTIPATER THE IDUMAEAN

But there was a certain friend of Hyrcanus, an Idumaean called Antipater, who, being very rich and by nature an active and seditious man, was at enmity with Aristobulus and had differences with him because of his [Antipater's] good will towards Hyrcanus. It is true that Nicolas of Damascus says that Antipater was of the stock of the leading Jews who came out of Babylon into Judaea. But that assertion of his was made to gratify Antipater's son Herod, who through certain revolutions of fortune became afterwards king of the Jews. . . .

This Antipater was suspicious of Aristobulus' power and feared harm from the latter's hatred for him. He therefore secretly incited the most powerful of the Jews against him, protesting the unjustness of Aristobulus' conduct in wrongfully obtaining the throne and ejecting his brother, who as the elder, should have kept what was his by right of birth. And he similarly incited Hyrcanus . . . telling him that Aristobulus' friends perpetually counseled him to kill Hyrcanus in order to assure retention of his power. A gentle man who did not readily listen to calumny, Hyrcanus gave no credence to these words. This temperament of his, indisposing him to meddling in public affairs, and his want of spirit made him appear degenerate and unmanly. Aristobulus, on the other hand, was of opposite temper, an active man and wide-awake. (Antt. XIV, 1:3.)

Antipater secured for Hyrcanus the alliance of the Nabataean king Aretas III in the fight for the throne of Jerusalem. Hyrcanus promised that, once victor-

*ious, he would restore to Aretas the twelve frontier
cities Alexander Jannaeus had wrested from the Arabs.
(1:4.)*

THE FIGHT BETWEEN THE BROTHERS
AND THE PRAYER OF THE HASID ONIAS
(APRIL 65 B.C.)

After Aretas obtained these promises, he marched
against Aristobulus with an army of fifty thousand
horse and foot soldiers, and defeated him in battle. So
many then deserted to Hyrcanus that Aristobulus was
left alone and fled to Jerusalem. The Arab king pursued with his army, assaulted the Temple, and besieged
Aristobulus. The people, supporting Hyrcanus, aided
in the siege, and only the priests stayed with Aristobulus. Aretas combined the Arab and Jewish forces
and pressed the siege vigorously. Since this took place
in the season of the feast of unleavened bread, which
we call the Passover, the leading Jews left the country
and fled into Egypt.

There lived at the time one Onias, a righteous man
and beloved of God, who once during a drought had
prayed to God to put an end to the intense heat and
whose prayers God heard, and sent rain. This Onias
was in hiding because he foresaw a civil strife of long
duration. But he was found and brought to the camp
of the Jews, who desired that as once he had put an
end to the drought by his prayers, he should now in
like manner put a curse on Aristobulus and his adherents.

When, despite his refusal and excuses, he was forced
to speak, he stood up in the midst of the multitude and
said: "O God, King of the whole world, since these
that stand now with me are Thy people, and those that
are besieged are also Thy priests, I beseech Thee that
Thou wilt neither hearken to the prayers of those
against these nor bring to effect what these pray for
against those." No sooner had he made this prayer

than he was stoned to death by the wicked among the Jews who surrounded him. (Antt. XIV, 2:1.)

The talmudic tradition (Mishnah Taanith III, 8) preserves the childlike prayers of the pious Onias (or Honi, called the "circle-drawer" because he prayed standing in a magic circle). The murder of Onias, says Josephus, was soon punished by a violent storm "which destroyed the fruits of the entire country" (Antt. XIV, 2:2). The struggle between the brothers is referred to in a talmudic story (Sotah 49b). Aristobulus (first favored by Scaurus, Pompey's general) and Hyrcanus brought their dispute before Pompey, who was engaged in his campaign in Asia. He had subdued Mithridates, king of Pontus, and Tigranes, king of Armenia, and after defeating various princes in the Lebanon came, in spring 63, to Damascus (Antt. XIV, 2:3-3:2).

THE INTERVENTION OF ROME

POMPEY AND THE END OF JUDAEAN INDEPENDENCE (63 B.C.)

Pompey [was in Damascus when he] heard the case of the Jews; their leaders, Hyrcanus and Aristobulus, who were fighting each other; and the people who because they did not wish to be ruled by a king, opposed both of them. The government bequeathed from their forefathers, they argued, was one of submission to the priests of the God they worshipped; but Hyrcanus and Aristobulus, though descendants of priests, wished to change that government in order to enslave them.

Hyrcanus complained that, though he was the elder brother, he had been deprived of the prerogative of his birth by Aristobulus and ruled but a small portion of the country, Aristobulus having wrested the remainder from him by force. He also held Aristobulus responsible for the sorties that had been made into the neighboring countries and for the piracies at sea,

and said further that his nation would not have revolted were not Aristobulus a man of violence and
disorder. A thousand Jews of the highest rank confirmed this accusation—a confirmation procured by
Antipater.

But Aristobulus contended that Hyrcanus' own temperament . . . was the cause of his losing the throne.
As for himself, he was forced to take over the government for fear lest it be transferred to others. And as
for his title [king], it was but that of his father. He,
too produced witnesses—some men who were both
young and insolent, and whose purple garments, fine
heads of hair, and other adornments were detested by
the court. So clad, they did not look like men come to
plead their cause in a court of justice, but like march-
ers in some pompous procession.

Having heard the two [rivals], Pompey condemned
Aristobulus for his violent conduct. He then spoke
civilly to both and sent them away, saying that he
would settle all their affairs when, after he looked over
the affairs of the Nabataeans, he returned to their
country. (Antt. XIV, 3:2-3.)

*Although Aristobulus promised to admit the Romans
into Jerusalem, he denied entry to Pompey's general
Gabinius; for this he was imprisoned. Hyrcanus' men
then opened the gates of the city and admitted Pompey's army. But Aristobulus' faction, concentrated in
the strongly fortified Temple mount, was determined
to resist. (3:3-4:2.)*

Pompey pitched his camp on the north side of the
Temple, where it was easiest to strike. But even on that
side stood great towers; a ditch had been dug, and a
deep valley surrounded it. There were precipices on the
city side, and the bridge through which Pompey came
was broken. However, with materials gathered from
the vicinity, the Romans, day by day and after much
toil, raised a bank. When this bank was sufficiently
high and the ditch filled up, though but poorly because

of its immense depth, Pompey brought his siege engines and battering rams from Tyre, placed them on the bank, and battered the Temple with stones. But had it not been our ancient practice to rest on the seventh day, this bank could never have been completed because of the battle the Jews would have put up; for though our law permits us to defend ourselves on that day against attacks and assaults, it does not permit us to fight against an enemy while he's engaged in other labors.

On becoming aware of this, the Romans shot no missiles at the Jews on the days that we call the Sabbaths, nor did they engage in pitched battles with them, but raised instead their earthen banks and focused their engines for battle on the following days. How great is our piety towards God and the observance of His laws can be learned from the fact that fear, throughout the siege, did not keep the priests from their sacred ministrations. Twice a day, in the morning and around the ninth hour [3 P.M.], they offered their sacrifices on the altar; not even when some grave accident befell them from the stones thrown at them did they neglect these sacrifices. Nor, though the city was taken in the third month [of the siege] . . . and the enemy fell upon the Jews and cut the throats of those who were in the Temple, could the men offering the sacrifices be forced to run away, either by fear for their lives or by the numbers already slain. They preferred to suffer whatever was to be inflicted upon them at their very altars rather than neglect anything that their laws required them to do. . . .

When the battering engine was brought close, the largest of the towers was shaken, and fell, crushing part of the fortifications; so the enemy poured in. . . . Now all was slaughter, some of the Jews being killed by the Romans, some by each other. Others, unable to endure their miseries, threw themselves down precipices or set fire to their houses and burned them.

Twelve thousand Jews fell in the holocaust, but only a few Romans. . . .

Great sacrileges were committed in the Temple, which in former ages had been inaccessible, and seen by none. Pompey and many of his men entered it and gazed upon what was unlawful for any other men but the high priests to see. In the Temple were the golden table, the sacred candlestick, the pouring vessels, a great quantity of spices, and among the treasures, two thousand talents of sacred money. Yet Pompey because of his high esteem for religion touched none of these; in this he acted in a manner worthy of his virtues.

The following day he ordered the men in charge of the Temple to cleanse it and to bring what offerings the law required. He restored the high priesthood to Hyrcanus, both because the latter had been useful to him in other respects and because he had kept the Jews within the country from aiding Aristobulus in this war. The initiators of the war Pompey beheaded. . . . He made Jerusalem tributary to the Romans, took away the cities of Coele-Syria that Judaea had subdued [7] and put them under a Roman governor, and confined the whole nation, which had raised itself so high, within its own limits. . . .

Non-Jewish cities conquered by the Hasmonaeans, Pompey joined to the newly formed Roman province of Syria.

Hyrcanus and Aristobulus, who had revolted against each other, are to be blamed for the misery that now afflicted Jerusalem. We lost our freedom, became subject to the Romans, and were deprived of the territory we had won from the Syrians by our arms and compelled to restore it to them. Moreover, the Romans exacted of us, within a short period, over ten thousand talents. And the royal authority, formerly bestowed on those who were high priests by right of birth, became the property of common men. . . .

Pompey committed Coele-Syria as far as the river

Euphrates and Egypt, to Scaurus and two Roman legions, then went to Cilicia, and hastened to Rome. He carried with him, bound, Aristobulus and his children—two daughters and as many sons. The older son, Alexander, escaped, but the younger, Antigonus, was brought to Rome together with his sisters. (Antt. XIV, 4:2-5.)

In the Roman triumph of 61 B.C., Aristobulus, scion of the Maccabean rebels, marched in front of Pompey's chariot. The prisoners of war, later freed, whom Pompey brought to Rome became the nucleus of the still extant Jewish community of Rome (Philo, Embassy to Gaius, 23). Aristobulus' son Alexander, who had escaped Pompey, tried, in 57 B.C., to organize resistance to the new overlords in Judaea; but the new Roman governor of Syria, Gabinius, defeated him. On the other hand, Gabinius gave orders to rebuild the demolished cities in Judaea (Antt. XIV, 5:2-4).

THE ADMINISTRATION OF JUDAEA

Gabinius, a follower of Pompey and an oppressive administrator, came to Syria in 57 B.C. One of his tasks was the reorganization of Judaea.

[Gabinius] . . . brought Hyrcanus to Jerusalem and committed the care of the Temple to him. He ordained five councils [synhedria] and divided the nation into the same number of parts. These councils governed the people; the first was in Jerusalem, the second in Gadara, the third in Amathus [east of the Jordan], the fourth in Jericho, and the fifth at Sepphoris in Galilee. So the Jews were freed from monarchic authority and governed by a [priestly] aristocracy. (Antt. XIV, 5:4.)

In 56 B.C., Aristobulus and his son Antigonus escaped from Rome to start a new revolt in Judaea; many joined him "because of his former glory." But although the Jews "fought valiantly and with alacrity, they were overborne by the enemy." For a second time

Aristobulus was sent to Rome and kept in chains; his children were released by order of the Senate and returned to Judaea. Later, his son Alexander rose in another rebellion against Rome and again suffered defeat at the hands of Gabinius (XIV, 6).

In 54 B.C., Gabinius was replaced by the triumvir Crassus as proconsul of Syria. The latter had risen high, as Plutarch says, "by fires, wars and public calamities." He is remembered for looting the treasures of the Jerusalem sanctuary, an act that heightened Jewish detestation of Roman rule (7:1). At this point Josephus appends a section on the material status of the Jews outside Judaea.

THE JEWS OUTSIDE JUDAEA

Let no one wonder at the great wealth in our Temple, since from antiquity the Jews throughout the habitable earth, as well as those [semiproselytes] who worshipped God, those even who resided in Asia and Europe, sent their contributions to it. . . . Many witnesses attest to this, and particularly Strabo of Cappadocia, who says: "Mithridates [VI Eupator] sent to Cos and took the money that Queen Cleopatra [III of Egypt] had deposited there [102 B.C.], as well as eight hundred talents belonging to the Jews." Now we have no public money but only what is God's; it is therefore evident that the Asian Jews removed this money from fear of Mithridates, for it is not likely that the Judaeans, who had a strong city and Temple, would send their money to Cos; it is just as unlikely that the Jews of Alexandria would do so, since they did not fear Mithridates. Strabo himself bears witness to the same fact in another place; where he states that Sulla as he passed into Greece to fight Mithridates, sent Lucullus [87 B.C.] to put an end to a revolt of our nation in Cyrene, he notes that the habitable earth was filled with Jews. This is what he says: "There were four classes of men in Cyrene: citizens, husbandmen,

strangers [metics], and Jews. The Jews have penetrated into all cities, and it is difficult to find a place
on the habitable earth that has not admitted this tribe
of men and is not occupied by it. And it has come to
pass that Egypt and Cyrene, who have the same
[Ptolemaic] governors—and many other nations too
—imitate their mode of life, maintain great bodies of
these Jews, grow to greater prosperity with them, and
observe their laws as well. In Egypt the Jews are
assigned special sections to live in. These are in addition to what is allotted to them at Alexandria, that
allotment constituting a large part of that city. There
is also an ethnarch allowed them, who governs the
people, administers justice, and takes care of contracts, as if he were the ruler of a free republic. In
Egypt, therefore, this nation is powerful because the
Jews were originally Egyptians and because the land
they have inhabited since they left that country is
close to Egypt. They also settled in Cyrene, because,
like Judaea, this land adjoined the realm of Egypt, or
rather, was formerly under the same government."
This is what Strabo says. (Antt. XIV, 7:2.)

THE POWER OF ANTIPATER

*Crassus, a member, with Pompey and Julius Caesar,
of the First Triumvirate (60 B.C.), was awarded the
province of Syria. He perished during the Parthian
campaign (53), whereupon the Judaeans rose under
Peitholaus, "who continued the revolt led by Aristobulus." Cassius, who succeeded Crassus in the procon-
sulship, captured the rebel and slew him. The power
behind the Roman activities was—Antipater.*

Antipater . . . was at that time in great repute
with the Idumaeans also. Out of that nation he married a wife, the daughter of one of their eminent Arab
men, named Cypros. By her he had four sons, Phasael,
Herod, who was afterwards made king [of the Jews],
Joseph, and Pheroras; and a daughter, named Salome.

Antipater cultivated friendly relations with other potentates, especially with the king of the [Nabataean] Arabs [Aretas]. . . . (Antt. XIV, 7:3.)

CAESAR AND THE JEWS

In 49 B.C. Caesar crossed the Rubicon, the limit of his province, and the Roman civil war began. In this period "the whole Roman history was reflected in the history of Syria and also in that of Palestine" (Emil Schürer). Caesar freed Aristobulus that he might fight in his behalf in Syria; but Pompey's partisans poisoned him and beheaded his son Alexander in Antioch. However, upon Pompey's defeat (at Pharsalus, 48 B.C.), Hyrcanus and Antipater, who formerly supported Pompey, changed sides and strengthened Caesar's position in the East. Antipater aided Caesar in his Egyptian campaign (48-47 B.C.) and won the Jews in Egypt to Caesar's side. Later, a grateful Caesar bestowed on Antipater the rare privilege of a Roman citizen with freedom from taxes, and made him an object of admiration by such honors and marks of friendship (Antt. XIV, 7:4-8:3; War I, 9:5). (It was during this Egyptian campaign that young queen Cleopatra fell in love with Caesar.)

ANTIGONUS MAKES CLAIMS FOR THE LEADERSHIP OF JUDAEA

At this time Antigonus, the son of Aristobulus, came to Caesar and lamented his father's fate. He complained that Aristobulus had been poisoned and his [Antigonus'] brother beheaded because of Caesar . . . and asked the latter to take pity on him who had been cast out of his principality. He also accused Hyrcanus and Antipater of governing the nation by violence and acting lawlessly towards him. (Antt. XIV, 8:4.)

On hearing this, Antipater [who was present] stripped his garment and exposed his numberless scars. Concerning his loyalty to Caesar, there was, he said, little need of words; his body, even were he silent, would proclaim it aloud. He marveled at the temerity of Antigonus. The son of an enemy of Rome and of a fugitive from its jurisdiction, and by inheritance an inciter of rebellion and sedition, dared to accuse others to the Roman governor and ask for favors when he should be grateful to remain alive! Nor was it out of indigence that he coveted the government [of Judaea], but out of desire to incite rebellion among the Jews and to take advantage of what he had gained from the Romans to do them harm. (War I, 10:2.)

[Having heard these conflicting claims] Caesar appointed Hyrcanus high priest, and offered Antipater whatever power he himself should choose. The latter left the final decision to Caesar, who appointed him procurator of Judaea. He also granted Hyrcanus' request to restore the walls of his city [Jerusalem], which had been demolished by Pompey, and sent the following edict to the consuls in Rome, to be engraved in the Capitol. . . .

Josephus quotes a Roman decree of friendship with Judaea.

Because he had on many occasions been useful to them, the people of Athens also honored Hyrcanus. They sent him the following decree: ". . . Whereas Hyrcanus, son of Alexander, high priest and ethnarch of the Jews, continues to bear good will to our people as a whole and to each of our citizens individually, and treats them with all manner of kindness; and whereas any Athenians come to him, either as ambassadors or on some private errand he receives them cordially and insures their safe conduct home—as has been testified on several occasions—it is now decreed . . . to honor him with a crown of gold, the customary reward decreed by the law, to erect his statue in brass in the temple of Demos and the Graces, and to publicly proclaim this gift of a crown in the theater at the Dionysian shows, as the new tragedies are being presented, as well as at the Panathenaean, Eleusinian, and gymnastic shows. It is further decreed that, as long as he continues his friendship and preserves his good will towards us, the commanders should take care to requite his affection and generosity with all possible honor and favor, that it may be demonstrated by this treatment how kindly our people receive the good and how they repay them with commensurate rewards, and that he may be impelled to continue in his affection towards us by the honors we have bestowed on him. Let ambassadors be chosen out of all the Athenians to carry this decree to him and petition him to accept the honors we bestow on him and to strive always to do good to our city." . . . (Antt. XIV, 8:5.)

ANTIPATER AND HIS SONS—HEZEKIAH AND THE JUDAEAN REBELS

After settling the affairs of Syria, Caesar sailed away, while Antipater, as soon as he had conducted Caesar out of Syria, returned to Judaea. There he at once raised the wall that had been demolished by Pompey, and by both threats and counsel, allayed the turbulence that had been raging in that country. He promised the people that if they sided with Hyrcanus, they would live happily and undisturbed in the enjoyment of their possessions; but that if they harbored hopes of revolt, and aimed to profit thereby, they would find in him a severe master instead of a gentle governor, in Hyrcanus a tyrant instead of a king, and in the Romans and Caesar bitter enemies instead of rulers. For the latter would never tolerate the overthrow of the man they had appointed to govern. Having said this, Antipater settled the affairs of this country.

Because Hyrcanus was of a slow and slothful temperament, Antipater appointed Phasael, his own eldest son, governor of Jerusalem and surrounding places, but committed Galilee to Herod, his next son, who was then a very young man of [some twenty five] years.[8] Herod's youth, however, was no impediment to him; a man of great intelligence, he quickly found an opportunity to demonstrate his valor. A certain Hezekiah, leader of a band of brigands, overran the neighboring parts of Syria with a large troop. Herod captured and slew him, as well as many of his brigands. This deed won him the love of the Syrians; for they had longed to free their country from these brigands, and he had so freed it for them. They sang songs in his honor in their villages and cities, lauding him for having brought them peace and the secure enjoyment of their possessions. . . .

Phasael, Herod's brother, envying his fame, was moved to emulate his actions and grew ambitious to equal him in winning similar esteem; so he made the inhabitants of Jerusalem bear him the greatest good will. Though he alone ruled the city, he neither abused his authority nor managed its affairs improperly. Because of this conduct the nation accorded to Antipater the respect due to kings and the esteem given to absolute lords. Such glory did not, as frequently happens, diminish in the least his good will and loyalty to Hyrcanus. (Antt. XIV, 9:1-2.)

KING HEROD
THE GREAT

HEROD'S BEGINNINGS

THE TRIAL BEFORE THE JERUSALEM SYNHEDRION

But when the leading Jews saw Antipater and his
sons grow so greatly in the nation's good graces and
in the revenues they received from Judaea and from
Hyrcanus' personal wealth, they became ill disposed towards him . . . These Jews [also] feared Herod, because they recognized in him a bold and violent man
with tyrannical inclinations. They came to Hyrcanus
and accused Antipater openly, saying: "How long will
you stay quiet in the light of such deeds? Don't you
see that Antipater and his sons have already taken
over the government and that you have only the name
of king? [9]. . . . Herod, Antipater's son, has slain
Hezekiah and his followers, thus transgressing our
law, which forbids the slaying of any man, even an
evil one, unless he has first been sentenced to death
by the Synhedrion.[10] Yet he has been so insolent as to
do this, and without authority from you."

Hyrcanus lent ear to their complaints. The mothers
of Herod's victims also incited his indignation; each
day, in the Temple, they implored him and the people
to try Herod before the Synhedrion for what he had
done. Moved by these pleas, Hyrcanus summoned
Herod to trial on the charges against him. Herod
obeyed, but came, as his father had persuaded him to,

not as a private citizen, but with a guard, for the security of his person. . . .

But Sextus Caesar,[11] governor of Syria, wrote to Hyrcanus, threatening reprisals if he did not clear Herod and dismiss him at his trial. This epistle gave Hyrcanus an excuse to rescue Herod, whom he loved as his own son, from suffering any harm from the Synhedrion. However, when Herod appeared before the Synhedrion with his body of men, he frightened everyone, and not one of his accusers dared bring charges against him; there was instead deep silence, and no one knew what to do.

At this point, one Sameas,[12] a righteous man and therefore above all fear, rose and said, "O you that are judges with me and you who are our king, never have I known such a case, nor do I think that any one of you can name its parallel, wherein one called to be tried by us appeared in such a manner before us. Whoever comes to be tried by this Synhedrion presents himself in a submissive manner and like one in fear of himself, endeavoring to move us to compassion with disheveled hair and black and mourning garment. But this admirable man Herod, who is accused of murder and called to answer so heavy an accusation, stands here clothed in purple, with the hair of his head finely trimmed, and with his armed men about him so that if we condemn him by our law he may slay us, and by being too strong for justice, escape death. Yet I do not blame Herod for being more concerned for himself than for the laws; I blame you and the king, who give him license to do so. However, know that God is great, and this man whom you are going to absolve and dismiss, for the sake of Hyrcanus, will one day chastise both you and the king."

Sameas was not mistaken in this prediction. When Herod obtained the kingdom he slew all the members of this Synhedrion, and Hyrcanus also. He excepted only

Sameas, because he honored him greatly for his righteousness and because when Jerusalem was later besieged by Herod and Sosius, Sameas persuaded the
people to admit Herod by telling them that for their
sins they would not be able to escape him. . . .

When Hyrcanus saw that the Synhedrion was ready
to pronounce sentence of death upon Herod, he put off
the trial to another day, and secretly warned him to
flee from the city, for by this means he might escape
danger. Herod retired to Damascus, as if fleeing from
the king. After seeing Sextus Caesar and securing
his affairs, he resolved not to obey if he were again
summoned before the Synhedrion. The members of
the Synhedrion were greatly aroused by this and tried
to convince Hyrcanus that Herod's actions were directed against him. Hyrcanus was not ignorant of
this, but he was so unmanly by nature and so foolish
that he was incapable of doing anything about it.
When Sextus made Herod governor of Coele-Syria
[and Samaria], having sold him that post for money,
Hyrcanus feared that Herod would make war against
him. What he feared was not long in coming. Angry
at the trial he had been summoned to undergo before
the Synhedrion, Herod came with an army.

However, his father, Antipater, and his brother
[Phasael] met him and stopped him from assaulting
Jerusalem. They appeased his vehement temper and
persuaded him to commit no overt action, but only to
threaten and to proceed no further against the man
who had given him the stature he had . . .

They asked him to consider that since it is God who
turns the scales of war, there is great uncertainty in
the issue of battles and that, therefore, he could not
be sure of victory when fighting one who was both his
king and the man who had supported him and conferred many benefits upon him. . . .

Herod was convinced by these arguments and be-

lieved that it was sufficient for his future hopes to
have made a show of his strength before the nation. . . . (Antt. XIV, 9:3-5.)

*Here Josephus appends a series of Roman letters
and declarations of friendship and leagues of mutual
assistance with the Jewish nation, "that all the rest of
mankind may know the regard the kings of Asia and
Europe had for us, and that they were abundantly
satisfied as to our courage and loyalty." He concludes
the quotations by pointing to these epistles as "evident
marks of our former friendship with the Romans."
Especially important is Caesar's decree restoring to
Judaea the harbor city of Jaffa (taken away by Pompey). Caesar also conferred Roman citizenship on the
Jews of Alexandria, and assured freedom of religion
to the Jews of Asia Minor (XIV, 10).*

*After the assassination of Caesar on the Ides of
March 44, the conspirators went East, and Cassius
Longinus (one of them) became master of Syria;
Antipater and Herod aided him in raising the heavy
tribute imposed on the country. For his services Herod
received from Cassius confirmation of his appointment
as governor (strategos) of Coele-Syria and a promise
of the royal title after the war with Antony and
Octavian was over. Around 43 B.C., Antipater became
the victim of a plot instigated by a certain Malichus
who aspired to Antipater's position. Herod, authorized
by Cassius, quickly avenged his father's death (XIV,
11:2-6).*

HEROD'S FAMILY

Through espousal with a descendant of the House of
Hyrcanus, Herod established affinity with that family.
For this reason Herod took the greater care of him.
He was about to marry the daughter of Aristobulus'
son Alexander and granddaughter of Hyrcanus, by
whom he eventually became the father of three sons

and two daughters. He also had a previous wife, from a lower family of his own nation, whose name was Doris and who bore him his eldest son, Antipater. (Antt. XIV, 12:1.)

MARK ANTONY AND HEROD

After the assassination of Caesar, Mark Antony obtained control of Roman affairs. With Lepidus and Octavian he formed the Second Triumvirate, with the aim of establishing a state. The decisive battle at Philippi, Macedonia, in 42 B.C., between Antony and Octavian on one side and Cassius and Brutus on the other ended with the victory of the first. Now that Antony was master of Asia, Hyrcanus, Herod, and Phasael, former supporters of Cassius, were in a critical position.

Antony and Caesar [Octavian] defeated Cassius near Philippi, as others have related. After the victory Caesar [Octavian] went into Italy, and Antony marched for Asia. When he arrived at Bithynia, he was met by ambassadors from everywhere. The leading Jews came also [41 B.C.], to bring charges against Phasael and Herod. Though on the surface, they complained, Hyrcanus seemed to reign, in reality these two men had all the power. Antony, however, paid great respect to Herod, who came to defend himself against his accusers. His adversaries could not obtain as much as a hearing, a favor Herod obtained from Antony by money. Nevertheless, when Antony came to Ephesus, the high priest Hyrcanus and our nation sent an embassy to him. This embassy brought him a crown of gold and requested him to write to the governors of the provinces to set free those Jews who, though they had not fought against him, had been made captive by Cassius and to restore to them the land that had been taken from them in the days of Cassius. Antony considered these requests just and

at once wrote to Hyrcanus and the Jews [to this ef-
fect] and sent a similar decree to the Tyrians. (Antt.
XIV, 12:2.)

*Josephus quotes Antony's letters to Hyrcanus and
to the magistrates and people of Tyre concerning Jewish rights, as proofs "of the fact that the Romans had
great concern for our nation" (12:3-6.)*

*After Caesar's death, Cleopatra [VII] returned to
Egypt. In 41 B.C., Antony ordered her to meet him in
Tarsus, Cilicia; she was under suspicion of having
supported Cassius.*

When . . . Antony came to Syria, Cleopatra met
him in Cilicia and caused him to fall in love with her.
One hundred of the most representative Jews once
more[13] came to level charges against Herod and his
retinue, with the charges entrusted to the most elo-
quent among them. But in the presence of Hyrcanus,
who was already Herod's father-in-law, Messala [a
Roman statesman] impugned their assertions against
the young men. After hearing both sides at Daphne
[near Antioch], Antony asked Hyrcanus who were the
best rulers of the nation. "Herod and his friends,"
said Hyrcanus. Whereupon Antony, influenced by the
affectionate friendship he had established with Herod's
father [Antipater] when he was with Gabinius,[14] appointed both Herod and Phasael tetrarchs and entrusted the public affairs of the Jews to them, writing
letters to that effect. He also bound fifteen of their
foes and would have killed them had not Herod obtained their pardon. (Antt. XIV, 13:1.)

*The Jewish envoys who "were for making revolu-
tions" were punished by order of Antony, who wanted
to secure Herod's authority. (13:2.)*

THE INVASION OF THE PARTHIANS (40 B.C.)
—KING ANTIGONUS

*While Antony enjoyed his affair with Cleopatra, or
was busy with Italian politics, the Parthians invaded*

Syria; they were supported by Antigonus, who in turn, was aided by them in his aspirations of winning the throne of Jerusalem and freeing Judaea from the Romans and from Herod. The citizens of Jerusalem favored Antigonus the Hasmonaean. Hyrcanus and Phasael fell into the hands of the Parthians; Phasael committed suicide (by smashing his head against the wall); Hyrcanus was exiled to Babylon, after his ears were mutilated to prevent his reassumption of the priestly office. Herod brought his family to the fortress of Masada (after the Nabataean king Malchus I refused to give him protection) and went to Rome. Cleopatra, by the way, made an unsuccessful attempt to detain Herod in her service. From 40 to 37 B.C., Antigonus (his Hebrew name was Mattathiah) was king and high priest of the Jews, the last Hasmonaean to hold this office. His patrons, the Parthians, "plundered all Jerusalem and the palace," but a "great deal of Herod's money escaped" (Antt. XIV, 13:3-14:2).

HEROD MADE KING OF JUDAEA

Herod appeared in Rome in 40 B.C., after the agreement at Brundisium between Octavian and Antony by which the latter was awarded the Eastern provinces and married Octavian's sister, Octavia.

[Herod] related to Antony what had befallen him in Judaea, and how Phasael, his brother, had been seized and slain by the Parthians, and Hyrcanus was held captive by them. He told also how they had made Antigonus king in return for his promise to them of a large sum of money, no less than a thousand talents, and five hundred women of Jewish lineage and daughters of the leading families, and how he [Herod] had carried off the women by night and, by undergoing many hardships, had escaped from the hands of his enemies. He said further that his relatives were in danger of being besieged, and that he had sailed through a storm, scorning its fearful perils in order to reach Antony, his only hope and succor, as quickly as possible.

This account made Antony commiserate the change in Herod's fortunes. Reasoning that such changes were a common occurrence among those in high places, and that such men are more susceptible than others to fortune's vagaries, he was ready to give Herod the aid he desired. In this he was also motivated by the friendship he had had with Antipater and by the money Herod offered him for making him king—as he had formerly given it for making him tetrarch—but chiefly by his hatred of Antigonus, whom he considered to be a seditious man and an enemy of the Romans.

Caesar [Octavian] was also ready to restore Herod's rank and to give him the desired aid, as much because of the rigors of war he had shared with Antipater, Herod's father, in Egypt and the generosity and good will Antipater had always shown him, as to gratify Antony, who was a most zealous partisan of Herod's. The Senate was therefore convoked; and first Messala, then [the augur] Atratinus, introduced Herod and enlarged upon the benefits the Romans had received from his father, recalling also the good will he had borne them. At the same time they censured Antigonus and declared him to be an enemy, not only because of his former opposition to them, but also because he had now ignored the Romans and accepted the government of Judaea from the Parthians. This provoked the Senate. Whereupon Antony came forward and argued that it would be to Rome's advantage in the Parthian war that Herod should be king. The notion seemed a good one to all the Senators and they so decreed.

It was the greatest proof of Antony's affection for Herod that he not only procured him a kingdom he did not expect . . . but that he had procured it for him so suddenly that by so speedily obtaining what he had not anticipated, Herod was able to leave Italy within only seven days. . . . When the Senate adjourned,

Antony and Caesar [Octavian] left with Herod between them, preceded by the consuls and other magistrates, in order to offer sacrifices and to deposit their
decrees in the Capitol. On this, the first day of his
reign, Antony also feasted Herod. . . . (Antt. XIV,
14:3-5.)

Herod returned to Judaea, collected an army, and
started on the reconquest of the country. He took
Jaffa, then Masada, where his family had been be-
sieged, and then turned to Galilee to capture some of
the sites held by the garrisons of Antigonus and to
attack the seats of the rebels and freedom fighters
(15:1, 3).

THE REBELS OF GALILEE

Herod went in haste against the [Galilean] rebels
in the caves. These caves lay in mountains that were
exceedingly steep; in the center were only precipices,
with hidden entrances into the caves. In these caves,
which were surrounded by sharp rocks, the rebels lay
concealed with their families. Herod had special chests
made in order to destroy them. These chests, bound
with iron chains, were to be lowered by an engine
from the summit of the mountains, since the sharp
ascent of the mountains made climbing up to the caves,
or creeping down from above, an impossibility. The
chests were filled with armed men carrying long hooks
with which to pull up those who resisted them, then
throw them down the precipices, and by so doing kill
them.

Even though the men had provisions in the chests
for so doing, lowering the chests proved to be a most
dangerous feat because of the vast depth into which
they were to be lowered. When the chests were finally
lowered, not a single man hidden in the mouths of the
caves dared come near them; all lay still out of fear.
Whereupon some of the Roman soldiers, impatient at
the delay occasioned by the rebels' fear, girded their

armor, took hold with both hands of the chain by which the chests had been lowered, and entered the mouths of the caves. When they reached these mouths, they first with their javelins killed many of those who were there, then with their hooks pulled up those who resisted, and threw them down the precipices; afterwards the men went inside the caves, killing many more. This accomplished, they re-entered their chests and lay still there. Terror seized the rest [of the rebels] when they heard the lamentations, and they despaired of escaping. But night put an end to the slaughter. And since the king proclaimed pardon by a herald to those who surrendered, many did so.

The same method of assault was used the following day. On that day the men in the chests went farther, fought the rebels at their doors, threw flames among them, and there being much combustible matter inside, set their caves on fire. One old man was caught inside a cave with his wife and seven children; they implored him to give them leave to go out and surrender to the enemy, but he stood at the cave's mouth and slew whatever child went out, until he killed them all. Then he slew his wife and threw all the dead bodies down the precipice and himself after them, preferring death to slavery. First however, he reviled Herod for his meanness, though Herod (who saw what he meant to do) stretched out his hand and offered him every kind of assurance for his life. By such means [as those described] were all the rebels in the caves finally subdued. (Antt. XIV, 15:5.)

Herod continued his pursuit of the forces of Antigonus. Joseph, Herod's brother and a leader in the campaign, fell in one of the battles. In time, Herod was in control of the country, with the exception of Jerusalem. He also helped the army of Antony, who was fighting the king of Commagene, a confederate of the Parthians. Antony seized the occasion to em-

brace Herod and "salute him in a most affectionate manner." (15:6-12).

THE SIEGE OF JERUSALEM (37 B.C.)—
HEROD'S MARRIAGE WITH MARIAMNE

The rigor of winter having abated, Herod hastened to Jerusalem. It was the third year since he had been declared king in Rome. He led his forces up to the walls and encamped before the Temple, for the city was assailable from that quarter, and from that vantage point Pompey had on a former occasion captured it. Dividing his army for the execution of the work, he leveled the environs, and raising three mounds, ordered towers to be erected on them. Leaving the most efficient of his men to superintend these labors, he proceeded to Samaria, to meet [Mariamne] the daughter of Aristobulus' son, Alexander, to whom, as we have stated, he was betrothed. To show his contempt for his antagonists, he made his wedding an interlude to the siege.

The wedding over, he returned to Jerusalem with a more effective force. Here Sosius [governor of Syria] [15] joined him with a formidable body of horsemen and foot soldiers, having sent that army to precede him through the interior, while he himself took the Phoenician route. Herod's entire army—amounting to eleven battalions of infantry and six thousand of cavalry, exclusive of the Syrian auxiliaries, who formed no inconsiderable part of his force—being now assembled, he encamped near the north wall. Herod relied on the decree of the Senate, which had constituted him king; Sosius on Antony, who sent the army under his command to Herod's support.

Throughout the city, meanwhile, the Jewish populace was troubled in various ways. The feeble, congregating around the Temple, called those people happy and most fortunate who had reached their end in happier times.

The more daring, now that sustenance remained neither for horses nor men, organized into bands and committed every sort of depredation, plundering mainly the environs of the city. Of those capable of bearing arms however, the better trained, who were appointed to repel the besiegers, endeavored from the walls to check the men who were raising the mounds, and continually invented new devices to impede the engines. But they excelled the enemy above all in their underground mines.

To curb the pillage, Herod contrived ambuscades; and to relieve the wants of his army, he took measures to procure supplies from afar. Because of the military skill of the Romans he proved superior in every conflict, even though his opponents displayed the very acme of valor. The Jews did not, it is true, meet the Romans in open battle, for that would have been certain death; but with the aid of their underground mines they would appear suddenly in their midst, and even before one portion of the [Jerusalem] wall was battered down, erected another in its stead. In a word, the Jews, flagged neither in courage nor ingenuity, resolved to hold out to the last. Indeed, though surrounded by so great a force, they sustained the siege for five months —until the flower of Herod's army ventured upon the wall and rushed into the city, followed by Sosius' centurions.

First the environs of the Temple were captured, then, when the troops poured in, a horrible massacre ensued. Both the Romans and the Jews of Herod's party, exasperated by the length of the siege, endeavored to exterminate every opponent. Multitudes were butchered in the narrow streets, as they crowded together in the houses, and as they fled to the sanctuary. There was no pity for infancy, for age, or even for woman's helplessness. Though the king sent messages in all directions entreating them to spare the people, none could stay his hand; like madmen they assailed old and

young alike. So great was the slaughter that Antigonus, disregarding both his former and his present
high status, descended from the citadel and threw himself at the feet of Sosius. But the Roman, having no
pity for his reverses of fortune, only roared with
laughter and called him Antigone.[16] He did not, however, let him go free, as if he were indeed a woman,
but detained him in bonds and held him in custody.

Herod, now master of his foes, pondered next how
he could be master also of his foreign auxiliaries, for
the mob of aliens evinced the most ardent curiosity to
examine the Temple and the holy objects of the
sanctuary. With some the king expostulated; others he
threatened; still others he restrained by force, considering victory worse than defeat if they cast eyes on
anything forbidden to be seen. He finally stopped the
pillage of the city as well, hotly demanding of Sosius
whether the Romans, by emptying Jerusalem of men
and money, wished to leave him king of a desert. He
would count the sovereignty of the world too dearly
bought with the slaughter of so many of his people.
When Sosius replied that he had justly allowed the
soldiers to plunder as compensation for the rigors of
the siege, Herod promised to distribute rewards out
of his private revenues.

Having thus redeemed what remained of the capital,
he fulfilled his promise, magnificently remunerating
every soldier, the officers according to their rank, and
Sosius with truly royal munificence; so no one departed devoid of wealth. Sosius, after dedicating a
golden crown to God, withdrew from Jerusalem, leading Antigonus in chains to Antony. Clinging to life
and to the last cherishing a miserable hope, Antigonus
fell beneath the axe, an end worthy of his ignoble
mind! (War I, 17:8-18:3.)

Thus ended the rule of the Hasmonaeans, one hundred and twenty-six years after it was first set up. This
dynasty had been a splendid and illustrious one, both

in nobility of lineage and in dignity of the high priesthood, as well as in the glorious deeds of their progeni-
tors on behalf of our nation. But these men lost the
rule through mutual dissensions, and it passed to
Herod, the son of Antipater, descendant of a common
family of no eminent extraction and subject to other
kings. Such, so history tells us, was the end of the
Hasmonaean dynasty. (Antt. XIV, 16:4.)

Now that all Judaea was his, Herod promoted those
citizens of Jerusalem who had supported him and re-
lentlessly pursued with his vengeance the adherents
of his enemies. Pollio, the Pharisee, and Sameas, his
disciple,[17] he honored above all others, because when
he besieged Jerusalem they counseled the citizens to
admit him—a counsel for which they were well re-
warded. At the time Herod was on trial for his life
[before the Synhedrion] [18] this Sameas prophesied
that if Hyrcanus and the other judges suffered him to
escape, he would subsequently take revenge on all of
them. This prediction was in time fulfilled, when God
made good the words Sameas had spoken.

Being now master of Jerusalem, Herod also carried
off all the royal ornaments and despoiled the wealthy
of their possessions. When he had by these means
gathered much silver and gold, he gave it all to Antony
and to his friends. Furthermore, he executed forty-
five of Antigonus' principal adherents and set guards
at the gates of the city to see that nothing was carried
out with their dead bodies. . . . (Antt. XV, 1:1-2.)

ARISTOBULUS III, BROTHER
OF MARIAMNE (35 B.C.)

*Hyrcanus II was set at liberty by the Parthians in
36 B.C., and returned to Jerusalem, where Herod "received him with all possible respect . . . calling him
father," etc. Nevertheless, Herod took care to keep the
Hasmonaean family powerless. Since Hyrcanus no
longer qualified to be high priest and Herod wished to*

avoid appointing Mariamne's brother, Aristobulus, to
that post, he chose an obscure priest from Babylon,
Ananelus [Hananel], for this high office. This appoint-
ment was deeply resented by Alexandra, daughter of
Hyrcanus and mother of Mariamne and Aristobulus.
She wrote to her friend Cleopatra "to desire her inter-
cession with Antony" on behalf of her son. Antony re-
ceived pictures of the beautiful Hasmonaeans; he
would have liked to see Mariamne, but "refrained,
fearing Cleopatra's reproaches," and asked to see Aris-
tobulus instead. Herod, knowing the most powerful
Roman's strange sexual inclinations and that he
"openly indulged in unbridled pleasure," prevented
this. However, in the hope of satisfying Alexandra
and Mariamne, he dismissed Ananelus and appointed
the seventeen-year-old Aristobulus high priest. (2:1-
3:1.)

[With this appointment] Herod presumably healed
the breach in his family. Nevertheless, he remained
suspicious, as is frequently the case with people seem-
ingly reconciled to each other, because he feared that
since Alexandra had already made attempts tending to
rebellion, she would continue doing so if she found
the opportunity. He therefore ordered her to live in the
palace and to refrain from meddling in public affairs.
She was, in addition, spied on by her guards so that
not a single daily act of her private life was hidden
from Herod.

This treatment exasperated her, and she began to
hate Herod. A woman of great pride, she was highly
indignant at the spying guards, preferring whatever
catastrophe might befall her to being deprived of freedom of speech, and living, under the pretense of being
given an honorary guard, in a state of slavery and terror. She therefore sent a long complaint of her circumstances to Cleopatra, entreating her to do her utmost
for her assistance. Cleopatra advised **immediate flight**
to Egypt, together with her son.

Herod detected Alexandra's plot to escape and caught her in the very act of flight. Though outwardly he forgave her in order not to antagonize Cleopatra, he made up his mind to get rid of both his mother-in-law and her son.

On the approach of the feast of Tabernacles, a festival highly honored by us, Herod refrained from immediate execution of his plans, and both he and the people celebrated merrily. But the jealousy aroused in him at this time provoked him to hasten what he was about. When the seventeen-year-old Aristobulus, wearing the insignia of his high priesthood, ascended the altar to offer the sacrifices according to the law, he, being taller than most men of his age, looked so handsome as he performed the sacred offices and bore so great a likeness to the noble family whose scion he was that warm zeal and affection for him sprang in the hearts of the people, and the memory of the deeds of his grandfather, Aristobulus, leaped fresh to their minds. Mastered by their emotions, they could not refrain from demonstrating their feelings. . . .

Whereupon Herod resolved to carry out his design against the young man. When the festival was over and he was celebrating at Jericho with Alexandra, who was entertaining him there, he was most cordial to young Aristobulus. Playing amusing adolescent games with him, he drew him to a lonely spot. Since it was very hot they went . . . to cool themselves bathing. At first they merely looked on as Herod's servants and friends swam; then at Herod's suggestion, Aristobulus joined them in the water. Those of Herod's friends whom he had chosen to execute his orders first ducked him as he was swimming, then in the dark of the evening, thrust him under the water, as if only in sport. They did not release him until he was completely suffocated. Thus was Aristobulus murdered, having lived but eighteen years and having kept the high priesthood only one. After his death Ananelus was reappointed high priest.

When this sad "accident" was revealed to the women, their merriment quickly changed to lamentation at sight of the dead body that lay before them and they grieved immoderately. Jerusalem, too, when the news spread, grieved greatly. Every family regarded the calamity not as one that had befallen a stranger but as if a kinsman had been slain. Alexandra was even more deeply affected . . . because she knew that Aristobulus had been murdered. However, fearing still greater evils, she had to endure her sorrow. Though she often contemplated suicide, she restrained herself in the hope that she would live long enough to avenge the unjustified murder so ingeniously committed. . . .

Herod, to allay any suspicion outside Judaea that he was responsible for Aristobulus' death, exhibited not only the customary signs of grief, but shed excessive tears and displayed genuine confusion. Possibly he was overcome by emotion when he saw the boy's countenance, so young and beautiful in death, even though that death tended to insure his [Herod's] own security. To this extent at least his grief served to exonerate his guilt. Moreover, he gave Aristobulus a magnificent funeral, ordering a resplendent sepulcher for his body, providing a great quantity of spices, and burying many ornaments with him, so that the very women who grieved so deeply were amazed at his conduct and somewhat consoled by it. (Antt. XV, 3:2-4.)

Alexandra, who could not be deceived, reported Herod's treacherous deed to Cleopatra. Egypt's queen "made the case her own" and persuaded Antony to call Herod to judgment. Antony, who at that time resided in the East, summoned Herod to Laodicea, south of Antioch. Herod came with gifts and persuasive arguments and soon regained Antony's friendship. Before leaving for Laodicea, Herod had ordered his uncle (and brother-in-law) Joseph to kill Marianne if he failed to return from the dangerous meeting with Antony. Upon his return to Jerusalem he learned that his orders had been communicated to his beloved wife and that the latter was suspected of adultery with Joseph. It was Herod's sister, Salome, who slandered her husband, Joseph, and caused his execution (3:5-9).

HEROD AND CLEOPATRA

Antony, already enamored of Cleopatra to distraction, was an utter slave to his passion. She, having ruthlessly exterminated her own kin, now thirsted for the blood of foreigners. As an easy method of obtaining their possessions, she slandered the men of authority in Syria and persuaded Antony to kill them. She then extended her cupidity to Judaea and Arabia, and secretly devised measures for the destruction of their respective kings, Herod and Malchus.

Antony complied with her overt demands only in part. Considering the killing of two innocent and eminent princes unjustifiable, he, as the closest approach to her wishes, renounced their friendship.

Because of Cleopatra's constant urging that Antony appropriate everybody's domain, the affairs of Syria were at this time in chaos. She kept insisting that he should take their realms away from the various princes who headed them and bestow them upon her, and because of his passion for her, she wielded great influence over him. She was, besides, very covetous, and cringed from no iniquity. . . . Indeed, if there was hope of getting money, she violated even temples and sepulchers. There was no holy place, however inviolate, that she did not denude of its treasures. . . .

Still this extravagant woman, who was a slave to her lusts, was not sated, but craved everything she could think of and did her utmost to gain it. . . . When she accompanied Antony to Syria, she plotted to gain possession of it. . . . She petitioned him to give her

Judaea and Nabataean Arabia also, desiring him to expropriate these countries from their present kings. As for Antony, he was so completely enthralled by this woman that their intimacy could not alone account for it, and one would rather have thought him prey to some witchcraft designed to make him a slave to her wishes. . . . He gave her the cities on this side of the river Eleutherus [north of Tripolis] as far as Egypt, except Tyre and Sidon, which he knew to have been free cities since antiquity, although she pressed him very often to give her these also.

Having obtained this much and having accompanied Antony on his expedition to Armenia as far as the Euphrates [34 B.C.], Cleopatra turned back, came to Apamea and Damascus, and passed on to Judaea, where Herod met her and leased from her the Arab lands Antony gave her, as well as her revenues from the region around Jericho. That region yields the most precious balsams, which are to be found only there, and also grows numerous and excellent palm trees. While in Judaea, she spent much time with Herod and tried to have sinful intercourse with him. She made no secret of her indulgence in this type of pleasure. It is possible that Herod aroused her passion, but more probably she was laying a treacherous snare for him were adulterous intercourse with him consummated. On the surface, however, she appeared overcome with love for him.

Herod had for some time been ill disposed towards Cleopatra, knowing how troublesome she was to everybody; at the moment he found her particularly hateful if her attempt [to seduce him] was occasioned by lust. To stop her intrigues, if such were her motives, he even considered killing her. Rejecting her propositions, he called a council of friends to advise him on the wisdom of such an act now that he had her in his power. He argued that by her death he would free her victims from a multitude of evils, both present and future, and that Antony too would benefit greatly, because she was sure not to remain loyal to him were some crisis or need of his to necessitate such loyalty.

But Herod's friends dissuaded him. They argued that it was rash to court danger by attempting so perilous a deed and implored him to do nothing recklessly, for Antony would never countenance it, not even if convinced that the deed was committed for his benefit; the loss of Cleopatra in so violent and treacherous a manner would, in fact, only inflame his love for her. [They said also that] Herod could offer no tolerable defense, his contemplated deed being directed against a woman of higher rank than any other in the world. As for any advantage to be derived from his scheme, assuming any resulted, that advantage would be outweighed by the insolence of the act, and therefore condemned. These arguments convinced Herod that the murder of Cleopatra would fill his reign with great and lasting perils both to himself and to his posterity and that it was still in his power to avoid these perils and at the same time preserve his honor by rejecting Cleopatra's adulterous overtures. By pointing out the hazards he would almost certainly bring upon himself with his scheme, and thus alarming him, his friends restrained him from carrying it out. He therefore paid court to Cleopatra, loaded her with gifts, and conducted her on her way to Egypt. (War I, 18:4-5; Antt. XV, 4:1-2.)

Herod dutifully paid his tribute to Cleopatra, but Malchus I, the king of the Nabataean Arabs, for whose tribute Herod had assumed responsibility, "became niggardly and dilatory in his payments" (Antt. XV, 4:4.)

THE WAR WITH THE ARABS (32 B.C.)

When the battle of Actium was expected, "in which Antony and Octavian (Augustus) were to fight for the sovereignty of the world," Herod was ready to lead an army to Antony's aid. But Cleopatra persuaded Antony to entrust to Herod the war against the Nabataean Arabs instead. "If he won, she might become mistress of Arabia; if he lost, of Judaea." "She thought it would be to her advantage for these two kings to weaken one another." (War I, 19:1; Antt. XV, 5:1.)

This policy proved fortunate for Herod. Because after some merely predatory incursions into the enemy's territory, he eventually mustered a powerful body of cavalry, charged the foe near Diospolis [in Coele-Syria], and after a severe battle defeated them. Greatly upset by this defeat, the Arabs massed immense forces at Canatha, in Coele-Syria, and there awaited the Jews. In an effort to run this war circumspectly, Herod, on reaching Canatha, ordered his camp to be fortified. But, flushed with their prior victory, his troops disregarded his commands and rushed on the Arabs, whom they overthrew at the first onslaught and chased from the field.

During the pursuit a trap was laid for Herod by Athenion, one of Cleopatra's generals, who, always inimical to him, suddenly dispatched a native force against him from Canatha. Encouraged by this charge, the Arabs renewed the fight, assembled their numerous forces in rocky territory that was difficult to approach, routed Herod's troops, and committed dreadful slaughter among them. . . .

Shortly after this catastrophe Herod arrived with reinforcements—too late. . . . However, he subsequently avenged the slaughter by ceaseless ravaging of Arab territory as retribution for their single victory.

But while he was avenging himself on his enemies, another fateful disaster struck him—in the seventh year of his reign, when the war of Actium was at its height. In the early spring an earthquake destroyed countless cattle and thirty thousand people; however, the soldiers, lying in the open fields, were uninjured. But rumor, ever inclined to exaggerate misfortune, pictured Judaea as a scene of total desolation, thereby inspiring the Arabs with increased confidence. In the belief of gaining easy possession of a devastated country, they advanced towards it by rapid marches and invaded it, after first massacring the envoys the Jews sent to them. Dismayed at this invasion, the people, their spirit broken by the magnitude of their successive disasters, sank into despair. Herod, therefore, convened his army and endeavored to arouse its spirit of resistance.

Here follows Herod's exhortatory address, ending with his promise to precede his army when danger threatened.

Having reanimated his troops, Herod, seeing their ardor, sacrificed to God, then crossed the Jordan with his army. Encamping in the neighborhood of Philadelphia [Rabbath Ammon], not far from the enemy, and eager to provoke the latter to action, he skirmished with them for the possession of a fort situated between their lines. The Arabs sent a detachment to occupy it; a contingent dispatched by Herod drove them back and took possession of the hill. Daily Herod drew up his troops in battle array and challenged his adversaries. When, seized by such dread that their general, Elthemus, stood frozen with terror among his troops, none accepted the challenge, Herod attacked and demolished their entrenchments. Impelled by necessity, the Arabs then sallied forth in great disorder, cavalry and infantry intermixed in their haste, reckless in their boldness because despairing of victory.

As long as they fought, their losses were not too great; but as soon as they retreated, many perished, some by the hands of the Jews, others trodden down by their own men. Five thousand fell in the flight; the rest avoided instant death by crowding into their entrenchments. Here Herod surrounded and besieged them. But the destruction that menaced them by arms was anticipated by thirst, their supply of water failing.

The king treated their messengers with scorn; though they offered five hundred talents as ransom, he pressed the siege with still greater vigor. Parched with thirst, many came out and surrendered to the Jews; so in five days, four thousand were made prisoners. On the sixth, the remaining Arabs, in despair, came out to give battle. Herod attacked and again defeated them, slaughtering some seven thousand. With this disastrous defeat Herod avenged himself on Arabia and broke the spirit of its people so completely that he was chosen by the nation for its Protector. (War I, 19.)

OCTAVIAN AUGUSTUS AND HEROD

The battle of Actium, September 2, 31 B.C., marked the fall of Antony; Herod, friend of Antony, found himself in a precarious position before the victor, Octavian Augustus. Herod's visit to Octavian at Rhodes took place in the spring of 30 B.C.

Because of his friendship for Antony, recently defeated by Octavian Augustus at Actium, Herod was uneasy about the security of his power. Yet he was more alarmed than hurt, since Octavian did not consider his victory complete so long as Herod continued to aid his rival. Resolving to confront the danger, Herod sailed for Rhodes, where Octavian was staying, and appeared before him without his diadem and in the dress and character of a private man, but with the spirit of a king. He concealed nothing of the truth, addressing Octavian candidly:

"I was made king of Judaea by Antony, and I acknowledge, Caesar, that I have, as king, in all things studied his interests; I unhesitatingly avow that had not the Arabs prevented me, you would most certainly have found me in arms, an inseparable companion of Antony. According to my ability, however, I supplied him with troops and with many thousands of measures of grain; nor did I desert my benefactor even after his defeat at Actium. When I could no longer help him as an ally, I gave him the most prudent counsel; I told him that there was but one remedy for his disasters— to kill Cleopatra. I promised him money, ramparts for his security, an army, and myself as his confederate in the war against you were she to be destroyed. But his passion for Cleopatra, and God, who has granted you the victory, closed his ears. Together with Antony, therefore, I too have been conquered, and with his ruin lay down my crown. To you, however, I come, founding my hope of safety on my integrity, foreseeing that it will be asked how firm a friend, rather than whose friend, I have been."

To this Octavian replied: "Live in safety and reign henceforth under surer auspices. For thus standing forward in defense of friendship you deserve a ruler's pre-eminence. Endeavor to remain as faithful to those who have been more fortunate; for I too entertain the most splendid hopes anent your noble spirit. It is my good fortune that Antony yielded to Cleopatra's persuasions rather than to yours; we have gained you by his infatuation. . . . For the present, therefore, I ensure you the throne by decree, and I shall endeavor to be of service to you in the future also, that you may not feel the loss of Antony."

Having addressed the king in this cordial manner, Octavian placed the diadem on his head, and announced this grant [of the throne] by a decree in which he lauded him in most flattering terms. . . .

Later, when Octavian was passing through Syria on the way to Egypt [30 B.C.], Herod received him with royal magnificence. He accompanied him on horseback during a review of his troops at Ptolemais [Acco] and entertained him and his whole entourage. He also provided the soldiers with every requisite for a feast. In addition, he supplied the army with ample water, both on its march, through a dry country, to Pelusium and on its return; the troops lacked no necessaries.

It then occurred to Octavian and his soldiers that compared with the services he had rendered, Herod's domains were too confined. Cleopatra and Antony being dead now, the Roman ruler, on his arrival in Egypt not only conferred new honors on Herod but also added to his kingdom the territory of which Cleopatra had deprived him,[19] and also Gadara, Hippos, Samaria, the maritime towns of Gaza, Anthedon, Jaffa, and Strato's Tower [the later Caesarea]. In addition, he presented him with Cleopatra's bodyguard of four hundred Gauls. Nothing stimulated Octavian's liberality as much as the noble spirit of the man who was the recipient of it. (War I, 20:1-3.)

THE EXECUTION OF HYRCANUS II (SPRING 30 B.C.)

Herod, realizing that Hyrcanus was the sole survivor of royal rank, decided it would be to his advantage no longer to suffer him to be an obstacle in his path. He reasoned that if he himself survived [after seeing Octavian] . . . it would be safer to stop the man who was more worthy of the kingdom than he from making any attempt against him; and envy prompted him to want to kill the only man who would be king after him were he to be slain by Octavian.

According to the "Commentaries of King Herod" referred to by Josephus, Hyrcanus' ambitious daughter Alexandra induced her father to engage the help of the Nabataean king Malchus in anticipation of the Hasmonaeans' return to power. Herod discovered the plot and slew Hyrcanus.

Hyrcanus seems to have been a mild and moderate man who, as a rule, let others under him administer the affairs of state. He disliked business, nor had he the shrewdness to rule a kingdom. Both Antipater and Herod achieved their power through his mildness, and he finally met such an end at their hands as is not to be condoned either by justice or piety. (Antt. XV, 6:1-4.)

HEROD AND MARIAMNE

The initial tragic break between Herod and his Hasmonaean wife occurred when, after the battle of Actium, he went to see Octavian Augustus at Rhodes.

[When Herod] made haste to Octavian, he . . . feared that Mariamne's mother, Alexandra, might seize the opportunity to instigate a revolt against him. He therefore settled his mother, Cypros, his sister, Salome, and the rest of the family at Masada, and entrusted the kingdom to his brother Pheroras, charging him, should he hear bad news about him, to seize the government. Mariamne, his wife . . . he settled at Alexandrium, together with her mother, Alexandra, and left his treasurer, Joseph, and [a certain] Sohemus of Ituraea to guard that fortress.

These two men had been Herod's loyal adherents from the start, and were now, under pretext of paying them due respect, left to watch the two women. They were charged to kill both of them if they heard of any misfortune befalling Herod, and insofar as they were able, to preserve the kingdom for his sons and for his brother Pheroras.

When he returned, he found a most disordered household, and Mariamne and Alexandra greatly provoked. They had soon realized that they had been put into the fortress not for safety but as prisoners. . . .

Mariamne, suspecting Herod's love for her to be hypocritical, considered it feigned. And she was most unhappy that he should leave her no hope of surviving him should he himself come to harm. . . . She therefore tried to please her keepers, especially Sohemus, being well aware that everything was in his power.

At first Sohemus was loyal to Herod and neglected none of the tasks the latter had entrusted to him. But when the women, with kind words and liberal gifts, gained his affections, he was gradually won over and finally disclosed to them all the king's injunctions.

Josephus analyzes Sohemus' selfish motives for his action.

When she learned of the dangers threatening her from Herod, Mariamne was very uneasy. She hoped he would be granted no favors [by Octavian] and thought it unbearable to continue living with him. This state of mind she later showed openly, not concealing her resentment.

Herod sailed for home overjoyed at his unexpected success. He came first of all to his wife, as was proper, embraced her and out of love for her and the intimacy they had enjoyed, told her, and her only, the good news before informing anyone else. She, however, instead of rejoicing at his good fortune, regretted it. Nor was she able to conceal her resentment. Mindful of her status and the nobility of her birth, she groaned when he embraced her and clearly showed that she grieved rather than rejoiced at his success. Her conduct perturbed Herod, for it betokened not only suspicion of him but evident dislike. . . . Because he loved her, her attitude both angered and upset him. . . . Alternating between hatred and love, he suffered greatly. A conflict raged within him: he often wished to punish her for her contempt of him; at the same time, being deeply in love with her, he had not the heart to destroy this woman. In short, though he would gladly have chastised her, he feared that by her death he would punish himself more than her.

His state of mind provided Herod's sister and mother with an excellent opportunity to gratify their hatred of Mariamne. They aroused Herod's wrath with lengthy lies and calumnies about her designed to inflame both his hatred and his jealousy.

Though he heard their words willingly enough, Herod still lacked the courage to punish Mariamne as though he believed the slanders. However, his ill will towards her increased, and as she failed to conceal her dislike of him and his love for her turned into wrath against her, the evil passions of both became more and more inflamed. (Antt. XV, 6:5; 7:1-3.)

THE FINAL BREAK WITH MARIAMNE (29 B.C.)

When Herod returned [from his visit to Octavian in Egypt, end of 30 B.C.], his family distresses—particularly in the Mariamne affair wherein he had formerly appeared to have been most fortunate of all—increased as greatly as his prosperity had been augmented by the additions to his kingdom. For his passion for Mariamne was as great as the passions famous in history, and justly so.

As for her, she was chaste and faithful to him; but she had a woman's caprices, was haughty by nature, and treated her husband imperiously, because she saw he loved her well enough to be her slave. Nor did she heed the fact that she lived under a monarchy and was subject to her king, but assumed instead a haughty manner towards him. Most of the time he concealed his vexation and bore her tantrums good-naturedly. She also openly jeered at his mother and sister and cast aspersions at the lowliness of their birth. There had therefore been quarrels and deadly hatred among the women even before this break, and now the mutual recriminations were greater than ever.

These hatreds festered for a year after Herod's return, then flared into the open on the following occasion. Lying down for a rest one afternoon, Herod, still in love with her, called for Mariamne. She came, but would not lie with him, though he craved her, thus showing her contempt for him. In addition, she accused him of instigating the murder of her [grand-] father and her brother.

Inflamed by this insult, Herod was ready to use violence on her. Observing that he was more than ordinarily upset, his sister, Salome, sent in his cupbearer, who had for some time been prepared for this plot, and bid him tell the king that Mariamne had asked him to help her prepare a love potion for him. If Herod showed suspicion and asked what the love potion contained, the cupbearer was to tell him that he had it with him and was asked to give it to him. But if Herod showed no suspicion, the cupbearer was not to pursue the matter, and would suffer no harm.

Having given the cupbearer these instructions, Salome sent him in. He told Herod in a convincing and earnest manner that Mariamne had given him presents and had urged him to give the king a love potion. Seeing Herod touched by this, he said further that Mariamne's love potion was a poison, whose effects he did not know. This being so, he had resolved to reveal the truth to the king as the safest course for both himself and Herod.

On hearing this, Herod, already ill-disposed towards Mariamne, became more wrathful than ever. Aware that nothing, great or small, could be accomplished without him, he ordered Mariamne's most devoted eunuch to be tortured about this potion. The eunuch, even under torture and suffering the greatest agony, could reveal nothing about the potion. He did reveal, however, that Mariamne's hatred for Herod was occasioned by something Sohemus had told her.

As he disclosed this, Herod cried out, contending that Sohemus, who had at all other times been most faithful to him and his rule, would not have revealed the injunctions he had given him had he not been unduly intimate with Mariamne. He therefore ordered Sohemus' arrest and immediate execution. But Mariamne he put on trial. (Antt. XV, 7:4.)

MARIAMNE'S TRIAL AND EXECUTION

He assembled his most loyal adherents and formally charged Mariamne with responsibility for the love potion and its composition (falsely attributed to her). He was intemperate in his accusations and in too great a passion to judge rightly. When at length the court became convinced that this was what he desired, they sentenced Mariamne to death. However, when this sentence was passed, Herod himself, as well as some other judges, suggested that she should not so hastily be executed but be instead imprisoned in one of the kingdom's fortresses. But Salome and her party worked hard to have the poor woman slain, and persuaded the king to do so by insisting that the people would riot if she were suffered to live. And so Mariamne was led to execution.

When Alexandra, her mother, saw the course events were taking, and that little hope remained that she herself would escape similar treatment from Herod, she shamelessly reversed her former bold behavior. In her eagerness to prove her uninvolvement in the crimes charged against Mariamne, she jumped up and publicly rebuked her daughter. She accused her of having been ill-tempered and ungrateful to her husband and declared death to be a just punishment for her insolent behavior, for her not having properly recompensed the man who had been their mutual benefactor. She behaved in this hypocritical manner for some time, and even went so far as to tear Mariamne's hair.

As was to be expected, this indecent dissembling was condemned by the rest of the spectators. Mariamne, the poor woman who was to suffer, did not address a single word to her, nor did she seem upset at Alexandra's vituperations; in the greatness of her soul, she showed instead concern for her mother's offense, and especially for making such a shameful spectacle of herself. She herself went to her death unshaken in the firmness of her mind and without changing the color of her face, manifesting even in the last moments of her life the nobility of her descent.

So died Mariamne, a superior woman both in chastity and greatness of soul. However, she lacked moderation and was overly contentious. In beauty of body and majesty of bearing she surpassed all women of her day. . . .

After Mariamne's death the king's passion for her was rekindled. His love for her had never been a calm one, nor as simple as the usual love of husbands for their wives. Their long years together and their free conversations had not diminished its initial ardor. And now that she was dead that love affected him in so peculiar a manner that it seemed like divine vengeance for taking away her life. He continually called for her and unceasingly lamented her passing in a most unseemly manner. Though he made every attempt to divert his mind from thinking of her, contriving feasts and other entertainments, nothing sufficed. Neglecting the public affairs of state, he was so overcome by his passion that he kept ordering his servants to call Mariamne, as if she were still alive and able to hear them.

A pestilence arose in this period. It killed many people and a number of his best friends. All suspected that this plague was a manifestation of God's anger at the injustice meted out to Mariamne. This misfortune affected the king still more. At length he forced himself to go into the desert. There, while pretending to go hunting, he mourned bitterly. There, too, before many days passed, he became dangerously ill. Inflammation and a pain in the back of his head was joined with madness. The remedies employed, instead of helping, aggravated his case so that his life was finally despaired of. . . . (Antt. XV, 7:4-7.)

ALEXANDRA'S EXECUTION (28 B.C.)

When informed of Herod's condition, Alexandra, who now resided in Jerusalem, endeavored to obtain possession of the city's fortifications. . . . She told the commandants of these strongholds that they ought to transfer them to her and to Herod's sons, lest on

Herod's death some outsider should usurp the government. And if Herod recovered, she argued, none could hold them more safely for him than members of his own family.

These words met with hostility. Having been faithful to Herod in the past, the commandants resolved to continue being so, now more than ever, both because they hated Alexandra and because they considered it an impiety to despair of Herod's recovery while he was yet alive. . . . They therefore dispatched messengers to Herod to inform him of Alexandra's designs. Delaying no longer, he ordered her execution.

He was still sorely afflicted, both in mind and body, so that he was exceedingly morose, and readier than ever to penalize, whenever the occasion arose, all who fell into his power. (Antt. XV, 7:8.)

Two years later Herod ordered the execution of Costobarus, governor of Idumaea (and second husband of Herod's sister, Salome), for having attempted to win Idumaea for himself and for having given protection to two sons of Babas, distant relatives of the Hasmonaeans. The two princes were also murdered. "Now there were none at all left of the kindred of Hyrcanus, the kingdom was wholly in Herod's power, and there remained no one so highly placed that he could challenge his actions against the Jewish laws" (7:9-10).

A NEW MARRIAGE (ABOUT 25 B.C.)

Herod fell in love again and took another wife, not suffering anything to stop him from living as he pleased. This marriage came about as follows. There lived at the time a certain Simon, a native of Jerusalem, the son of one Boethus, an Alexandrian and a priest of great note there. Simon's daughter was considered to be the most beautiful woman of her day. When the fame of her beauty spread in Jerusalem, Herod was greatly affected by what he heard about her. And when he saw the young woman he was much taken with her beauty. Nevertheless, he completely rejected the notion of taking advantage of his authority to violate her, believing, rightly, that such an act would condemn him for violence and tyranny. He thought it best therefore to marry her. And since Simon was of too low a rank to be allied to him, but too highly placed to be despised, he solved the problem most prudently by raising the status of Simon's house and ennobling it. Accordingly, he deprived Jesus, the son of Phabes, of the high priesthood, conferred that dignity on Simon, then married his daughter. (Antt. XV, 9:3.)

The name of this second wife is given in War I, 28:4, as Mariamne (called Mariamne II, to distinguish her from the Hasmonaean Mariamne). She gave birth to Herod Philip. This union was followed by marriages to seven more women, "polygamy being permitted by Jewish laws and the king delighting in this privilege" (War I, 24:2). Among them were the Samaritan Malthace (who became the mother of Archelaus and Herod Antipas) and Cleopatra of Jerusalem (who became the mother of Philip the Tetrarch).

The story of Herod's new marriage is preceded by a reference to "five hundred picked men of his bodyguards" whom Herod sent as auxiliaries to the expedition of Aelius Gallus, Roman governor of Egypt, against Arabia.

BETWEEN JERUSALEM AND ROME

Octavian, from 27 B.C. on bearing the title Augustus, exercised proconsular command over frontier provinces and needed strong and loyal Roman or native administrators. Herod's ability to serve the cause of Rome secured him the friendship of Augustus and of the latter's principal aide and favorite, Marcus Agrippa.

HEROD'S SONS

Herod . . . resolved to send his sons Alexander and Aristobulus to Rome to enjoy the company of Augustus. There they stayed at the house of [Asinius] Pollio,[20] a man very proud of Herod's friendship. They were also allowed to stay in Augustus' own palace, for he received these sons of Herod with all possible kindness, and he granted Herod permission to leave his kingdom to whichever one of his sons he pleased. In addition, he bestowed on him [23 B.C.] Trachonitis, Batanaea, and Auranitis. (Antt. XV, 10:1.)

THE NORTH TRANSJORDAN DISTRICTS

Herod managed to subdue the fierce inhabitants of these north Transjordan districts; he "put a stop to their nefarious plunders, and gave peace and quiet to the neighboring people." Especially troublesome was Zenodorus, leader of the rebels of Trachonitis. Augustus, who happened to visit Syria, could well ignore the clamor of neighboring Gadara against Herod and assure him of his gratitude; he made Herod "one of the procurators of Syria." "Next to Agrippa, Augustus preferred no one more than Herod, and Agrippa made no one, except Augustus, a greater friend than Herod." At that same time Augustus granted Herod's wish to appoint his brother Pheroras tetrarch of Peraea (Antt. XV, 10:1-3).

THE KING AND THE PEOPLE

At this time Herod released his subjects from a third of their taxes. The dearth they had recently suffered served as his overt pretext for so doing. His chief motive, however, was his desire to regain their good will, for he had antagonized them by the innovations he had introduced in their usages, his disruption of their religion, and his abandonment of their customs; people everywhere talked against him. . . . To forestall any opportunity for the discontent to flare into a disturbance, he enjoined them to be ever at work, deprived them of freedom of assembly—they could not even walk or eat together—and watched their every action. When caught in disobedience they were severely punished, and many . . . were put to death. Spies were everywhere, both in the city and on the roads, watching those who assembled together. It is reported that Herod himself often put on the garb of a commoner and mingled with the people at night in order to find out their views of his administration.

Those whom nothing could induce to acquiesce in his methods of governing, he prosecuted in manifold ways; on the rest he imposed an oath of allegiance to him. . . . Either to please him or out of fear of him, most of the people yielded to his demand; the spirited who rebelled at force, he destroyed by various means.

He endeavored also to persuade Pollio the Pharisee, Sameas,[21] and most of their followers to take this oath; they refused, but because of Herod's reverence for Pollio, were not punished with the rest. The Essenes too . . . were excused from this oath. These men lead the same kind of life as those whom the Greeks call Pythagoreans. . . . It is but fit to set down here the reasons why Herod held these Essenes in such honor and thought more highly of them than their mortal nature warranted; nor is this account unsuited to the nature of this history, since it will show the opinion men held of this sect.

One of these Essenes, whose name was Menahem, not only lived an exemplary life, but was reputed to have been granted by God foreknowledge of the future. This Essene once met Herod, when he was still a schoolboy, and saluted him as king of the Jews; Herod, assuming that Menahem either did not know who he was or was jesting, reminded him that he was only a commoner; but Menahem smiled, clapped him on the backside, and said:

"However that may be, thou wilt be king, and wilt begin thy reign happily, for God finds thee worthy of it. And do thou remember the blows that Menahem hath given thee as a token of the change of thy fortunes. And truly this will be the best resolve for thee to make, that thou love justice and exercise piety toward God and clemency toward thy citizens; yet I know thy whole future conduct, that thou wilt not be such a man. For thou wilt excel all men in good fortune and earn everlasting fame, but thou wilt forget piety and justice. And these crimes will not be hidden from God, for at the conclusion of thy life thou wilt find that He will be mindful of them, and punish thee for them."

At that time Herod paid no attention to what Menahem said, entertaining no hopes of the prophesied advancement; later, however, when he was so fortunate as to progress to the rank of king and was at the height of his power, he sent for Menahem and asked him how long he would reign. When Menahem gave no answer to his question, he asked whether or not he would reign ten years. "Yes," Menahem replied, "twenty years, nay, thirty years." But he did not reveal the precise duration of his reign. Herod was satisfied with this answer; he gave Menahem his hand and dismissed him. From that time on he continued to honor all the Essenes. I have thought it proper to relate these facts to my readers . . . because many of the Essenes because of their superior virtue have been deemed worthy of such knowledge of divine things. (Antt. XV, 10:4-5.)

AGRIPPA VISITS JERUSALEM (15 B.C.)

Agrippa, Augustus' friend and "representative in the countries beyond the Ionian Sea" (Antt. XV, 10:2), was sent to Syria in 23 B.C. and retained the position of governor for ten years (Antt. XVI, 3:3). He did not spend all this time in the East.

Herod . . . on hearing that Marcus Agrippa had again sailed from Italy to Asia Minor, hastened to him and beseeched him to come to his kingdom, there to receive the welcome he might justly expect from one who had been his guest and was his friend. He earnestly pressed his plea, and Agrippa accepted his invitation and came to Judaea. Herod left nothing undone that might please him. He entertained him in his newly built cities,[22] showed him the edifices he had erected, and provided the best and most costly delicacies for him and his friends. He also showed him Sebaste, the port he built at Caesarea, and the fortresses he had erected at great cost, Alexandrium, Herodium, and Hyrcania.

Then he conducted him to Jerusalem, where the people, in festive attire, received him with acclamations. In return, Agrippa sacrificed a hundred oxen to God and feasted the people, omitting none of the greatest delicacies. He enjoyed himself so much that he stayed many days in Jerusalem, and would willingly have stayed longer had not the season of the year hastened his departure. With winter coming, he thought it unsafe to postpone sailing for Ionia, this being the country to which he had to return. (Antt. XVI, 2:1.)

In the following spring, 14 B.C., Herod rejoined Agrippa, who was engaged in a campaign in Asia Minor. "Herod was an invaluable aide and counselor to Agrippa in the conduct both of the war and civil affairs. He was also a pleasant companion for Agrippa when he relaxed himself." During this visit, Jewish residents of Ionian cities came to complain about "the injuries they suffered, for they were not permitted to live according to their laws and were deprived of the money they used to send to Jerusalem." Herod assigned Nicolas of Damascus to plead their cause. Agrippa decreed that "their privileges were not to be abrogated and that they were to continue in the observance of their own customs" (Antt. XVI, 2:2-5). Josephus ends a list of several epistles by Augustus and Agrippa affirming the right of the Jews in the Empire to adhere to their ancestral institutions (6:1-7) with a dissertation on Jewish laws, which follows.

IN DEFENSE OF JEWISH LAWS

I have felt compelled to set down these decrees, because this history of mine will circulate among the Greeks. By quoting these decrees, I have shown them that we were formerly held in great esteem and not forbidden by the governors whose subjects we were from keeping any of the laws of our forefathers and that we were supported by them in following our own religion and worship of God. I often point to these decrees in an effort to reconcile other people to us and to remove any grounds for the hatred unreasonable men have for us. As for our customs, no nation observes the same practices as another; in nearly every city we encounter different ones. But justice is a universally admired practice and advantageous to all men equally, whether Greek or barbarian. And for justice our laws have the greatest regard. These laws therefore, if we observe them rightly, make us charitable and friendly towards all men. For this reason we have a right to expect similar treatment from others and to tell them that they ought not to hold difference of institutions sufficient cause for antagonism but should base their attitude on the possession of virtue and probity, for these all men honor equally, and are sufficient reason for the safeguarding of human life. (Antt. XVI, 6:8.)

THE EXPEDITION AGAINST THE NABATAEAN ARABS (CA. 9 B.C.)

The formerly subdued people of Trachonitis (a territory given to Herod in 23 B.C.) found it difficult to adjust to a civilized life under Herod's rule (Antt. XV, 10:1).

When [Herod] sailed for Rome . . . the Trachonites spread a rumor that he was dead; revolted, and resumed their customary plunder of their neighbors. The king's commanders subdued them during his absence, but some forty of the leaders, terrified at the punishment meted out to their comrades, escaped into [Nabataean] Arabia, where Syllaeus [procurator of king Obadas II] entertained them . . . and provided them with a stronghold in which to live. These overran and pillaged not only Judaea but all Coele-Syria as well, with Syllaeus providing them with safe and protected hideouts while they indulged in these criminal raids.

When Herod returned from Rome, he found that his dominions had suffered greatly at their hands. Unable to reach the plunderers because of the secure retreat the Arabs had given them, he, enraged at the harm they had inflicted on him, slew their relatives throughout Trachonitis. Their law exacting revenge at all costs on slayers of their kin, the brigands, more furious than ever, retaliated by continuing to ravage all of Herod's domains with impunity. Herod finally complained to Saturninus [the governor of Syria] and Volumnius [the Roman general], demanding that these brigands be punished. But they only waxed stronger and more numerous. Chaos reigned because of their revolt. Some one-thousand strong by this time, they laid waste the countries and villages of Herod's kingdom and butchered the men they captured, until at length their criminal forays differed little from war. Filled with wrath at this turn of affairs, Herod demanded of king Obadas both the surrender of the brigands and the overdue sixty talents he had lent him through Syllaeus. But Syllaeus, who had pushed Obadas aside and usurped his authority, denied the brigands' presence in Arabia and delayed payment of the debt. The case was brought before Saturninus and Volumnius. . . . Syllaeus, in obedience to their ruling, finally agreed to repay Herod within thirty days, and to an exchange of each other's subjects. But whereas it was proved that the brigands were indeed in Arabia, not a single Arab subject was found to be in Herod's kingdom. . . .

When the due date for payment of his debt to Herod

was passed, Syllaeus, without fulfilling any part of his agreement, set out for Rome. Once more demanding payment of his money and deliverance of the brigands, Herod, with the permission of Saturninus and Volumnius, took the law into his own hands and led his army into Arabia. In three days, by forced marches, he arrived at the garrison where the brigands were stationed, took it by storm, and captured the whole band. He demolished the place, called Raepta, but harmed no other city. However, when the Arabs, led by their captain Nacebus, came to the aid of the brigands, a battle ensued. A few of Herod's soldiers, Nacebus, and some twenty of his men fell; the rest fled. Having punished them, Herod settled three thousand Idumaeans in Trachonitis, thus restraining the brigands that were there. . . . (Antt. XVI, 9:1-2.)

In Rome, Syllaeus complained to Augustus about Herod's intervention and succeeded in gaining the Roman's favor. Augustus wrote to Herod that "whereas of old he had treated him as his friend, he would now treat him as his subject." The inhabitants of Trachonitis, informed of Syllaeus' success, rose against the Idumaean garrison. A first Herodian embassy to Rome failed to conciliate Augustus. Herod then sent a second, headed by Nicolas of Damascus. Nicolas succeeded in reconciling Augustus to Herod and in restoring their friendship (9:3-4; 10:8-9).

ALEXANDER AND ARISTOBULUS, SONS OF MARIAMNE, AND ANTIPATER, SON OF DORIS

In 18 or 17 B.C., the sons of Mariamne, after a five year stay in Rome, were brought home by Herod. Antipater, the son of Doris, Herod's prior wife (Antt. XIV, 12:1), lived in exile with his mother, until recalled by Herod in 14 B.C.

Mariamne's sons inherited their mother's resentment towards Herod, and because of the enormity of his guilt, had even earlier, when studying in Rome, regarded him as an enemy. Their antagonism increased on their return to Judaea and waxed ever stronger with the years. On reaching the marriage age, one of them [Aristobulus] took [Berenice], daughter of his aunt Salome, their mother's accuser, for wife; the other [Alexander] married [Glaphyra], daughter of Archelaus, king of Cappadocia. They now manifested their hatred of Herod in speech, as well as in thought. Taking advantage of this rashness, their slanderers told the king that his sons were conspiring against him and that the son-in-law of Archelaus [Alexander], relying on his father-in-law, was preparing to flee in order to accuse Herod before Augustus. These calumnies prompted Herod to recall Antipater, his son by Doris, to act as bulwark against the children of Mariamne, and to honor him with every mark of favor.

This change in their affairs was intolerable to the young men. In their pride of birth they could not restrain their indignation on seeing the son of a woman of no standing exalted above them. Nor did they hide their chagrin. In the meantime, as each day they gave fresh offense, Antipater zealously promoted his own cause. Remarkably clever in flattering his father, he was similarly clever in inventing calumnies against his brothers. Some of these slanders he himself related to Herod; others were circulated by the agents he employed. He was so successful that he finally cut off his brothers from any hope of succeeding to the crown. For both by testament and open acknowledgment he was now Herod's successor, and invested with the decorations and other insignia of royalty except the diadem, he was sent to Augustus as sovereign prince. He also succeeded in bringing his mother back into Mariamne's bed. And with his two weapons of flattery and slander, he at last brought matters to such a pass that Herod contemplated putting his sons to death.

He dragged Alexander to Rome and charged him

at Augustus' tribunal with attempts to poison him. With difficulty the young man summoned confidence to reveal his distress. Nevertheless, though facing a judge more skillful than Antipater and more rational than Herod, he, while modestly avoiding any imputation against his father, ably exculpated himself from the charges. Establishing as well the innocence of his brother, his partner in danger, he complained of Antipater's treacherous conduct and of the dishonor suffered by him and by his brother. A clear conscience aided his power of words, for he was a most impressive speaker. When he concluded that it was in Herod's power to punish him and his brother with death if he proved his charge against them, he moved all to tears. And so deeply did he affect Augustus that the latter dismissed the charges and reconciled Herod to his sons on the following terms: they were to render full obedience to their father; the latter at the same time remained free to leave his kingdom to whomever he pleased. (War I, 23:1-3.)

The journey to Augustus took place in 12 B.C. Back in Jerusalem, Herod declared all three sons successors to his throne. But Antipater, aided by Salome and Pheroras, continued to plot against his half brothers and to feed Herod's suspicions. Many members of the court, including servants, were involved in the intrigue. Alexander was arrested. His father-in-law, the king of Cappadocia, effected a reconciliation between father and son, but the peace did not last (23:4-26:5).

THE TRAGIC END

Salome further whetted Herod's cruelty towards his sons. Because she was both his mother-in-law and his aunt, Aristobulus wished to involve her in the perils he and his brother faced. Accordingly, he cautioned her about her safety, warning her that Herod was planning to kill her on charges brought against her that she had, when she had been anxious to marry the

[Nabataean] Arab Syllaeus, disclosed to the latter, an avowed enemy, the king's secrets.

This warning proved to be the last storm that overwhelmed the young men, already sorely tossed by the tempest. For Salome ran to the king and informed him of Aristobulus' warning. Herod, no longer master of himself, threw his sons into chains and confined them in separate prisons. He then, with all haste, sent to Augustus the military tribune Volumnius and his friend Olympus with a letter of information about the latest events. . . . Augustus was greatly distressed by the plight of the young men, but he did not think he should deprive the father of authority over his sons. In a return letter to Herod, he therefore gave him full powers of discretion in the case, adding, however, that he would do well to hold an inquiry into the conspiracy before a general council composed of his own kin and of the governors of his provinces. If his sons were convicted, he could inflict the extreme penalty; but if they had merely meditated flight, a less severe punishment was called for.

The trial at Berytus (about 7 B.C.) took place in the absence of the accused sons; "this was done very cunningly, for Herod knew that their mere appearance would have excited universal compassion."

Rising from his seat, the king inveighed against his sons as if they were present. He did not stress conspiracy, lacking evidence to prove it; but his sons' invectives, jests, insults, and a thousand other offenses against him, which, he said, were worse than death, he presented in detail. Since no one contradicted him, he called for a vote, lamenting at the same time, that, though he had gained a bitter victory over his sons, he, rather than they, was the victim.

The first vote was that of Saturninus [governor of Syria]. He condemned the young men, but not to death, arguing that it would not be proper for him, whose own three sons were present, to vote for the

destruction of another's children. His two legates concurred in his decision, and a few others followed their
example. Volumnius [the procurator] was first to
recommend the severest penalty, and all who followed
him condemned the young men to death; some to curry
favor, others out of hatred for Herod, none from indignation at the youths. All Syria and Judaea was now
in suspense, awaiting the last act of the drama. But
no one expected Herod to be so cruel as to murder his
children. He, however, carried them off to Tyre, then
sailed to Caesarea, there to deliberate the kind of death
they should suffer.

*From an old soldier, Tiro, Herod learned more of
the nation's sentiment in favor of Alexander and
Aristobulus, and from his barber Trypho of a plot to
kill him. He then decided to act.*

Herod sent his sons to Sebaste [Samaria], which is
not far from Caesarea, and ordered them to be
strangled. This order was executed and direction given
to convey their bodies to the fortress of Alexandrion,
there to be buried with Alexander, their maternal
grandfather. Such was the end of Alexander and Aristobulus. (War I, 27.)

It may perhaps not seem unnatural to some that
Herod's deep-seated hatred for his sons grew so great
as to suppress all natural feeling. But a just appraisal
of his action must take into consideration these
factors: whether his sons' behavior was such as to
feed his anger, inciting him to do what he did . . . ;
whether the deed was perpetrated because Herod was
so cruel and so dominated by his craving for power
. . . that he could not tolerate any possible rivals . . . ;
or whether Fortune is not more powerful than all
prudent reasonings. We must indeed assume that man's
actions are predetermined by some inevitable necessity, which we call Fate, because nothing is done without it. This view, however, should be weighed against
the one that attributes events in part to ourselves and

holds men responsible for the conduct of their lives—
which is the teaching of our ancient law. . . . (Antt.
XVI, 11:8.)

THE LAST YEARS

THE GOLDEN EAGLE (4 B.C.)

There lived in Jerusalem two men of learning, Judah,
son of Sepphoraeus, and Matthias, son of Margalus,
reputed to possess thorough knowledge of the laws of
their country and held accordingly in the highest
esteem by the entire nation. Many young men came
to listen to their exposition of the laws, and a small
army almost of those who had reached manhood assembled every day. Hearing that the king was wasting
away with melancholy and disease, these men of learning dropped hints to their disciples that this was a
propitious moment to uphold the honor of God by
pulling down the works put up contrary to the laws
of their country, for it was unlawful to place in the
Temple statues, busts, or any other representation of
living creatures.

The king had erected a golden eagle over the great
[Temple] gate. The learned men exhorted their listen-
ers to cut this eagle down. It was honorable, they said,
to die, if such danger threatened, for the laws of
one's country—the soul was immortal and eternal happiness awaited those who died in this manner. Only
the ignoble and those unskilled in wisdom clung in
ignorance to life and preferred death from disease to
death attained through virtue.

As they held forth in this vein, a rumor spread that
the king was dying; consequently the disciples boldly
set about their work. At midday, when many were
busy inside the Temple, they lowered themselves from
the roof with ropes and hacked off the golden eagle.

The deed was instantly communicated to the king's
captain, who hurried to the spot with a great body of

soldiers, arrested some forty young men, and brought them to the king. Had they indeed dared to cut down the golden eagle? Herod asked them. They confessed the deed. "Who ordered you to do so?" he inquired. "The law of our fathers," was their reply. He asked: "Why are you so joyful when you are to be put to death?" "Because greater happiness awaits us after death," they answered.

So great was the king's wrath then that disregarding his disease he went before the people. In a lengthy speech he accused the men of sacrilege and of plotting, under cover of their law, still other crimes, and he demanded punishment for their impiety. Fearing added victims of his anger, the people implored him to confine his punishment to the instigators of the deed and those who were caught at it and to forego his wrath against the rest. With difficulty the king complied. He burned alive the chief perpetrators and the learned men; the rest of the seized men he delivered to the officers for execution. (War I, 33:2-4.)

ANTIPATER'S PLOT AND HEROD'S END

After the execution of Mariamne's sons, Antipater plotted against Herod's life in order to hasten his succession to the throne. The king eventually became aware of his beloved son's designs. After a court trial in the presence of Varus, the governor of Syria, Antipater was imprisoned and messengers sent to lay the case before Augustus. Herod "was now nearly seventy; his spirit was broken by the miseries his children had brought him . . . and his malady aggravated by the thought that Antipater was still alive" (War I, 28:1-33:1).

Herod's disease [now] spread over his entire body, and he was racked with complex pains. He suffered from continuous fever, though in a mitigated form, intolerable itching of his entire body, constant pain in the intestines, dropsylike tumors in his feet, inflammation of the abdomen, and an ulceration of his genitals which bred maggots. In addition, he had difficulty in breathing, and convulsive spasms in all his limbs. The diviners pronounced his maladies a judgment for his treatment of the learned men.

Yet despite these aggregate pains, Herod still clung to life, cherishing hope of recovery and devising various cures. He crossed the Jordan to try the hot baths of Callirrhoe. . . . There physicians advised the bathing of his entire body in warm oil. When they immersed him in a vessel filled with such oil, his eyes failed him and he suddenly fell back as if dying. He was revived by the commotion this caused among the physicians. Despairing now of recovery, he ordered fifty drachmas to be given to every soldier and large sums of money to be distributed among his friends and his commanders.

Filled with gloom, he reached Jericho on his return journey. There, as if defying death, he contrived a horrible atrocity. Having assembled the noblest men from every village of Judaea, he commanded them to be shut up in the hippodrome. Then he sent for his sister Salome and her husband Alexas, and said: "I know that the Jews will celebrate on my death; but if you will obey my commands, I will have both a vicarious mourning and a splendid funeral. Upon my death, surround the men now in custody with soldiers and kill them instantly. All Judaea and every family in it will then shed unwilling tears at my death."

Herod scarcely finished when letters arrived from his ambassadors in Rome, informing him that . . . Antipater had been condemned to death. However, if Herod preferred to banish him, Augustus granted him permission to do so. This news a little longer revived Herod's desire to live; but once more overcome with pain and already wasted from lack of nourishment and wracked by a convulsive cough, he attempted to anticipate death.

Taking an apple, a fruit he usually sliced before eating, he called for a knife. Then after looking around to see that there was no one to stop him, he raised his hand to stab himself. But Achiab, his cousin, rushed forward and stayed his hand. As if the king had really died, loud wailing instantly filled the palace. The clamor reached the ears of Antipater; his spirits revived, and elated with joy, he tried to bribe the guards to free him from his bonds and let him escape. However, the captain not only forbade acceptance of the bribe, but rushed to inform the king of Antipater's plot. The latter, with greater strength than was to be expected from a man in his condition, called to his spearmen to slay Antipater. This accomplished, he had the body interred at Hyrcanium. Amending his will once more, he named Archelaus, his eldest son, and brother of Antipas, successor to the throne; and Antipas, tetrarch.[23]

Herod survived the execution of his son by only five days. He had reigned thirty-four years from the time when, on Antigonus' execution, he became king; but from the date of his being declared king by the Romans, thirty-seven years. Though in all other respects he was favored by fortune—if ever a man prospered he was such a man, for born a commoner, he ascended a throne, occupied it a long time, and bequeathed it to his own children—he was most unfortunate in his family life.

Before news of Herod's death reached the soldiers, Salome and her husband hurried from the palace to free the prisoners he had ordered to be slain, stating that Herod had changed his mind and now wished these men to be returned to their homes. Only after the men were gone, did Salome inform the soldiers of Herod's death and assemble both them and the people in the amphitheater of Jericho. Here [Herod's friend] Ptolemy [of Rhodes], to whom Herod had entrusted his signet ring, came forward, blessed the memory of the king, and comforted them. Then he read to the troops the letter Herod had left, which earnestly exhorted them to be loyal to his successor. The reading of the codicil followed. It left Trachonitis and the neighboring territories to Philip [son of Cleopatra of Jerusalem], and as already noted, named Antipas tetrarch [of Galilee and Peraea], and Archelaus king. The latter was also enjoined to carry to Augustus Herod's ring, together with the sealed documents relating to the administration of his dominions, because Herod had vested in Augustus the control of the arrangements and the ratification of the will. The remaining particulars were to be governed by the prior testament.

Congratulatory acclamations immediately greeted Archelaus; and the soldiers, marching in companies, together with the people, promised their good will and prayed to God to bless his reign. Preparations were then made for the funeral of the king. Archelaus, sparing nothing that would augment its magnificence, brought forth all the regalia to grace the procession in honor of the deceased. The bier was solid gold, studded with precious stones, and the bed was of variegated purple. On it lay the body, also covered with purple. A diadem was on Herod's head, and over it a crown of gold. At his right-hand side lay a scepter.

Herod's sons and numerous kin surrounded the bier. Next came the guards, the Thracian bands, the Germans, and the Gauls, all of them equipped as for war. The rest of the army, preceded by its commanders and subordinate officers, marched in front, armed and in order. They were followed by five hundred of Herod's servants and freedmen, bearing sweet spices. The body was conveyed to Herodium, a distance of two hundred furlongs, Herod having left orders to be buried there. So ends the history of Herod. (War I, 33:5-9.)

HEROD'S BUILDINGS, FOUNDATIONS, AND ENDOWMENTS

"With the possible exception of the Emperor Hadrian, Herod the Great was the most passionate builder of antiquity" (Steward Perowne). *The most prominent of his buildings, the reconstructed Temple, is described in greater detail in Antt. XV, 11. According to that description, the work began in the eighteenth year of Herod's rule, i.e., in 20 B.C. The building of Caesarea started two years earlier. For a parallel description see Antt. XV, 9:6.*

In the fifteenth year of his reign[24] Herod, at incalculable expense, restored the Temple, unsurpassed in splendor. A wall encircling the area around it enlarged it to twice its former size. Great colonnades, which encompassed the holy place, and the fortress on its north side added to its sumptuousness. The colonnades, Herod built from the foundations; the fortress, not in anything inferior to a palace, he restored at immense cost, and named it Antonia, in honor of Antony. He also built a palace for himself in the Upper City. Its two buildings surpassed even the Temple in beauty and spaciousness. These he named after his friends, one Caesareum, the other Agrippeum.

"In addition, Herod built for his own use an underground passage leading from Antonia to the inner Temple at its eastern gate. Above it he erected a tower in order to provide himself with an underground ascent to the Temple as safeguard against a possible people's revolt against their kings" (Antt. XV, 11:7).

Herod honored the memory and names of his friends not only with buildings; his generosity extended to whole cities. In the district of Samaria he encircled a town with a superb wall twenty furlongs long, and settled there six thousand colonists, to whom he allotted a highly fertile piece of land. In the center of that town he erected a large temple to Augustus, with a furlong and half of consecrated ground around it. He named the city Sebaste, and he bestowed an enviable charter on its inhabitants.

He also erected improved and more spacious buildings at Jericho, between the fort of Cypros [named after his mother] and the former palace, and named them after the same friends [Augustus and Agrippa]. In short, no suitable spot in his domain lacked some memorial to the emperor. And when his own territories were filled with temples, he lavished on the provinces testimonials of his regard and erected monuments to Augustus in many cities.

He observed among the maritime towns one, called Strato's Tower, that had fallen into decay. Its advantageous position being suited to the display of his zeal, he rebuilt it throughout with white stone and adorned it with splendid palaces. This work gave striking proof of his magnanimity. There was not a single good harbor throughout the seashore from Dora to Jaffa, midway between which lay Strato's Tower; so vessels sailing from Phoenicia to Egypt were forced to face the perils of the sea when menaced by the southwest wind. . . . But the king, even nature yielding to his lavishness and enterprise, constructed a harbor larger than the Pyraeus [the harbor of Athens]. . . .

Adjacent to the harbor, to which the equidistant streets of the town led, were dwellings built also of white stone. Facing the entrance of the harbor, upon an elevation, stood the temple of Augustus, distinguished for beauty and magnitude. Inside it were two colossal statues: one of Augustus, not inferior in size to the Olympian Zeus, after which it was modeled; the other of Rome, equaling that of Hera at Argos. The city Herod dedicated to the province; the port, to those sailing to it; but the honor of the founding of the city he ascribed to Caesar Augustus, and named it Caesarea accordingly.

The rest of Caesarea's edifices—amphitheater, theater, and market place—he built in a style worthy of its name. He held games there every fifth year. These too he named after Caesar Augustus. He inaugurated them [10 B.C.] in the one hundred and ninety-second Olympiad, and he was the first to offer prizes of great value. And not only the victors, but those as well who obtained second and third places shared in the royal munificence.

He also rebuilt Anthedon, a maritime town [near Gaza] destroyed in the wars, and called it Agrippium. So warm was his regard for this friend [Agrippa] that he engraved his name on the gate he erected in the Temple [of Jerusalem].

Herod also loved his father, as much as any man ever did. As a monument to him, he built a city in the most pleasant plain of his dominion, a plain rich in rivers and trees, and called this city Antipatris [Ras el-Ain]. To his mother he dedicated a fortress above Jericho, remarkable for strength and beauty, which he walled and named Cypros. His brother Phasael he honored by a tower in Jerusalem, giving it that brother's name. . . . Still another city, which he built in the valley leading north from Jericho, he also named Phasaelis.

While thus immortalizing his family and friends, he did not neglect to leave a memorial of himself. Erecting a fortress on a mountain near Arabia, he called it Herodium. He also gave his name to an artificial mound, shaped like a woman's breast and lying sixty furlongs from Jerusalem. . . . At immense cost he conveyed to it an ample supply of water from a great distance, and since the mound was very high and completely artificial, he eased its ascent with two hundred steps of the whitest marble. At the base he erected other palaces, large enough to accomodate his furnishings and his friends. In the diversity of its accommodations, this stronghold resembled a town; in its circumscribed territory, a royal residence.

Having completed these various works, he lavished his munificent bounty on many alien cities. He erected gymnasia at Tripolis, Damascus, and Ptolemais [Acco]; constructed a wall for Byblus; town halls, colonnades, temples, and market places, for Berytus and Tyre; theaters for Sidon and Damascus; an aqueduct for Laodicea on sea; baths, costly fountains, and a peristyle, admirable both in workmanship and magnitude, at Ascalon. To some cities he dedicated groves and meadows. Numerous other cities received grants of land, as if they were part of his kingdom. Others, like Cos, he endowed in perpetuity with annual revenues to maintain the office of keeper of the gymnasium and to ensure that prizes should never be wanting. On many occasions and at various places he granted subsidies to the people of Rhodes for the equipment of a navy. At his own expense he rebuilt the Pythian temple, destroyed by fire, in a style superior to its former glory.

And need I speak of his gifts to the people of Lycia and Samos, or of his generosity throughout Ionia, where he gave to each according to his need? Are not the Athenians and Lacedaemonians, the Nicopolitans, and Pergamum in Mysia, laden with his bounty? Did he not also, though it was twenty furlongs long, pave with marble that broad street in Antioch of Syria that was shunned by all because of the mud imbedded in it? And did he not adorn it with a colonnade of equal size as protection against the rain?

It may be argued that only individual communities benefited by Herod's generosity. But his bounty to the people of Elis benefited not only the whole of Greece but the entire world as far as the fame of the Olympic games reached; since when he saw that these games were dying for want of funds and that this sole relic of ancient Greece was fast disappearing, he not only accepted the office of president at their quinquennial celebration, at which he happened to be present during his journey to Rome [12 B.C., or 8 B.C.], but he allocated in perpetuity revenues for their support so that the memory of him would never cease, as it were, to occupy that presidency. . . . (War I, 21:1-12.)

HEROD'S PERSONALITY

By introducing alien practices Herod betrayed the laws of his country and corrupted its ancient constitution, which should have been preserved inviolate. Accordingly, we became guilty of great wickedness because the religious practices which used to guide the multitude to piety were now being neglected. . . . The theater at Jerusalem and the great amphitheater on the plain were indeed costly works, but contrary to Jewish custom, since no such spectacles were handed down to us by our tradition. . . .

He also made proclamation to the neighboring countries and called men together out of every nation. Wrestlers also, and all others who vied for prizes in such games were invited from every land. . . . Because of the great rewards promised for victory, not only to those who performed naked but to professional musicians as well, Herod succeeded in assembling the most renowned athletes. . . . He offered large rewards also to those who contended for prizes in chariots drawn by two or four pairs of horses.

In his ambition to give public demonstration of his grandeur, Herod also imitated all the practices of other nations, though not in so costly and magnificent a fashion. Throughout the theater hung inscriptions of Augustus' great victories and trophies, all of purest gold and silver, from the nations he had defeated. . . . Herod also assembled many wild beasts—lions in great abundance and such other beasts as were either unusually powerful or rare. These were trained to fight either each other, or men condemned to death.

Foreigners were greatly surprised and delighted at the vast expense of the shows and the great danger of the spectacles. But the Jews saw them only as a tangible abrogation of the customs they so greatly venerated. They also thought that to throw men to wild beasts for the delight of spectators was barefaced impiety, and it seemed no less impious to them to abandon their laws for such alien practices. . . . (Antt. XV, 8:1.)

Herod had a body suited to his mind. He was an excellent hunter and skilled horseman. The land being rich in wild boars, and richer still in deer and wild asses, he at times captured forty wild animals in one day. He was an overpowering warrior, and he excelled in sports. Many must have been astonished at the skill of his javelin throwing and his unerring bowmanship. In addition to his mental and physical superiority, he was fortune's favorite. In war he rarely met with any misfortune; when he did, not he but treachery or the rashness of his troops was responsible. (War I, 21: 13.)

Some men are amazed at the contradictions in Herod's nature and aims. When one considers his bounty and the benefits he bestowed on mankind, not even those who least admire him can deny that he was a generous man. But when one considers the punishments and suffering he inflicted, not only on his subjects but also on his closest kin, as well as his harsh and unrelenting character, he can only appear as a savage brute devoid of humanity. Some people therefore believe that his nature was at times at war with itself.

I myself hold another opinion. I believe that Herod's contradictory actions were guided by only one motive. Being a passionately ambitious man, he was compelled to lavishness whenever there was hope of perpetuating his memory or increasing his present fame. Since this lavishness exceeded his means, it led to repressive measures against his subjects. . . . Though aware of their hatred, he did not mitigate his harshness, since that would have reduced his income, but strove instead to exploit their ill will for further gains.

From the people at court, he demanded obsequiousness and slavishness. Recalcitrants and those who appeared to be considering some revolutionary changes in his government . . . he prosecuted and punished as if they were enemies, even when these were friends or members of his family. He committed these offenses out of craving that he alone be honored. The honors he lavished on Augustus, Agrippa, and other friends are proof of my assertion about this passion of his; he wanted others to honor him as he himself honored his superiors. . . .

But the Jewish nation is through its law a stranger to such acts, preferring righteousness to glory. That is why that nation did not please him; it could not flatter the king's ambition with statues, temples, or similar objects. This, it seems to me, was at one and the same time the cause both of Herod's crimes against his own courtiers and counselors and of his bounty to aliens and strangers. (Antt. XVI, 5:4.)

THE HEIRS OF
HEROD AND THE
ROMAN PROCURATORS

JUDAEA UNDER ARCHELAUS
(4 B.C.-A.D. 6)

To ascend the throne, Archelaus, designated by his father, Herod, as his successor in Judaea, needed the consent of Augustus. Riots had broken out in Judaea; they increased in strength when Herod's unpopular heir left for Rome. The plunder of the Temple by Sabinus, temporary administrator of Herod's territory, further inflamed the Jews. Varus, governor of Syria, intervened in this explosive situation. He burned Sepphoris in Galilee, and in his pursuit of Jewish rebels wherever found, crucified two thousand men (War II, 1-5). Soon after Archelaus arrived in Rome, a Jewish embassy appeared before Augustus.

THE JEWISH EMBASSY BEFORE AUGUSTUS

In Rome . . . a charge was now brought against Archelaus by certain Jews who came . . . to plead for the autonomy of their nation. There were fifty of them, but they were supported by over eight thousand Roman Jews. Augustus convened a council, composed of Roman officials and of his friends, in the temple of the Palatine Apollo. . . . The [Roman] Jews were grouped with the Judaean ambassadors; Archelaus and his friends faced them.

The accusers, on being given permission to speak,

began with a recapitulation of Herod's crimes, asserting that he had been not a sovereign but the most cruel of tyrants. The miseries endured by the survivors of the thousands murdered by him had been so great that they envied the victims who were dead. He had tortured the bodies of his subjects, dismantled the cities of his own kingdom while beautifying those of other nations, and shed the blood of his people for the sake of foreign states. Poverty replaced Judaea's former prosperity, and iniquity, its ancient laws. In a word, Herod had in but a few years inflicted more miseries on the Jews than their forefathers had suffered during the entire period that had elapsed since their return [under Ezra] from Babylon to their own country in the reign of Xerxes.

But so great was the submissiveness and acceptance of misery to which he had reduced them, that they endured even a self-imposed continuation of their bitter servitude. Accordingly, though he was the son of so great a tyrant, they had, on his father's death, gladly acknowledged Archelaus as king, had mourned Herod's death with him, and had prayed for the prosperity of his reign. He, however, as if to leave no doubt of the stock from which he sprang, had prefaced his reign by the slaughter of three thousand citizens, offering to God as many sacrifices for his rule as he had with corpses filled the Temple at a festival. . . .

The Jews then implored the Romans to have pity on the remnants of Judaea and no longer to expose it to those who had so barbarously rent it but instead to unite their country to Syria and administer it with their own officials. They [the Jews] would then prove that, though now slandered as seditious and war-hungry people, they knew how to obey authority when mildly exercised. With this plea the Jews closed their charges.

At this point, Nicolas of Damascus rose and accused

the Jewish nation of being "difficult to rule and by nature insubordinate to kings."

Having heard both sides, Augustus dissolved the council. A few days later, however, he gave one half of the kingdom to Archelaus, with the title of ethnarch, promising to make him king should he prove himself deserving. The other half he divided into two tetrarchies, which he conferred on two other sons of Herod, Philip and Antipas, who had disputed the throne with Archelaus. Antipas received Peraea and Galilee, whose revenue was two hundred talents. Batanaea, Trachonitis, Auranitis, and certain districts of Zeno's [Zenodorus'] domain in the vicinity of Panias, yielding a revenue of one hundred talents, were subjected to Philip. To the ethnarchy of Archelaus were assigned Idumaea and Judaea, together with Samaria, one quarter of whose taxes were remitted in consideration of its nonparticipation in the general revolt.

Archelaus' authority extended also to the cities of Strato's Tower, Sebaste, Jaffa, and Jerusalem. The Greek towns Gaza, Gadara, and Hippos, Augustus severed from the kingdom and annexed to Syria. The revenues of the district bestowed on Archelaus amounted to four hundred talents. . . . (War II, 6:1-3.)

ARCHELAUS' END

On taking possession of the ethnarchy, Archelaus, mindful of former feuds, inflicted great cruelties both on Jews and on Samaritans. Both groups brought charges against him, through deputies, before Augustus; and in the ninth year of his administration [A.D. 6], he was banished to Vienne, a town in Gaul, and his property was confiscated by the imperial treasury. It is said that the following dream preceded his summons by Augustus: he thought he saw nine ears of corn, full and large, devoured by oxen. He asked the

diviners and some Chaldaeans to expound the portent
of this dream. After several different interpretations
had been given, Simon, a member of the Essene sect,
said that in his opinion the ears of corn denoted years,
and the oxen, changes in the state of affairs, for in
plowing the land, oxen altered it. Archelaus therefore
would reign as many years as there were ears of corn
and then would meet with various vicissitudes. Five
days later Archelaus was summoned to his trial. (War
II, 7:3.)

JUDAEA UNDER THE FIRST ROMAN
PROCURATORS

THE "ENROLLMENT" UNDER QUIRINIUS AND THE
REVOLT OF JUDAH THE GALILEAN

*In A.D. 6, Augustus abolished the rule of Archelaus
and made his territory a Roman province (Antt. XVII,
13:2 and 5). At that time Sulpicius Quirinius was
governor of Syria; Coponius was sent to Judaea as
its first procurator.*

At this time Quirinius, a Roman senator, who after
passing through other offices, rose to be consul and
was a man of great eminence in other respects as well,
was, with others, sent by Augustus to Syria to serve
as a judge of that nation and to appraise its property.
Coponius, a man of equestrian rank, was sent with him
to be governor, with supreme powers, of the Jews.
Quirinius, too, came to Judaea, which was now added
to the province of Syria, to appraise the property of
the Jews and to dispose of Archelaus' estate.

Although at first indignant, the Jews, at the persuasion of the high priest Joazar, son of Boethus, refrained from further opposition to the taxation and
peaceably accounted for their estates. But a certain
Judah, a Gaulanite from the city of Gamala, and
Zadok, a Pharisee, were eager to instigate a revolt.
Both said that this valuation was but a direct intro-

duction of slavery and exhorted the nation to assert its freedom. . . .

Men listened gladly, and the bold attempt reached great heights. Countless misfortunes sprang from these men, and the nation was infected by them to an incredible degree. One violent war succeeded another, and we lost the friends who used to alleviate our suffering. . . . Faction eventually reached such heights that the very Temple of God was burned by the enemies' fire. In consequence, the customs of our fathers were altered . . . for Judah and Zadok, who introduced among us a fourth philosophic sect, which had numerous followers, filled our state with increasing turmoil and laid the foundations of future miseries with their system of philosophy, a system formerly unknown among us. . . . (Antt. XVIII, 1:1.)

"A Galilean named Judah provoked the inhabitants to a revolt, denouncing them as cowards if they tolerated payment of tribute to the Romans and bowed to mortals as their masters after having had God as their lord. He was leader of a sect he had founded that was wholly unlike all the other sects" (War II, 8:1). In Acts 5, 34-40, the Pharisee Gamaliel mentions Judah of Galilee, who "in the days of the enrolling drew away people after him." Judah has been identified with Judah, son of Hezekiah, the Galilean rebel whom king Herod had executed (Antt. XIV, 9:2; War I, 10:5). The sons of Judah, James [Jacob] and Simon, were crucified by order of the procurator Tiberius Alexander (Antt. XX, 5:2).

THE "FOURTH PHILOSOPHY"

The fourth sect of Jewish philosophy was founded by Judah the Galilean. Though in all other respects its followers accept the Pharisaic notions, they differ from that sect in their inordinate attachment to liberty, saying that God alone must be their ruler and their lord. They make light of dying, whatever the

death may be, nor are they cowed by executions of
their kin and friends. Fear cannot force them to call
any man lord. Since this unshakable resolution of
theirs is well known to many, I shall say nothing
more. Nor have I any fears that anything I have said
about them will be disbelieved. I fear, rather, that
what I have said does not do justice to their fortitude
under pain. (Antt. XVIII, 1:6.)

PONTIUS PILATE

*The procurator Coponius was followed by Marcus
Ambivius, Annius Rufus, and Valerius Gratus, of
whom not much is known (Antt. XVIII, 2:2). The
fifth procurator was Pontius Pilate (A.D. 26-36).*

Pilate, sent by Tiberius as procurator to Judaea,
secretly and under cover of night brought into Jerusalem the images of Caesar known as standards. This
act, when day broke, engendered a fearful tumult
among the Jews; those close to the standards were
seized with dismay, their laws, as it were, being
trampled underfoot, for these laws permitted no image
to be placed in the city. The city's indignant crowds
were augmented by vast multitudes pouring in from
the countryside. Hastening to Pilate at Caesarea, they
implored him to remove the standards from Jerusalem
and to preserve their ancestral laws. When Pilate rejected their pleas, they fell prostrate on the ground
and stayed so for five days and nights.

On the following day Pilate ascended his tribunal in
the great circus and summoned the people, as if to
give them the answer they craved; then he gave a
prearranged signal to a body of armed troops to surround the Jews. Encircled by three-deep rings of
soldiers, the Jews were dumbfounded at the unexpected sight. Pilate, declaring that he would cut them
down if they refused to admit the standards of Caesar,
signaled to the soldiers to draw their swords. As if by
preconcerted agreement, the Jews fell prostrate in a

mass, and offering their necks, cried that they would rather die than transgress the law. Amazed at the force of their devotion to their religion, Pilate ordered the immediate removal of the standards from Jerusalem. (War II, 9:2-3.)

On a later occasion Pilate used the treasures of the Temple for the construction of an aqueduct and beat down the crowds angered by the sacrilege (9:4). Luke 13:1 has a reference to the unrest of the period: "There were present at that season some that told Jesus of the Galileans, whose blood Pilate had mingled with their sacrifices." Pilate was the judge of Jesus.

JESUS OF NAZARETH

Now about this time lived Jesus, a wise man, if indeed he should be called a man. He was a doer of wonderful works, a teacher of men who receive the truth with pleasure, and won over many Jews and many Greeks. He was the Christ. And when Pilate, at the information of the leading men among us, sentenced him to the cross, those who loved him at the start did not cease to do so, for he appeared to them alive again on the third day as had been foretold— both this and ten thousand other wonderful things concerning him—by the divine prophets. Nor is the tribe of Christians, so named after him, extinct to this day. (Antt. XVIII, 3:3.)

"For twelve hundred years, from the time of Eusebius down to the sixteenth century, the words were . . . treasured by Christians as the testimony of an outsider . . . to the main articles of their creed" (Thackeray). However, words like "He was the Christ" could have been written only by a Christian; Josephus was a Pharisee. The tenor of the passage and the fact that Origen (d. ca. 254) did not find it in his text of Josephus has led many historians to consider it either a Christian revision of an original Josephus reference to Jesus or an interpolation in-

*jected in the period between Origen and Eusebius (d.
ca. 340).*

JOHN THE BAPTIST

*Archelaus' brother, the tetrarch Herod Antipas, who
ruled over Galilee and Peraea (4 B.C. to A.D. 39), fell
in love with Herodias, wife of one of his half brothers;
Herodias left her husband to marry Herod Antipas
(Antt. XVIII, 5:1), and John the Baptist reprimanded
the tetrarch (Mark 6:17-18). The following passage
refers to the defeat of the tetrarch's army in the war
against the Arab king Aretas, father of Herod Antipas' castoff first wife (Antt., l.c.).*

Some Jews thought that the destruction of Herod's
army came from God, and very justly so, as punishment for his treatment of John, who was called the
Baptist. For Herod [Antipas] had John executed,
though he was a good man and commanded the Jews
to exercise virtue through justice towards one another
and piety towards God and by so doing to arrive at
immersion, for immersion would be acceptable to God
only if practiced not to expiate sins but for purification of the body after the soul had first been thoroughly
purified by righteousness.

Because, affected by his words, many flocked to him,
Herod feared that John's great influence over the
people might lead to revolt (for the people seemed
likely to do whatever he counseled). He therefore
thought it best to slay him in order to prevent any
mischief he might engender, and to avoid possible
future troubles by not sparing a man who might make
him repent of his leniency when too late. Accordingly,
because of Herod's suspicious nature, John was imprisoned in the fortress Machaerus, and there put to
death. The Jews held the opinion that the destruction
of Herod's army was God's punishment on him, and
a mark of His displeasure. (Antt. XVIII, 5:2.)

The end of John the Baptist as brought about by

Herodias and her daughter (Salome) is related in Mark 6:21-28.

AGRIPPA I
Aristobulus, executed in 7 B.C. by command of his father, Herod, left two sons, Agrippa (born 10 B.C.) and Herod (king of Chalkis), and a daughter, Herodias (wife of the tetrarch Herod Antipas). At the age of six, Agrippa was sent to Rome for his education. He remained there until A.D. 23, consorting with members of the Roman aristocracy. After a stay in the East, including Palestine, he returned to Italy, in A.D. 36, where the emperor Tiberius appointed him tutor of his grandson Tiberius. (Antt. XVIII, 6:1-4.)

IN ROME
Agrippa . . . courted men of importance, especially Germanicus' son Gaius, who was as yet a private citizen. Once Agrippa climaxed an entertainment for Gaius, during which he paid him many honors, by lifting his hands in open prayer that he might soon behold him master of the empire, when [the emperor] Tiberius should be no more. A servant related this incident to Tiberius, who, indignant, threw Agrippa into prison. He kept him there six months, treating him with great harshness, until he himself died [A.D. 37], after a reign of twenty-two years, six months, and three days.

Gaius [Caligula], when proclaimed emperor [A.D. 37], freed Agrippa and appointed him king of the tetrarchy vacated by the death of Philip. Agrippa's rise to kingly rank inflamed the ambitions of the tetrarch Herod [Antipas]. Herodias, his wife, was the chief instigator of his hopes for a throne. She upbraided him for his inactivity, alleging that only his unwillingness to go to Rome deprived him of a kingship. If, she argued, the emperor made Agrippa, a private individual, king, would he not all the more willingly advance him, a tetrarch, to the throne? Influenced by these arguments, Herod [Antipas] presented himself to Gaius, who punished his ambition with banishment to Spain, for an accuser had followed him to Rome in the person of Agrippa, to whose territories Gaius annexed his rival's tetrarchy. Herod died in Spain, whither his wife had accompanied him. (War II, 9:5-6.)

THE STATUE IN THE TEMPLE

The emperor Gaius' abuse of fortune's favors became so excessive that he considered himself a god, desired all to address him as such, and cut off from his country men of noblest blood. His impiety extended even to Judaea. Accordingly, he sent Petronius [legate of Syria] with an army to Jerusalem to place his statues in the sanctuary. If the Jews refused to admit them, Petronius had orders to slay all who opposed him and to enslave the rest.

But God was not heedless of these commands. Petronius marched from Antioch towards Judaea at the head of three legions and a large body of Syrian auxiliaries. Some of the Jews discredited the rumors of war; others believed them to be true but despaired of making any defense. The panic quickly became universal, for the [Roman] army was already at Ptolemais.

A description of Ptolemais (Acco) follows.

With their wives and children the Jews assembled on the plain near Ptolemais and supplicated Petronius: first, to spare the laws of their fathers; secondly, to have mercy on them. Yielding to their numbers and their entreaties, he left his army and the statues at Ptolemais, while he himself proceeded to Galilee. There he summoned the people and their most important men to Tiberias, where he depicted to them the power of Rome and the vengeance of the emperor, and pointed out the unreasonableness of their request.

That they alone should oppose the act when every city in all of Rome's subject nations had placed the images of the emperor among their gods was little less than rebellion, augmented by affront.

The Jews, on the other hand, insisted on their law and national customs and pleaded that they were forbidden to set up any image of God, and still less of man, not only in the Temple but even in the most casual spot of their land. To this Petronius replied: "But am I, too, not compelled to observe the law of my master? If I disobey him and spare you, I shall justly perish. Not I, but he who sent me will levy war against you; for I, like you, am subject to his authority." Whereupon the multitude cried out in unison that they were prepared to suffer for their law.

Petronius, having quieted the clamor, rejoined: "Will you then make war against the emperor?" They answered: "For the emperor and the Roman people we sacrifice twice a day. But if he wishes to erect these statues, he must first sacrifice the entire Jewish nation; and we herewith present ourselves, with our children and wives, ready for the slaughter." Astonished at their exceeding devotion to their religion and at their unflinching readiness to die, and pitying the Jews, Petronius dismissed them, leaving matters as they were.

In the days that followed, he assembled the nobles privately, and the people publicly, now entreating, now counseling, but most often threatening. He enlarged on the power of Rome, the anger of Gaius, and his own predicament. Since, however, they yielded to none of his efforts, and he realized that the country was in danger of remaining unsown—for it was seedtime and the people had been idle fifty days—he finally assembled them and said: "It is better that I should endanger my own self. Either, God aiding me, I shall persuade the emperor and thus gladly save myself and you, or if he continue in his rage, I shall, for the lives of so many, cheerfully surrender my own." He then dismissed the multitude, who invoked many blessings on him, withdrew his army from Ptolemais, and returned to Antioch.

From there he immediately wrote to the emperor, acquainting him with his expedition into Judaea and the nation's entreaties, and adding that unless he was prepared to destroy both the country and its inhabitants, he should forego his orders and permit the Jews to observe their law. Gaius' answer was couched in most immoderate terms, threatening Petronius with death for being so tardy in executing his commands. It so happened, however, that the messengers carrying these dispatches were detained three months at sea by tempestuous weather, while others, announcing the death of Gaius, had a favorable voyage. Petronius, accordingly, received the news of Gaius' death twenty-seven days before he received the threats against himself. (War II, 10.)

On the anti-Jewish outbreaks in Alexandria and the embassy to Caligula (in A.D. 40) headed by the philosopher Philo, see Philo, Embassy to Gaius *and* Against Flaccus *(the Roman governor); on the rival embassy, led by the writer Apion, see Josephus,* Against Apion. *Religious freedom was restored by Claudius, A.D. 41-54.*

EMPEROR CLAUDIUS, KING AGRIPPA I, AND THE ROMAN SENATE

Gaius having been treacherously slain after a reign of three years and eight months [A.D. 41], the troops in Rome [the Praetorian Guard] hastened to proclaim Claudius emperor. But the Senate, on a motion of the consuls . . . assembled in the capitol, and remembering the tyranny of Gaius, decreed war against Claudius; they were determined either to restore the ancient rule by an aristocracy or to elect by suffrage a man worthy of the empire.

Agrippa, who happened to arrive in Rome at this juncture of events, was invited by the Senate to participate in their counsels. At the same time Claudius, from his camp, asked his help as circumstances might require. Perceiving that Claudius was virtually emperor, Agrippa repaired to him. Claudius sent him to the Senate as his envoy to present his case, namely, that he had been reluctantly hurried of by the soldiers; that he considered it unjust to desert these soldiers, who had shown such zeal for him, and unsafe to gamble with his own fortune, since merely to have received a call to the empire was not without its dangers; and that he would administer the government not as a tyrant but as a virtuous prince, content with the honor of being called emperor and granting to all permission to counsel him on every measure of state. For even if he were not naturally inclined to moderation, the fate of Gaius was sufficient warning for him to exercise his authority with sobriety.

To this message, delivered by Agrippa, the Senate replied that, relying on the army and the wisdom of their counsels, they would not submit to voluntary servitude. On receipt of this answer Claudius again sent Agrippa to inform the Senate that, though those against whom he was reluctantly going to war were men with whom he least wished to quarrel, he could not endure betraying those who had by oath bound themselves to his fortunes. Some spot, however, outside the city should be selected for the conflict, for it was not agreeable to piety to pollute the sacred precincts of that city with native blood, and this only because of their obstinacy. With these instructions Agrippa returned to the Senate.

In the midst of these negotiations one of the soldiers who sided with the Senate drew his sword and cried: "Fellow soldiers, what injury has been inflicted on us to induce us to murder our brothers and to attack our kinsmen who have followed Claudius, while we have an emperor with whom no fault can be found and are united by so many legitimate ties to those against whom we are preparing to take the field?" With this, he rushed through the Senate, carrying with him all his comrades. The patricians were struck with dismay at this desertion. But knowing no other refuge to turn to, they followed the soldiers and hastened to present themselves to Claudius. Those who had paid earlier court to fortune met them outside the walls, swords in hand. The lives of the group's leaders would have been imperiled before Claudius became aware of this contemplated attack had not Agrippa run to inform him of the danger and [to warn him] that if he did not restrain the impetuosity of his troops, who were infuriated with the patricians, he would lose the men who gave luster to the throne and be left monarch of a desert. (War II, 11:1-4.)

KING OF JUDAEA

On hearing this, Claudius curbed the fury of his soldiers. Admitting the Senators into the camp, he addressed them courteously, then at once went with them to offer thanks sacrifices to God on his accession to the throne. On Agrippa, he bestowed all of his grandfather's domains, annexing to them, in addition to the districts given by Augustus to Herod, Trachonitis and Auranitis, as well as the principality called the kingdom of Lysanias. He announced this bestowal to the people by an edict and directed the magistrates to have the grant engraved on brass tablets to be deposited in the Capitol. On Agrippa's brother, Herod —who by his marriage with Bernice [Agrippa's daughter], was also his son-in-law—he bestowed the kingdom of Chalcis.

Much wealth soon accrued to Agrippa from these extensive territories. Instead of spending it on unimportant matters, he proceeded to encircle Jerusalem with a wall so vast as, had it been completed, would have rendered ineffectual the [subsequent] Roman siege. But before it attained its intended height he died in Caesarea [A.D. 44], three years after his accession to the throne, and six from his appointment to the tetrarchy. (War II, 11:5-6.)

Antt. XIX, 8:2: "He reigned four years under Gaius Caesar, three of them over Philip's tetrarchy only, but in the fourth he had that of Herod [Antipas] added to it. And he reigned three years also under the reign of Claudius Caesar, during which time he reigned over the aforementioned countries and also had Judaea, Samaria, and Caesarea added to them." The same chapter in Antt. tells the moving story of his end.

AGRIPPA I'S PIETY AND CHARACTER

The golden chain given him[25] by Gaius [Caligula], a chain of the same weight as the iron one with which his royal hands had been bound, Agrippa hung in the Temple, over the treasury, as a memorial of the grievous fate he once suffered, a testimony of its change for the better, and a demonstration of how the most fortunate may fall and that God can raise again what has fallen. This chain, so dedicated, reminded all that king Agrippa, though once bound in chains for a small cause, regained his former stature and rose, shortly after being freed from his chains, to be a more illustrious king than he had been before. This reminder, therefore, was meant to teach all people that whoever partakes of the nature of man, however great he may be, may fall; and that those who fall may regain their former glory.

King Agrippa was a man of bounty, lavish in his gifts and desirous of pleasing people with large donations. He gained fame by his many gifts, took delight in giving, and rejoiced in his good name. He was most unlike the Herod who reigned before him. Herod had been ill-natured, cruel in punishment, and merciless to those he hated. It is admitted that he favored the Greeks more than the Jews, for he enriched foreign cities with large grants of money and adorned them with baths and theaters. In some he erected temples, in others porticoes, but he did not raise a single edifice, however small, in any Jewish city, nor did he favor such cities with any donation worth mentioning. But Agrippa was a mild man, and uniformly liberal to all. Humane and generous to foreigners, he was equally kind to his own countrymen, but more sympathetic. Accordingly, he preferred staying in Jerusalem most of the time and was strict in the observance of his country's laws. He therefore kept himself wholly pure, nor did he let a day pass without making its appointed sacrifices. (Antt. XIX, 6:1; 7:3.)

Jewish tradition preserves references to the king's piety (Mishnah Bikkurim III, 4; Mishnah Sota VII, 8), his humaneness (Ketuboth 17a), and his interest in the Jewish law (Pesahim 88b).

JUDAEA UNDER THE LATER ROMAN PROCURATORS AND AGRIPPA II

[Agrippa] left three daughters, Bernice, Mariamne, and Drusilla, the fruit of his union with Cypros, by whom he also had a son, Agrippa. The latter being still a minor, Claudius again reduced the kingdom to a province and sent first Cuspius Fadus as its procurator [*ca.* 44-45]; then Tiberius Alexander [*ca.* 46-48], who, introducing no change into the national customs, preserved the country at peace. . . . (War II, 11:6.)

Agrippa II, son of Agrippa I, became king of Chalcis, and later, king of Trachonitis and other provinces. The procurator Tiberius Alexander, a nephew of the Alexandrian philosopher Philo, was succeeded by Ventidius Cumanus (48-52), and the latter was succeeded by Antonius Felix (52-60); the frictions between Jews and Romans led to acts of open hostility. (War II, 12:1-8.)

THEUDAS THE FALSE PROPHET

When [Cuspius] Fadus was procurator of Judaea, a certain impostor named Theudas, claiming to be a prophet, urged the people to follow him, with their possessions, to the river Jordan, which, so he said, would by his command divide in two, thus enabling them to cross it easily. Many were deluded by his words. But Fadus prevented them from reaping any benefits from their folly. He dispatched against them a troop of cavalry, which in an unexpected attack, slew many and captured others. They also captured Theudas, cut off his head, and carried it to Jerusalem. (Antt. XX, 5:1.)

In his speech, Acts 5:34-39, Gamaliel is quoted as mentioning, somewhat anachronistically, the rise of Theudas together with the rise of Judah of Galilee.

THE CONVERSION OF KING IZATES OF ADIABENE AND OF HIS MOTHER, HELENA

The kingdom of Adiabene (Hadiab) in north Mesopotamia bordered on the Roman and the Parthian territories. Izates ruled in the period of the Emperor Claudius (41-54).

During Izates' stay at Charax-Spasini [at the Arabian Gulf], a Jewish merchant, whose name was Ananias, got among the king's women and taught them to worship God according to the Jewish faith. Through them he became known to Izates and persuaded him too, to embrace that religion; he also, at Izates' earnest entreaty, accompanied him to Adiabene when Izates' father sent for him. Helena [mother of Izates] was similarly instructed by another Jew, and she also was converted. . . .

On learning that his mother was highly pleased with the Jewish customs, Izates hurried to adopt all of them. Assuming that he could not be thoroughly a Jew unless he were circumcised, he was ready to do so. But his mother, when she heard of his intention, endeavored to stop him. She said that circumcision would endanger him, for as king he would be detested by his subjects when they learned how fond he was of ways strange and alien to them, and that they would never submit to being ruled by a Jew. . . . Ananias, when Izates informed him of his mother's opinion, agreed with her. . . . He told the king that even though he had resolved to follow the Jewish law in its entirety, he could worship God without being circumcised, because the worship of God was more important than circumcision. God would forgive him [his noncircumcision] since necessity and fear of his subjects were responsible.

Later, however, the king, under the influence of a certain Eleazar of Galilee, was circumcised. Helena and Ananias expected the people to censure him for his zeal for a "strange religion."

But God himself prevented what they feared from coming to pass. He preserved both Izates and his sons from the many dangers they encountered and delivered them from peril when such deliverance seemed impossible, proving thereby that the rewards of piety are ever with those who honor Him and pin their faith on Him alone. . . .

When she saw that, owing to God's providence, the kingdom was at peace and that her son was a happy man and admired by all, even by foreigners, Helena wished to go to Jerusalem, to worship and make her thanks offerings at that Temple of God which was so famous among all men. She asked her son to give her leave to do so. He gave it most willingly, made great preparations for her departure, supplied her with much money, and escorted her a great part of the way to Jerusalem.

A famine oppressed Jerusalem at the time. To relieve it, Helena imported corn from Alexandria and

figs from Cyprus and distributed food to the needy,
while Izates sent large sums of money.

On seeing how Izates' piety towards God and his
inherent goodness had won him the esteem of all men,
his brother Monobazus and the rest of his kinsmen
also desired to abandon the religion of their country
for that of the Jews, and they carried out their intention. But this act of theirs was discovered by Izates'
subjects. The nobles were greatly displeased, but concealed their anger for the time being, planning to
chastise them when the opportunity presented itself.

The nobles arranged with Abias, King of the Arabs,
to undertake a warlike expedition against Izates. Abias
lost and to avoid capture by Izates, committed suicide.
The nobles then invited the king of Parthia to make
war on Izates. However, upon receiving news of dis-
turbances at home, the invading Parthian was forced
to return. This miraculous delivery Izates attributed
to divine providence.

Shortly afterwards Izates died, at the age of fifty-
five, and after he had ruled his kingdom twenty-four
years. He left twenty-four sons and twenty-four
daughters. He gave orders that his brother Monobazus
should succeed him as king, as reward for having faith-
fully preserved the kingdom for him after his father's
death when he himself was absent. When she heard of
her son's death, Helena was oppressed by grief, as
was only natural after the loss of a most dutiful son,
but it was a comfort to her that the succession came
to her eldest son. Accordingly, she hastened to him.
After reaching Adiabene, she did not long outlive her
son Izates, being worn out from old age and sorrow.
Monobazus sent both her bones and those of his brother
Izates to Jerusalem, with orders that they be buried
in the pyramids that Helena had erected. These pyramids were three in number, and three furlongs from
the city of Jerusalem. . . . (Antt. XX, 2:3-5; 4:1-3.)

Rabbinic tradition refers to queen Helena as having

undergone Nazarite vows (Mishnah Nazir III, 6). According to Josephus, she had a palace in Jerusalem (War V, 6:1). Her tomb has been identified with the so-called Tombs of the Kings, north of Jerusalem. The Greek traveler Pausanias compared this tomb with the one of Mausolus in Halicarnassus, one of the seven wonders of the world (Descr. Graeciae VIII, 16). After Trajan's conquest, Adiabene became the Roman province Assyria.

THE RISE OF NERO

After administering the empire thirteen years, eight months, and twenty days, Claudius died [A.D. 54], leaving Nero as his successor. He had been prevailed upon by the wiles of his wife, Agrippina, to adopt Nero as heir to the throne, though he himself had a son, Britannicus, by Messalina, his former wife, and also a daughter, Octavia, whom he had given in marriage to Nero. . . .

How often Nero, frenzied with excess of prosperity and wealth, abused the favors of fortune, in what manner he slew his brother, wife, and mother, his subsequent cruelty to those of highest rank, and how finally he madly flung himself upon the stage and into the theater, I shall pass without notice, as acts of which the world has heard enough. I shall recall, however, those events of his reign which pertain to the Jews. (War II, 12:8; 13:1.)

AGRIPPA II'S KINGDOM, THE SICARII, AND THE FALSE PROPHETS

The kingdom of the Lesser Armenia, Nero conferred on Aristobulus, son of Herod [of Chalcis]; to the territory of Agrippa [II] he annexed four cities with their districts, Abila and Julias in Peraea, Tarichaeae and Tiberias in Galilee; to govern the rest of Judaea he [re-]appointed Felix as procurator [52-60]. Felix captured Eleazar, the rebel leader who with his companions had for twenty years ravaged the country, and sent him to Rome. The number of rebels he crucified, and the number of men discovered to be their allies, that he punished, was incalculable.

Of Antonius Felix, a freedman who had risen to the procuratorship with military command, Tacitus says: "With all manner of cruelty and lust he exercised royal functions in the spirit of a slave" (History V.9). *The Apostle Paul was imprisoned by Felix in Caesarea, about 58-60 (Acts 23-24). Under Felix, Jewish uprisings, which so far had remained isolated occurences, became permanent; we have come to "the turning-point in the drama which . . . reached its close in the bloody conflicts of the year 70"* (Schürer).

Rebels of another sort, called Sicarii,[26] sprang up in Jerusalem. They assassinated men in the broad light of day and in the very heart of the city. Chiefly at festival time, mingling with the crowds, they stabbed their enemies with the daggers concealed under their cloaks. Their victims dead, the murderers joined in the general expressions of indignation. This plausible behavior prevented their exposure.

Their first victim was the high priest Jonathan [son of Ananus]. After him many were slain each day. The state of fear engendered was more distressing than the calamity itself. As one does on the field of battle, hourly each man expected death. People kept watch at a distance from their enemies and did not trust even an approaching friend. Yet despite their suspicions and precautions, they were slain. So quick were the conspirators and so great their art of concealment.

Still another group of villains, whose hands were purer but whose intentions were more impious, disturbed the peace of the city no less than these assassins. Claiming divine inspiration but aiming at revolt and change, they persuaded the multitude to abandon reason and follow them into the desert by convincing them that there God would give them tokens of freedom. Felix, suspecting this to be but a prelude to insurrection, sent a detachment of cavalry and infantry against them and slew great numbers.

An Egyptian false prophet caused even greater suffering. A wily man, who arrogated to himself the authority of a prophet, he came into the country and gathered some thirty thousand dupes to be his followers. These he led through the desert to the Mount of Olives, from where he proposed to force entrance to Jerusalem, and after mastering the Roman garrison, to lord over the people with the aid of his spearmen, who poured in along with him. Felix, surmising his plan, intercepted him with the Roman forces, the entire population joining in the defense. In the ensuing conflict the Egyptian escaped with a few of his followers, but the majority of his adherents were either cut to pieces or taken prisoner. The rest dispersed, each to his own home, seeking safety in hiding.

As happens in a diseased body, no sooner had these disorders been suppressed than another part became inflamed. Several impostors and rebels, banding together, drew many into revolt by encouraging them to assert their liberty and threatening death to those who submitted to Roman authority; whoever willingly chooses servitude, they said, should be suppressed by force. Distributing themselves in companies throughout the country, they plundered the houses of the nobles, murdered the owners, and set fire to the villages. Their madness filled Judaea from end to end, and daily their war grew more malignant. (War II, 13:2-6.)

NEW PROCURATORS

Festus, who succeeded Felix as procurator [60-62], directed his efforts against the principal plague of the country. After apprehending large numbers of the rebels, he executed many of them.

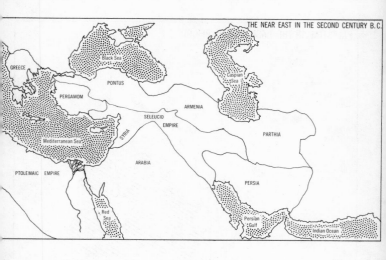

THE NEAR EAST IN THE SECOND CENTURY B.C.

GREECE

Black Sea

PONTUS

PERGAMOM

Caspian Sea

ARMENIA

SELEUCID EMPIRE

SYRIA

PARTHIA

Mediterranean Sea

ARABIA

PERSIA

PTOLEMAIC EMPIRE

Red Sea

Persian Gulf

Indian Ocean

THE WALLS OF JERUSALEM

Herod's Gate

Damascus Gate

Third Wall

BEZETHA

MT. of OLIVES

Antonia

North Wall ?

Second

Temple

Jaffa Gate

First Wall

Herod's Palace

UPPER CITY

LOWER CITY

Acra

Valley of Kedron

Valley of Hinom

PALESTINE IN THE HASMONAEAN PERIOD

Sidon

Damascus

PHOENICIA

ITURAEA

Tyre

Giscala

Acco

GALILEE

Sea of Galilee

Gamala

Sepphoris

Gadara

Dor

SAMARIA

Jordan

Shechem

Gerasa

Yaffa

Beth Horon

Rabbath Ammon

Jericho

Jerusalem

Ascalon

JUDAEA

Gaza

Dead Sea

Machaerus

NABATAEA

IDUMAEA

NABATAEA

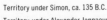 Territory under Simon, ca. 135 B.C.

Territory under Alexander Jannaeus, ca. 76 B.C.

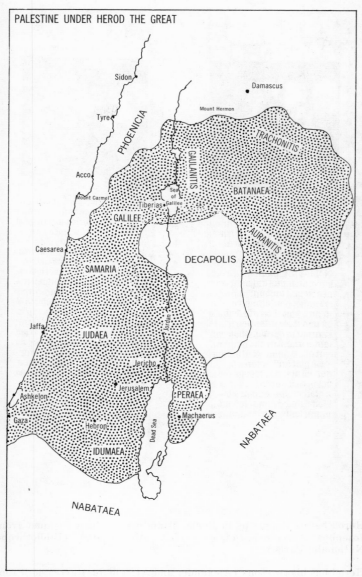

PALESTINE UNDER HEROD THE GREAT

Sidon

Damascus

Tyre

PHOENICIA

Mount Hermon

TRACHONITIS

Acco

GAULANITIS

BATANAEA

Mount Carmel

Sea of Galilee

Tiberias

GALILEE

AURANITIS

Caesarea

SAMARIA

DECAPOLIS

Jaffa

JUDAEA

Jordan

Jericho

Jerusalem

PERAEA

Ashkelon

NABATAEA

Gaza

Machaerus

Hebron

Dead Sea

IDUMAEA

NABATAEA

:::::::: Territory under Herod the Great, ca. 10 B.C.

Herod before Augustus in Rome. Miniature by Jean Fouquet from
Josephus' *Antiquités Judaïques* (fifteenth century). (Bibliothèque
Nationale, Paris.)

Herod has his two sons (Alexander and Aristobulus) arrested. From
Antiquités Judaïques.

Greek inscription from the Temple of Herod. The text reads: "Let no alien enter within the balustrade and the enclosure surrounding the sanctuary. Whoever is caught so doing, on himself shall be put blame for the death which will ensue." (New Museum, Istanbul.)

Josephus before Vespasian. From a Josephus manuscript, Wein-
garten Abbey. (Courtesy Landesbibliothek Fulda, Germany.)

Top Left: Silver shekel inscribed "Shekel of Israel" and dated "Year 3" (i.e., A.D. 68). Obverse. *Top Right:* "Jerusalem the Holy." Reverse.

Bottom Left: Bust of Vespasian. Obverse. *Bottom Right:* Jewish couple under a palm tree. Inscription reads "JUDAEA CAPTA" and "SC" *(senatus consulto).* Reverse.

The rock of Masada. (Courtesy Keren Hayesod, Jerusalem.)

Festus sent the Apostle Paul to Rome (Acts 25:1-27:2).

Festus' successor, Albinus [62-64], was a different kind of man. There was no crime he did not commit. In his official capacity he purloined and pillaged private property and burdened the nation with taxes. In addition, he allowed robbers, imprisoned either by their respective magistrates or by former procurators, to be ransomed by their kinsmen, and only those who paid nothing remained incarcerated as malefactors.

The audacity of the Jerusalem revolutionaries was given a new impetus. For by giving him money, their leaders obtained license from Albinus to continue their seditious practices with impunity. . . . Surrounded by tyrants, none dared to speak his mind. The seeds were now sown which brought the city to destruction. (War II, 14:1.)

A PROPHET OF DOOM

Four years before the war [that followed] . . . a certain Jesus, son of Ananus, a farmer of humble parentage, appeared at the feast of Tabernacles. Standing in the Temple, he suddenly cried: "A voice from the east, a voice from the west, a voice from the four winds; a voice against Jerusalem and the sanctuary, a voice against bridegrooms and brides, a voice against all the people."

Day and night he traversed all the streets with this cry. Some of the citizens, incensed at so ominous a voice, apprehended the man and severely scourged him. Uttering no word of defense or reproach, he continued his cry as before. Rightly assuming then that this man was under some supernatural impulse, the magistrates brought him before the Roman procurator. There, though bleeding from the lash, he neither sued for mercy nor shed a tear, but in the most mournful of voices cried at every stroke of the whip: "Woe, woe unto Jerusalem."

Nor did he cease his lament over the city to answer the procurator's questions as to who he was, whence he came, and why he uttered these words. Finally Albinus, concluding that he was a madman, set him at liberty.

During all the time that passed before the outbreak of the war, he neither associated with nor spoke to any of the citizens, but as though it were a prayer he had been meditating upon, daily uttered his lament: "Woe, woe unto Jerusalem." Nor did he curse those who beat him day after day or bless those who fed him; to all, the melancholy prophecy was his sole reply.

His voice rang loudest at the festivals. And, though for seven years and five months he continued his wail, his voice did not weaken, nor did he grow weary until, during the siege, when he beheld his prophecies come true, his voice was stopped. For then, as he was making his rounds on the wall, crying in a piercing voice, "Woe, woe once more, to the city, to the people, and to the Temple," and this time adding, "Woe, woe to myself also," he was struck by a stone shot from the ballista and killed on the spot, his dying lips still uttering the same portentous words. (War VI, 5:3.)

THE DEATH OF JAMES, THE BROTHER OF JESUS

Ananus . . . the high priest . . . was a bold and audacious man. He followed the sect of the Sadducees, who punish offenders more harshly than do any other Jews. . . . With Festus dead and Albinus still on the road, Ananus, being the man he was, saw an opportunity [to exercise his authority]. He assembled the Synhedrion of judges and brought before them James [Jacob], the brother of Jesus who was called Christ, and some other men whom he accused of breaking the law, and delivered them to be stoned. But those who seemed to be the most moderate of the citizens and strictest in the observance of the laws disliked the

deed and secretly sent a message to king Agrippa be-
seeching him to bid Ananus to refrain from similar
actions in the future, because what he had done was
not right. Some of them also went to meet Albinus as
he was journeying from Alexandria and told him that
it was illegal for Ananus to assemble a Synhedrion
without his consent. Albinus heeded what they said
and wrote in anger to Ananus, threatening punishment. And king Agrippa deprived him of the high
priesthood when he had ruled but three months, and
conferred it on Jesus, the son of Damnaeus. (Antt.
XX, 9:1.)

*James was the head of the Judeo-Christian com-
munity in Jerusalem and an antagonist of the high
priest in office. Our passage is quoted by Eusebius
(Church History II, 23). The fact, however, that
Origen read in Josephus a different account regarding
the death of James caused Schürer to suspect the au-
thenticity of the passage; Thackeray considers it genuine. It was Ananus who took part in the deliberation
in Jerusalem to remove Josephus from his military
leadership in Galilee (Life 38-39). On the assassination of Ananus, see War IV, 5:2.*

THE PROCURATOR GESSIUS FLORUS (64-66)

Gessius Florus, successor of Albinus, made the latter seem by comparison a man of virtue. Albinus dis-
sembled his villanies and perpetrated most of them
secretly; Gessius, on the contrary, made an ostentatious display of his outrages against the nation. As
though he were a public executioner commissioned to
carry out the sentence against condemned criminals,
he committed every species of rapine and depredation.
In a case which called for compassion, he was cruel in
the extreme. In matters of turpitude he was devoid of
shame. No one more ably smothered the truth, and
none was more ingenious in devising subtleties of de-
ception. To profit at the expense of an individual he

deemed a trifle; he despoiled entire cities, ruined populous communities, and practically proclaimed throughout the country that everyone was at liberty to rob, provided he might share in the plunder. Whole districts were desolated through his avarice, and many abandoned the homes of their fathers and sought refuge in foreign provinces.

So long as Cestius Gallus administered the province of Syria no one dared to send a deputation to him with complaints against Florus; but when he visited Jerusalem at the approach of the feast of unleavened bread [Passover], some three million people[27] came to implore him to take pity on the miseries of the nation and to denounce Florus as the bane of the country. Florus, who was present and stood at Cestius' side, ridiculed the outcry. Cestius, having calmed the excitement of the populace, pledged himself to take care that Florus should act with greater moderation in the future and returned to Antioch.

Florus escorted him as far as Caesarea and deluded him [with promises of change], though at that very moment he was laying plans for involving the Jews in a war—his sole hope of concealing his atrocities. He reasoned that if peace continued, the Jews would bring charges against him before the emperor, but if he engineered a revolt, the greater disaster would, he hoped, divert their attention from the lesser crimes. In order, therefore, to drive the nation into rebellion he daily aggravated their sufferings. (War II, 14:2-3.)

THE WAR
WITH ROME:
GALILEE

SEEDS OF THE WAR

PREFACE

The war of the Jews against the Romans—the greatest not only of our own age but of practically all past wars of which accounts have reached us . . . has attracted the attention of various writers.

Josephus criticizes the accounts of the Jewish war given by other historians of the period.

At the time of this momentous event, the Romans were occupied with their own internal disorders. Taking advantage of the turbulence of the period, the Jewish revolutionary party—a party deficient neither in strength nor resources—rose in rebellion. So great were the disturbances and so threatening the state of affairs in the East that the insurgents were encouraged to entertain hopes of its acquisition, while their opponents trembled for their loss. For the Jews expected all their people beyond the Euphrates to unite with them in revolt. The Romans, on the other hand, were harassed by their neighbors, the Gauls; the Celts, too, were restless and unquiet. In addition, the death of Nero [June, A.D. 68] threw everything into confusion. The opportunity created [by that death] induced many to aspire to sovereign power, while the soldiers, in the hope of plunder, looked eagerly for a change. . . .

Josephus promises to render an objective, unbiased presentation of the war.

But should anyone censure me for the reprehension with which I speak of the [Jewish] tyrants or their brigand bands, or for bewailing the misfortunes of my country, let him pardon my emotion, however contrary it may be to the rules for writing history. For of all the cities under the Roman sway, it was the lot of ours to attain the highest felicity, only to plunge in the end into the deepest miseries. . . . (Preface to War, 1-4.)

THE OUTRAGE IN CAESAREA (MAY 66)

The Greeks of Caesarea, having around this time won from Nero the government of that city, arrived with documents to that effect. From this event we may date the commencement of the war. . . . The incident that sparked this war was out of all proportion to the magnitude of its consequences.

The Jews of Caesarea had a synagogue close to some land owned by a Caesarean Greek. The former had more than once tried to buy this land, offering a price far exceeding its value. The owner not only disdained these tenders, but as further affront, erected on this land new buildings, which he converted into workshops, leaving the Jews only a narrow and most inconvenient passage to their synagogue. Exasperated by this, the more hot-blooded youths rushed to the spot and halted the builders. Since, however, [the procurator] Florus had prohibited violence, the more influential Jews—among whom was John, the tax collector—at a loss as to what measures to adopt, tried to induce Florus to stop work on the buildings by offering him eight talents of silver. Intent only on getting the money, Florus promised to co-operate fully; but he had no sooner obtained that money than he left Caesarea for Sebaste [Samaria], abandoning the sedition to its course, as if he had sold the Jews a license to fight it out.

The following day being a Sabbath, the Jews assembled in the synagogue. A hotheaded Caesarean placed an earthen vessel, inverted, at the entrance of that synagogue and sacrificed birds upon it.[28] This mockery of their laws and defilement of the site incensed the Jews beyond control. The more sober-minded and moderate among them thought it prudent to refer the matter to the authorities, but the rebellious spirits and those in the fervor of youth burned for a fight. The seditious among [the Gentiles of] Caesarea stood similarly ready, having by prearrangement dispatched the [bird] sacrificer; it therefore soon came to blows. Jucundus, the master of horse appointed to quell riots, hastened to the spot, removed the earthen vessel, and endeavored to stop the rioting, but he was overpowered by the violence of the Caesareans. Whereupon the Jews, taking the books of the Law with them, retired to Narbata, a Jewish district sixty furlongs distant from Caesarea. John, attended by twelve of his most influential associates, waited on Florus at Sebaste and complained bitterly of what had occurred, imploring his aid and delicately reminding him of the eight talents. But Florus, charging them with removing the books of the Law from Caesarea, seized the men and threw them into chains. (War II, 14:4-5.)

Florus further outraged the people of Jerusalem by taking money from the Temple treasury. A party of rioters scornfully carried around a basket to collect donations for the "poor" procurator. The incensed Florus then came to Jerusalem with an army. (14:6-7.)

FLORUS

Florus established his quarters in the palace. On the following day he erected a tribunal in front of it and took his seat. The chief priests, the men of power, and the rest of Jerusalem's men of eminence came and stood before that tribunal. Florus commanded them to surrender the culprits who had insulted him, threatening that if they did not, his vengeance would fall upon them. In reply, the leaders pointed out the peaceable disposition of the people and asked him to pardon those who had spoken unbecomingly. It was not to be wondered at, they said, that among so large a populace there should be some hotheaded and foolish youths; besides, with everyone expressing regret, and out of fear of the consequences denying any participation in the occurrence, it would be impossible to pick out the delinquents. It behooved Florus to insure peace for the nation and provide measures that would preserve the city for the Romans; rather than harrass a multitude of good men for the offenses of a few wicked ones, he ought, for the sake of the many innocent people, to forgive the few who had erred.

This speech only increased Florus' rage, and he ordered his troops to plunder [Jerusalem's] upper market, as a certain district was called, and to slay whomever they encountered. Their cupidity stimulated by their general's commands, the soldiers not only sacked the place against which they were sent, but broke into every house and massacred the inhabitants. Fugitives crowded the streets; the soldiers slew whomever they caught and indulged in every sort of plunder. Many of the moderate party were seized and brought before Florus, who first flogged, then crucified them. The total number slain on that day—including women and children, for not even infants were spared—came to some three thousand six hundred. This disaster was rendered the more grievous by a new cruelty of the Romans: Florus dared to do what no one had before, to lash in front of the tribunal and nail to the cross men of equestrian rank, who though of Jewish extraction, enjoyed that Roman dignity.

King Agrippa [II] was at this time on his way to

Alexandria to congratulate [Tiberius] Alexander[29] on having been appointed governor of Egypt by Nero. Agrippa's sister Berenice, who was in Jerusalem at the time and a witness of the soldiers' outrages, was deeply affected and frequently sent the masters of her horse, and her bodyguard, to Florus, imploring him to stop the slaughter. This prayer he rejected; intent only on the profit accruing him from the plunder, he was moved neither by the great numbers slain nor by the high rank of his suppliant. The rage of the soldiers did not spare the queen [Berenice] herself. They not only scourged and killed their prisoners before her eyes but would have killed her also had she not made a timely retreat to the palace, where she passed the night surrounded by her guards, dreading an attack from the soldiers.

Berenice was staying in Jerusalem in fulfillment of a vow to God, it being the custom that those who had been visited by illness or been otherwise afflicted should vow abstention from wine and [from] cutting off their hair for thirty days preceding the one designated for their sacrifice. While performing these rites, Berenice appeared barefoot before the tribunal, presenting her petition to Florus; she was not only treated disrespectfully, but narrowly escaped with her life. (War II, 14:8-15:1.)

Florus' cohorts refused to return the solemn greeting of the people, a proof of submission ordered by the procurator. The people, thus insulted, secured possession of the Temple and destroyed the connection between the Temple and the castle of Antonia. Cestius Gallus sent Neapolitanus, a tribune, to investigate the situation. At this time Agrippa II returned from Alexandria. (15:2-16:1.)

AGRIPPA II AND NEAPOLITANUS

The chief priests of the Jews, their leading men, and the council, arrived in Jamnia [Jabneh] to congratulate the king [Agrippa]. After paying their respects to him, they deplored their distresses and related Florus' cruelties. Though his indignation was aroused, Agrippa subtly transferred his resentment to the Jews, whom at heart he pitied, in order to lower their high opinions of themselves and, by appearing to disbelieve that they had suffered unjustly, to divert them from retaliation. Because they were of the upper class and, mindful of their property, desired peace, these men understood that the king's rebuke was dictated by kindness.

As for the people, they came sixty furlongs out of Jerusalem to welcome Agrippa and Neapolitanus. The widows of the slain ran ahead of them lamenting. Moved by their wails, the [rest of the] people soon joined in the lamentations and entreated Agrippa to succor them. They also loudly enumerated to Neapolitanus the many miseries they had endured under Florus. On entering the city, they showed them the desolated market place and the ruined houses. Then, through Agrippa, they persuaded Neapolitanus to walk around the city as far as Siloam, with but a single attendant, in order to assure himself that the Jews paid obedience to all the Romans, excepting only Florus, whom they abhorred for his excessive cruelty to them. Having traversed the city and ascertained the people's peaceable disposition, Neapolitanus went up to the Temple. There he assembled the people, warmly commended their loyalty to the Romans, and earnestly exhorted them to maintain peace. After participating, as far as was permitted [to a Gentile], in the divine worship at the Temple, he returned to Cestius.

The populace then turned to the king and the chief priests, requesting that envoys be sent to Nero against Florus lest their silence should arouse a suspicion that they were revolt-minded and had provoked such great slaughters by their conduct. If the true aggressor was not revealed in time, the belief might prevail that they had started the hostilities. It was clear that the people would not stay quiet if the embassy they wanted was denied them. Agrippa, although he felt that by appointing men to act as accusers of Florus the people invited danger, thought it best not to overlook their strong bent towards war. Accordingly, he convened them in a large gallery. Placing his sister Berenice in a conspicuous position on the roof of the Hasmonaean family's house, which overlooked the gallery on the opposite side of the Upper Town, where a bridge connected the Temple with the gallery, he addressed them (War II, 16:2-3).

AGRIPPA'S SPEECH ON THE UNIVERSAL POWER OF ROME

"Had I seen that all of you were bent on war with the Romans and not that the more upright and unprejudiced of the community were desirous of preserving peace, I would neither have appeared before you nor ventured to advise, for any discourse on proper measures is superfluous when all who hear it are by common consent resolved to pursue the less prudent course. Since, however, youth, inexperienced in the evils of war, kindles some of you, an unreasonable hope of freedom others, and still others are perhaps stimulated by avarice and hope of private aggrandizement in the general confusion at the expense of the weak, I have thought it my duty to assemble you and present what I conceive will be to your welfare, in the hope that these several categories of men may, when better instructed, alter their views, and in order that the virtuous may sustain no harm from the pernicious counsels of a few. And let no one interrupt me, albeit I touch on some displeasing topics. . . .

"I am well aware that many make tragic outcry about the injuries inflicted by the procurators and the blessings of freedom. Before inquiring who you are and against whom you undertake to wage war, I shall first separate these two pretexts for hostilities that you have intermingled. If your object be vengeance on those who have injured you, why speak so gravely of liberty? But if you think all servitude intolerable, complaints against your governors are superfluous. For even if they treated you with moderation, slavery would still retain its opprobrium.

"Consider each of these arguments separately and you will see how slight are the grounds for war. Let us take the charges against the procurators. Duty enjoins us to conciliate the authorities, not to irritate them. But when you complain overmuch about small offenses, you provoke those whom you reproach to become your enemies; so whereas they formerly ill-treated you covertly and with a sense of shame, they will now despoil you openly. Nothing so damps the force of blows as patient submission; the calm demeanor of the wronged serves as restraint on their oppressors. Granted that the Roman officials are harsh beyond endurance; still, not all the Romans wrong you, nor does the Emperor; yet it is against them that you will levy war. It is not by their command that cruel governors are sent to you; those who are in the west cannot see those who are in the east; nor is it easy to obtain in that quarter early intelligence from these parts.

"But it is absurd to wage war against many on account of one and against, for trivial reasons, so great a power, a power, moreover, that cannot know of what we complain. The evils with which we charge them [the procurators] may soon be corrected, for the same procurator will not remain forever, and his successor, it is probable, will be more moderate. War, however, once begun, is not easily put down, nor carried through without disaster.

"As for your longing for freedom, it is too late to indulge in it; you should have struggled earlier not to lose it. For servitude is bitter, and the struggle to avert its first approaches is just; but he who once sub-

dued, afterwards revolts is a refractory slave, rather
than a lover of liberty. There was a time for doing
your utmost to stop the Romans from gaining a footing; that was when Pompey made his first inroad into
this country.

"But our forefathers and their kings, who far excelled you in resources and in energy of both body and
mind, could not withstand a small division of the
Roman army. Yet you, who have for generations now
been accustomed to obedience and whose power is so
greatly inferior to those who first submitted to her,
wish to oppose the whole empire of Rome?

"The Athenians, who in order to preserve the liberty
of Greece, once consigned their own city to the flames;
who when he sailed the land and walked the sea, pursued the proud Xerxes, whom as he led an army too
vast for Europe, not even the deep could contain, and
forced him to flee in a single ship; and who off the
coast of the little [island] Salamis, broke the mighty
strength of Asia—these Athenians now serve the
Romans, and the supreme city of Greece obeys Italy's
commands. The Lacedaemonians also, after their victories at Thermopylae and Plataea and the ransacking
of Asia by [their king] Agesilaus, are content to
accept the same masters. So, too, do the Macedonians,
who still plume themselves on Philip and Alexander
who promised them the sovereignty of the world, submit to so great a change, and bow to those to whom
fortune has transferred her favors.

"Numberless other nations, with greater claims to
freedom than you, accept the yoke. You alone disdain
servitude to those to whom the entire world has submitted.

"On what troops, on what arms do you rely? Where
is your fleet to occupy the Roman seas? Where the
treasury sufficient for the enterprise? Do you think you
will be waging war against the Egyptians and Arabs?
Will you not reflect on the empire of the Romans? Will

you not evaluate your own weakness? Have not your
forces been frequently defeated even by nations on
your borders, whereas Rome's power has proved invincible throughout the habitable earth? Nay, they
seek for something even beyond that. The entire
Euphrates does not suffice them as boundary on the
east, or the Danube on the north, or Cadiz on the west;
nor does Libya on the south, though they have penetrated even into its uninhabited lands. They have
sought another world beyond the ocean and have carried their arms as far as the Britons, a people not
heretofore known to history.

"What then? Are you richer than the Gauls,
stronger than the Germans, more intelligent than the
Greeks, more numerous than all the people of the
habitable globe? What confidence emboldens you to
oppose the Romans?

"It is hard to endure slavery, you will say. But how
much harder is it for the Greeks, who though they
deem themselves to be the noblest people under the sun
and occupy so extensive a land, submit to the six
bundles of rods [fasces, symbol of Roman authority]
of a Roman magistrate! The same number preserves
the obedience of the Macedonians, who have a juster
claim to liberty than you. And what of the five hundred cities of Asia? Do they not, though ungarrisoned,
pay homage to a single governor and to the consular
fasces? And need I speak of the Heniochi, the Col-
chians [Black Sea region], the tribe of the Taurians
[Crimea], of the people who inhabit the shores of the
Bosphorus, or of the nations bordering on the Euxine
[Black Sea] and Maeotis [Sea of Azov]? The latter,
who once knew no lord of their own even, are now
held in subjection by three thousand soldiers, while
forty long galleys pacify that previously unnavigable
and inhospitable sea.

"How strong a plea for freedom may not be advanced by Bithynia, Cappadocia, the people of Pam-

phylia, the Lycians and Cilicians [Asia Minor]? Yet they pay their tribute without force of arms. And what of the Thracians, who are spread over a land five days' journey in breadth and seven in length, a land more rugged and more defensible than yours, and whose rigorous climate is sufficient to repel invaders? Do they not submit to two thousand Roman guards? And do not the Illyrians, who inhabit the adjoining region stretching as far as Dalmatia and bounded by the Ister, yield to but two legions, whom they join in repressing the incursions of the Dacians? As for the Dalmatians, who have so frequently made frantic efforts to regain their liberty and whose continued defeats only spurred them on to reassemble their forces for still another revolt, do they not now keep the peace at last under a single Roman legion?

"If great advantage could serve to provoke some people to insurrection, the Gauls, fortified as they are by nature—on the east by the Alps, on the north by the river Rhine, on the south by the Pyrenees, and by the ocean on the west—should certainly be tempted. Yet though protected by such formidable barriers, crowded with three hundred and five nations, and enjoying, as one might say, such fountains of internal prosperity that they irradiate with it practically the whole inhabited world, they are content to be tributary to the Romans and derive their prosperity from them. They tolerate this subjection not from effeminacy of mind or because they are of ignoble stock—they had for eighty years carried on a war for freedom—but out of awe for the might of Rome and for her fortune, which are of greater efficacy than their arms. They are therefore held in subjection by twelve hundred soldiers, a number scarcely equal to that of their cities.

"Nor did the gold of Iberia [Spain], wrought from her mines, suffice in the contest for freedom, nor yet her vast distance from the Romans, both by land and sea; nor the tribes of the Lusitanians and Cantabrians

whose passion is war; nor the neighboring ocean with
its surging tides—so terrible even to the inhabitants!
Extending their military operations beyond the Pillars
of Hercules and traversing the clouds over the Pyrenees, the Romans enslaved even these tribes. Though
conquered with such great difficulty and so remote
from Rome, a single legion suffices now to bridle them.

"Who amongst you has not heard of the hordes of
the Germans? Their strength and stature you have,
no doubt, often seen, since the Romans have captives
of that nation everywhere. Yet this breed of men, who
dwell in an immense land, who have minds greater than
their bodies, souls that despise death, and in rage are
fiercer than the wildest beasts, have the Rhine as
boundary to their ferocity and are tamed by eight
Roman legions. The captured among them submitted
to slavery, and the rest sought safety in flight.

"Reflect, also, on the rampart of the Britons, you
who depend on the walls of Jerusalem. Their land is
girded by the ocean and occupies an island no smaller
than the country we inhabit, yet the Romans sailed
there and subdued them; four legions hold that large
island.

"But why need I enlarge, when even the Parthians,
that most warlike of tribes, lords of so many nations,
and invested with so mighty a dominion, send hostages
to the Romans? Thus, in Italy, you can behold the
noblest of the East bending to the yoke for the sake of
peace.

"When, then, nearly every nation under the sun pays
obeisance to the Roman arms, will you alone maintain
hostilities, regardless of the fate of the Carthaginians,
who though they boast their great Hannibal and their
illustrious Phoenician ancestry, fell beneath the hand
of Scipio? Nor have the Cyrenians, of Spartan descent,
or the Marmaridae, a tribe that stretches to the regions
of drought, nor the Syrtes, whose very name strikes
terror, the Nasamons and the Maurians, or the count-

less multitudes of the Numidians checked the valor of
Rome.

"Moreover, Africa, the third part of the globe, whose
nations it is not easy to enumerate, and which, bounded
by the Atlantic Ocean and the Pillars of Hercules,
feeds numberless Ethiopians as far even as the Red
Sea—Africa, in her length and breadth, has Rome subdued. In addition to their annual produce, which sup-
ports the population of Rome eight months of the year,
its territories pay all sorts of other tributes and
furnish ready revenues for the needs of the empire.
Nor do their inhabitants deem it a disgrace, as do you,
to take orders from Rome, though but one Roman
legion is stationed among them.

"But why cite distant climes as instances of Rome's
power when Egypt affords an example at your door?
That country—which extends as far as Ethiopia and
Arabia Felix and borders upon India, and which, exclusive of the citizens of Alexandria, contains seven
million five hundred thousand souls, as may be learned
from the returns of the poll tax—that country does not
disdain the empire of the Romans, though Alexandria,
with its large population, wealth, and vast extent, being thirty furlongs in length and in breadth not less
than ten, offers so strong an incentive to revolt. The
monthly tribute of that city is greater than your yearly
one. In addition to this monetary tribute, it supplies
Rome with four months' corn. It is, moreover, protected on every side by almost impassable deserts, har-
borless seas, rivers, and morasses. Yet none of these
have proved too strong for Rome's fortune. Two legions
stationed in that city curb not only the wide reaches
of Egypt but the noble race of Macedonians as well.

"What help then will you obtain for this war? Will
it come from the uninhabited quarters of the earth?
For all the inhabited portion belongs to Rome. Or do
some of you, perhaps, extend your hopes beyond the
Euphrates, in the expectation that aid will come from

your kin in Adiabene? [30] But they will not for any
frivolous pretext allow themselves to become involved
in so serious a war; and if they were so ill-advisedly
disposed, the Parthian would stop them, for he is
careful to keep the truce with the Romans and would
consider it a violation of the treaty if any of his subjects rose in arms against them.

"Your last refuge, therefore, is divine assistance.
But even that is on the side of the Romans; without
God's aid it would not have been possible to consolidate so great an empire. Consider, too, that even if
you were contending against a less formidable foe, the
uncompromising character of your religious laws
would create difficulties. If you are forced to transgress
the very laws through which you hope to obtain divine
assistance, you will cause God to turn his face from
you. Should you observe the Sabbath laws and do no
work on that day, you will fall easy prey, as did your
forefathers to Pompey, who pressed his operations
most vigorously on the days when the besieged rested.[31]
But if in time of war you transgress the laws of your
country, I do not know for what then you would go to
war, since you have but one concern: not to violate any
of the teachings of your forefathers. How can you call
upon the Deity for aid, if you wilfully infringe on the
service due Him?

"Whoever engages in war relies either on divine or
human aid; since your going to war cuts off both, you
choose manifest destruction. What, then, hinders you
from slaying your children and wives with your own
hands and from surrendering your native city, so unsurpassed in beauty, to the flames? By such an act of
madness you would at least save yourselves the
ignominy of defeat.

"It would be well, O my friends, it would be well
indeed, to foresee the impending storm while the vessel
is still in harbor, and not borne from port into the
midst of the hurricane. We rightly pity those who en-

counter unforeseen misfortunes, but he who rushes into manifest destruction earns only rebukes.

"Or do you imagine that you will wage war against the Romans as if by agreement with them that when triumphant, they will be magnanimous? The contrary will be the case. As an example to other nations, they will burn the Holy City to the ground and destroy your nation in its entirety. Whoever survives will find no spot to flee to, since all have either already acknowledged Rome's supremacy or fear that they soon will have to do so. Moreover, the danger threatens not only us, the Jews who dwell here, but those as well who reside in other cities. There is not a nation in the world which does not contain some of you; all of these, should you go to war, will in retaliation be sacrificed by your foes. Through the evil counsels of a few, every city will be deluged with Jewish blood. And they who strike the blow will be pardoned. Let us, on the other hand, suppose that the Romans will pursue a milder course; how wicked then to take up arms against men so magnanimous.

"Have pity, therefore, if not on your children and wives, then on this your metropolis at least, and on its sacred boundaries. Spare the Temple and preserve this sanctuary and its holy objects for yourselves. If victorious, the Romans will no longer spare them should their past abstention be so ungratefully requited. And now, I call your sanctuary, the holy angels of God, and our common country, to witness that I have not kept from you anything that is for your preservation. If you adopt suitable measures, you will together with me enjoy peace; but if you are carried away by passion, you will invite hazards of which I shall be free."

Having spoken, Agrippa wept, as did his sister. Their tears restrained much of the people's violence. Nevertheless, they cried that they would take up arms not against the Romans but against Florus, to avenge the sufferings he had inflicted on them. To which king

Agrippa replied: "But your deeds are already acts of war against the Romans. You have not paid your tribute to the Emperor and you have cut off the [Temple] colonnades from joining to the Antonia fortress. If you but connect these again and pay the tribute, you will exonerate yourselves from blame for the insurrection. The fortress does not at present belong to Florus, nor to Florus will you pay the tribute money." (War II, 16:4.)

THE REBELS RISE

AGRIPPA'S POLICY FAILS—THE REBELS AND THE SICARII

Acquiescing in this counsel, the people, with the king and Berenice, proceeded to the Temple and began to rebuild the colonnades. At the same time, the magistrates and the members of the council dispersed throughout the villages and collected the tribute. They soon gathered the forty talents in which that tribute was deficient. Thus did Agrippa divert the threatened war. Later, however, when he endeavored to persuade the multitude to obey Florus until the Emperor sent a successor to replace him, they were so provoked that they not only rebuked him but by proclamation, banished him from the city. Some of the rioters even had the audacity to throw stones at him. Perceiving that the violence of the revolutionaries was not to be restrained, and incensed at the indignities offered him, the king sent the magistrates and influential men to Florus at Caesarea, in order for him to choose some among them to collect the tribute in the country. He then withdrew to his own dominions.

At this time some of the chief fomenters of hostilities assembled and assaulted the fortress called Masada [in the Dead Sea region]. Capturing it by stratagem, they massacred the Romans and replaced them with a garrison of their own. At the same time

Eleazar, son of Ananias the [former] high priest, a very daring youth, then captain of the Temple, persuaded those who officiated at the divine service to accept neither gift nor sacrifice from any foreigner. This was the true beginning of our war with the Romans, since the sacrifice offered on behalf of the latter and of the Emperor was thus rejected.[32] The chief priests, and men of note, earnestly implored them not to omit the customary offering on behalf of their rulers, but they remained inexorable. Supported by the most energetic of the revolutionaries, they placed great reliance on their numbers, but chiefly they relied on the military genius of Eleazar.

Whereupon the leading men, the chief priests, and those of note among the Pharisees assembled together. Realizing that everything was at stake and that their misfortunes were becoming incurable, they conferred on a plan for action. They thought it best to try to divert the revolutionaries from their intent by persuasion. Accordingly, they convened the people in front of the brassen gate—that of the inner Temple, which faced eastward. They first expressed their great indignation at this attempt at revolt and at inflicting so serious a war upon their country. Then they exposed the absurdity of the alleged pretext. Their forefathers, they said, had in great measure adorned the sanctuary with the offerings of foreigners, invariably accepting gifts from foreign nations; not only had they not prohibited the sacrifice of any—which would have been a most impious act—but they distributed the offerings throughout the Temple. Though they have been there for so long a time, these offerings are still to be seen. But these men, whose present conduct was provoking the might of the Romans and courting a war with them, introduced novel rules into the divine worship and not only invited danger but would, were the Jews alone to forbid strangers to sacrifice or worship, brand their city with impiety. If such a law were applied to but a single private individual, there would be indignation at so inhumane an act; yet there was indifference when the Romans and the Emperor were placed under the ban. Moreover, there was reason to fear that those who rejected the sacrifices offered on behalf of the Romans might be prohibited from sacrificing even on their own behalf, and that their city would come under the ban of the empire if they did not quickly adopt more prudent measures, restore the sacrifices, and repair the affront before news of it reached those so affronted.

While making these observations, they brought forth priests well versed in the traditions of their country, who asserted that all their ancestors had accepted the sacrifices of aliens. But the revolutionaries paid no attention. Even the officiating priests would not attend to their divine service but were instead preparing for the commencement of the war. Certain now of their complete inability to stop the insurrection and cognizant that they would be the first to feel Rome's resentment, Jerusalem's leading men took steps to exonerate themselves from blame by sending two deputations: one, headed by [a certain] Simon, son of Ananias, to Florus; the other, whose most eminent men were Saul, Antipas, and Costobar, all relatives of the king, to Agrippa.[33] Both Florus and the king were requested to come with an army and crush the revolt while it was still possible to do so.

To Florus this dire intelligence was good news. Eager to fan the flame of war, he dismissed the embassy without reply. Agrippa, on the other hand, was solicitous both for the rebels and for the nation against which hostilities were directed; he wished to preserve the Jews for the Romans, and the Temple and metropolis for the Jews; and he was conscious of the fact that continuation of the disturbances would not be to his advantage. He therefore dispatched three thousand

cavalry men out of Auranitis, Batanaea, and Trachonitis to the aid of the people.

Encouraged by this, the leading men, chief priests,
and those of the populace who favored peace, occupied
the Upper City, the Lower City and the Temple being
in possession of the insurgents. Stones and slings were
employed without intermission, and missiles hurled
incessantly from both quarters. Occasionally they
sallied forth in companies and engaged in close combat; the revolutionaries displayed greater daring, and
the royal troops, superior skill. The main object of the
latter was to gain possession of the Temple and to
expel those who were profaning the sanctuary; the
rebels, led by Eleazar, battled to add the Upper City
to what they already held. For seven days the mutual
slaughter continued uninterruptedly; but neither side
relinquished the quarter they occupied.

The eighth day was the festival of wood-carrying.[34]
It was the custom for every man to bring wood on
this day for the altar, whose fire was never allowed to
go out. The men within the Temple excluded their opponents from this observance. Having by this time
drawn to their side many Sicarii—as the brigands who
carried concealed daggers in their bosoms and who
now crowded among the more feeble of the people were
called—the rebels battled with still greater confidence.

Overpowered by their numbers and their boldness,
the royal troops gave way and retreated from the
Upper City. The insurgents then attacked the residence
of Ananias, the high priest, and the palace of Agrippa
and Berenice, and burned them to the ground. They
next carried flames to the public archives, hurrying to
destroy the contracts of the moneylenders and to prevent the exaction of debts, in order to win over the
numerous debtors and enable the poor to rise against
the rich without fear. The keepers of the record office
having fled, the rebels set fire to the building. After

burning these sinews of the state, they advanced against their opponents. Some of the leading men and chief priests hid in sewers; others fled with the royal troops to [Herod's] upper palace and instantly locked the gates. Among the latter were Ananias, the high priest, his brother Hezekiah, and the members of the deputation to Agrippa. Content with their victory and the conflagrations they had set, the insurgents paused for the present. (War II, 17:1-6.)

The rebels also stormed the fortress Antonia, and began to lay siege to Herod's palace, which was defended by the peace party (17:7).

MENAHEM

In the meantime one Menahem (son of Judah, called the Galilaean—a very able sophist, who in the days of Quirinius had upbraided the Jews for acknowledging the Romans as masters after having God for their master) accompanied by his associates, repaired to Masada with his companions. There he broke open king Herod's armory and armed not only his own adherents but other rebels as well. He employed the latter as a guard and returned in royal pomp to Jerusalem, where he became leader of the revolution and conducted the siege of the palace. . . .

Agrippa's troops give up the palace and are permitted to withdraw under safe conduct—granted to them, but not to the Romans.

On the following day the high priest Ananias was discovered hiding in a sewer of the palace, and with his brother Hezekiah, was executed by the rebels. The insurgents now laid siege to the towers, keeping close watch to prevent any [Roman] soldier from escaping. Menahem, inflated by the destruction of the strongholds and the death of Ananias, gave way to cruelty; imagining that he had no rival to dispute his leadership, he became an insupportable tyrant.

But Eleazar and his comrades, having interchanged ideas, rose against him, on the ground that after revolting against the Romans for freedom's sake, it was unbecoming to betray that freedom to one of their own people and bow to a master who even if he had not been guilty of violence, was still of humbler origin than they. They agreed also that should it be necessary to invest someone with supreme authority, Menahem was the last person to be so invested. Accordingly, they attacked him in the Temple, where he had gone in state to worship, arrayed in royal garb and attended by his armed zealots. When Eleazar and his companions rushed upon him, the rest of the populace, in sudden passion, snatched up stones and threw them at the sophist, in the hope that his fall would end the whole revolt.

For a time Menahem and his adherents resisted; but when they saw themselves assailed by the entire multitude, they fled whichever way they could. All who were caught were slain, and a search was made for those in hiding. A few escaped, having secretly made their way to Masada. Among them was Eleazar, son of Jairus [Yair], a kinsman of Menahem, who later acted the tyrant there.[35] Menahem himself retired to a place called Ophel and hid there abjectly; but he was found, dragged forth to public view, and after every variety of torture, executed. His officers, and Absalom, the principal instrument of his tyranny, met a similar fate. (War II, 17:8-9.)

The rebels, in possession of all Jerusalem, massacred the Roman garrison. At the same time, "as if by divine Providence," the people of Caesarea slew the more than twenty thousand Jewish residents of that city, an act that enraged the whole Jewish nation. Violent conflicts between Jews and Gentiles broke out in Syrian cities and spread as far as Alexandria. (17:10-18:8.)

THE VICTORY OVER CESTIUS GALLUS

Cestius [Gallus, governor of Syria] deemed it imprudent to remain inactive any longer while the Jews were everywhere up in arms. He therefore left Antioch with the twelfth legion in full complement, two thousand picked men from each of the other legions, six cohorts of infantry, and four squadrons of cavalry. Besides these he had with him the auxiliaries sent by the sovereign princes: [king] Antiochus [of Commagene] furnished two thousand horse and three thousand foot soldiers, all bowmen; Agrippa, an equal number of cavalry and a little less than two thousand infantry; [king] Soaemus [of Emesa] followed with four thousand men, a third of whom were cavalry, the rest archers. With these troops Cestius marched to Ptolemais [Acco]. Great numbers of additional auxiliaries were obtained from the [free] cities; they lacked the skill of the regulars, but compensated for that lack by their fervor and their hatred of the Jews. Agrippa himself came along with Cestius, both as guide and as director of what was fit to be done.

Cestius sent out various detachments to take Jaffa and then to subdue Galilee. With his entire army he entered Antipatris, northeast of Jaffa, and proceeded to Lydda; ascending through Beth-horon, he pitched his camp at Gabao (Gibeon), some six miles northwest of Jerusalem (around October 66).

The Jews, seeing that the war was now approaching the capital, abandoned the festival [of Tabernacles] and took to arms. Emboldened by their numbers, they rushed to battle in clamor and disorder, paying no heed to the seventh day of rest, though the Sabbath was a day especially revered by them. But the same rage that made them forget religious observance rendered them victorious in the conflict. So furious was their attack that they broke the Roman ranks and advanced through their midst, dealing death. Had not

the [Roman] cavalry with a tolerably fresh battalion
of infantry wheeled around to the support of the still
intact part of the ranks, Cestius and his entire army
would have been endangered. Five hundred and fifteen
Romans were killed, four hundred of them foot
soldiers, the rest cavalry. But the Jews lost only two
and twenty men. The most valiant of the latter were
Monobazus and Cenedaeus, relatives of Monobazus,
king of Adiabene. . . .[36]

Repelled in their advance, the Jews retreated to the
city. But Simon, son of Giora, who attacked the Roman
rear as it ascended the road to Beth-horon, routed
much of it and carried off many of the baggage-carry-
ing mules, which he brought into the city. While
Cestius tarried in the neighborhood for three days, the
Jews seized the heights, set watches at the approaches
to the city, and appeared openly resolved not to remain
inactive should the Romans begin to move.

*The insurgents ignore Agrippa II's plea to desist
from fighting.*

Cestius, realizing that internal dissensions offered
a good opportunity for attack, led out his entire force,
routed the Jews, and pursued them to the gates of
Jerusalem. Encamping at a place called Scopus,[37] seven
furlongs from the city, he suspended operations
against it for three days, in the hope that those within
might perhaps yield a little. In the meantime he sent
numerous foraging parties to the neighboring villages
to seize their corn. On the fourth day . . . he marshaled his troops and led them into the city.

The people had hitherto been restrained by the rebels
[from surrendering], but now the latter, greatly dismayed at the good order of the Romans, abandoned the
suburbs and retired to the inner city and the Temple.
Cestius, on entering, set fire to Bezetha, known also as
the New City, and to the so-called Timber Market. Proceeding to the Upper City, he encamped opposite the
royal residence. Had he at this precise moment chosen

to storm the walls, he would immediately have won the city and have ended the war right then and there. But bribed by Florus, Tyrannius Priscus, the camp prefect, together with the majority of the cavalry officers, diverted him from the attempt. That was the cause of the war's long duration and the irreparable disasters that befell the Jews.

In the meantime, persuaded by Ananus, son of Jonathan,[38] many of the leading citizens invited Cestius to enter the city, promising to open the gates to him. But partly out of resentment and partly because he did not fully believe them, he deferred accepting these overtures—until the insurgents, discovering the treason, chased Ananus and his accomplices from the walls, and pelting them with stones, drove them into their houses. They then posted themselves on the towers and showered their missiles on those who were attempting to get over the wall. For five days the Romans pressed the assault on all sides without success; on the sixth, Cestius, at the head of a large body of picked men and archers, attacked the north quarter of the Temple. The Jews assailed them from the colonnade and repulsed them several times as they advanced to the wall, until at length, overwhelmed by missiles, the Romans retreated. Then, however, their front rank fixed their shields firmly against the wall, the second joined theirs to those of the preceding one, and the next similarly to theirs, forming what they call a *testudo,* a tortoise. From this the missiles glanced off without effect. No longer harmed, the soldiers undermined the wall and prepared to set fire to the Temple gate.

A terrible panic seized the insurgents; many fled from the city, as if its capture were imminent. Emboldened by the flight of these miscreants, the people ran to open the gates and admit Cestius as a benefactor. Had he persevered in the siege a little longer, he would have taken the city. But God, so I suppose, already regarding even his sanctuary with aversion because of these wicked men [the rebels], prevented the war from ending that very day.

It happened then that Cestius, aware neither of the despondency of the besieged nor of the disposition of the people, suddenly recalled his troops. Though he had not met with the slightest reverse, he abandoned all hope, and contrary to all calculation, retired from the city. This unexpected retreat restored the confidence of the rebels. They sallied out upon Cestius' rear and slew considerable numbers of both cavalry and infantry. Cestius passed that night in the camp at Scopus. By withdrawing still further on the following day, he invited more attacks from his opponents. Pressing upon him, they cut the rear of his army; advancing also on both sides of his route, they showered their missiles on his flanks. In the belief that they were being pursued by countless numbers, the rear ranks dared not turn on those who wounded them from behind. Nor did they attempt to beat off those who were pressing their flanks. Heavily armed, they were afraid to break their lines lest the Jews, who were light-armed, should penetrate their ranks. That is why the Romans suffered severe damage without being able to retaliate.

Harassed throughout their route, thrown into disorder, they fell, and great numbers of them were slain. . . . With difficulty, and loss of much of their equipment, they finally reached their former camp at Gabao [Gibeon]. Here Cestius halted for two days, undecided about his next course. But on the third, perceiving that the enemy had greatly increased in numbers and that Jews had infiltrated into all the neighboring spots, he realized that the delay had been to his detriment and that if he continued to hesitate, he would have still more enemies to face.

To expedite his retreat he ordered whatever might hinder his army's march to be discarded. Accordingly, the mules and other beasts of burden were killed, except those that carried missiles and engines. These the Romans preserved for their own use, especially because they feared that if captured by the Jews, they would be turned against them.

Cestius and his army then marched toward Beth-horon. In the wider passes the Jews pressed them less closely; but when the Romans started their descent through defiles [to Lower Beth-horon], one group hurried ahead and hindered them from getting out of them, another drove their rear guard into the ravine, while the main body [of the Jews] spread above the gorge and showered the phalanx with missiles. Here, however perplexed the infantry was about means of protection, the cavalry was still more endangered. Assailed in the manner described, they were unable to preserve their ranks along the route, and a charge up the slopes was impracticable for horses. Losing their footing, the latter tumbled down the precipices and ravines by which they were surrounded. There was neither room for flight nor time to deliberate on defense. In their perplexity, the Romans surrendered to lamentation and wails of despair. The war cry of the Jews answered them, and a clamor of mingled joy and rage. It is likely that Cestius and his entire army would have perished had not night, during which they took refuge in [Lower] Beth-horon, intervened. The Jews in the meantime occupied the entire surrounding country and watched for their egress.

Despairing of open retreat, Cestius now took measures for flight. Picking four hundred of his bravest soldiers, he stationed them on the ramparts, commanding them to raise the beacons of the camp sentinels, in order to trick the Jews into thinking that the entire army was still on the spot. Then he himself, with the rest of his army, silently advanced thirty furlongs. When, in the morning, the Jews saw the night quarters of the army deserted, they rushed upon the four hundred men who had deluded them, threw their javelins at them, and hastened in pursuit of Cestius.

He, however, though it had been night, had already advanced a considerable distance, and now, by day, pushed still more rapidly forward. In their terror and consternation the soldiers abandoned their battering rams, catapults, and many other engines. These the Jews captured and later used against the very men who had relinquished them. The Jews continued the pursuit as far as Antipatris [Ras el-Ain, northeast of Jaffa]. Failing to overtake the Romans, they then returned, secured the [Roman] machines, stripped the dead bodies, collected the booty that had been left behind, and with songs of triumph, retraced their steps to the capital. In this whole affair they had lost but few men; but the Romans and their allies had five thousand three hundred foot and three hundred and eighty horse soldiers slain by them. . . . (War II, 18:9-19:9.)

"This reverse of Cestius' proved disastrous for our whole nation, for the advocates of the war were so elated with this success that they entertained hopes of remaining victorious to the end" (Life 6).

After this catastrophe of Cestius' many eminent Jews abandoned Jerusalem, as they would a sinking ship. . . .

Among those who were wholeheartedly attached to the Roman cause and who left the city were the brothers Costobar and Saul, relatives of Agrippa II (War II, 17:4); Antipas, another relative, remained and was later killed by the rebels (IV, 3:4).

In the meantime, the people of Damascus, informed of the Roman disaster, hastened to slaughter the Jews who resided among them. Since, being suspicious of them, they had, some time earlier, already imprisoned them in the Gymnasium, they thought they would have no difficulty in carrying out their design. However, they distrusted their own wives, nearly all of whom had become converts to the Jewish religion;

their main concern, therefore, was to keep these wives in ignorance of their intent. Attacking the Jews, thus cooped up and unarmed, they massacred ten thousand of them, unresisting, within a single hour. (War II, 20:2.)

PREPARATIONS FOR THE WAR

A PEOPLE'S ASSEMBLY IN JERUSALEM ELECTS WAR LEADERS, AMONG THEM JOSEPHUS

On their return to Jerusalem the Jews who had pursued Cestius induced—some by force, others by persuasion—those who favored the Romans to come over to their side, and assembling in the Temple, appointed additional generals for the war. Joseph, son of Gorion, and Ananus, the [former] high priest, were elected to the supreme authority of the city's affairs and charged with the special task of repairing the walls of the city. Because they saw that he was of a tyrannical temper and that his followers behaved like royal guards, they did not confer the administration on Eleazar, son of Simon, though he had in his possession the Roman spoils, the money taken from Cestius, and in addition, much of the public treasure. Shortly, however, want of money and Eleazar's intrigues succeeded in making his authority paramount in the state.

For Idumaea they appointed other generals: Joshua, son of Sapphas, one of the chief priests, and Eleazar, son of the high priest Neus.[39] They also instructed Niger [of Peraea], then governor of Idumaea . . . to obey their commands. Nor were the other districts neglected. Joseph, son of Simon, was sent as commander to Jericho; Manasseh, to Peraea; John, the Essene, to the district of Thamna; Lydda, Jaffa, and Emmaus were also allotted to the latter. John, son of Ananias, was appointed governor of Gophna and Acrabetta, and Josephus, son of Matthias,[40] was given the two Galilees. Gamala, the strongest of the towns in that section, was also placed under his authority.

Each of the other commanders administered the district entrusted to him according to his zeal and abilities. Josephus, however, proceeding into Galilee, made it his first care to gain the good will of the inhabitants, for he knew that by so doing he would, even if he failed on other scores, prove successful in the main. Realizing that he would win the friendship of the nobles by sharing his authority with them, and the friendship of the people if he conducted affairs through the medium of their countrymen, he chose from among the nation seventy men, of mature years and eminent in wisdom, and appointed them magistrates of Galilee. . . . And knowing that the Romans would invade Galilee, he fortified the most suitable posts.

Sepphoris and, headed by John, son of Levi, Gischala were authorized to build their own defenses.

When he considered the fact that the Roman army owed its invincible power chiefly to prompt obedience and military training, he despaired of a discipline pursued only in the moment of need. However, observing that the ready obedience of the Romans was due to the number of their officers, he partitioned his army more on the Roman model and increased the number of his captains. Moreover, he distributed the soldiers into various classes and placed them under [the command of] decurions, centurions, and tribunes; in addition, he appointed generals for the larger divisions. He also taught the soldiers to pass signals, to advance and retreat by trumpet calls, to bring the wings up to a charge and make them wheel about, and how the victorious are to relieve sorely pressed comrades and share the labors of the fatigued. He continually instructed them in all matters conducive to mental fortitude or hardiness of body. But chiefly he trained them for the war by detailed expounding of the Roman dis-

cipline and by telling them that they had to cope with
men who through strength of body and intrepidity of
mind had conquered almost the entire inhabited world.

He told them that he would consider it proof of
their discipline as warriors, even before they took the
field, if they abstained from the usual excesses—theft,
robbery, and rapine—and from defrauding their countrymen or regarding an injury to their nearest kin as
being to their own advantage. For the most successfully conducted wars [he said] are those in which the
soldiers preserve a clear conscience, since those who
are depraved at heart have as adversaries not only
their antagonists but God Himself. (War II, 20:3-7.)

*Josephus' army consisted of sixty thousand infantry,
three hundred and fifty cavalry, and four thousand
five hundred mercenaries. This army "he equipped with
old weapons that he had collected." He also had a bodyguard of six hundred men (20:6, 8).*

JOHN OF GISCHALA'S OPPOSITION

While Josephus was thus administering affairs in
Galilee, there appeared upon the stage a treacherous
character, a native of Gischala, John, son of Levi, in
craft and duplicity pre-eminently distinguished, and
unequaled in wicked practices. . . . A solitary rebel,
he subsequently drew associates in his daring; few
indeed, at first, but he daily widened their numbers.
He was careful to accept no one who would be easy
prey to an assailant, but picked men who excelled in
physical activity, intrepidity, and knowledge of the
arts of war. He assembled a band of four hundred
men, mainly fugitives from the district of Tyre and
the neighboring villages. With their aid he ravaged
the whole of Galilee and harassed a great many people
who were already in turmoil at the approaching war.

While thus aspiring to command and prosecuting
his schemes for advancement, John had been checked
by want of pecuniary resources. Perceiving that Jo-

sephus was highly pleased with his energy, he . . .
persuaded him to entrust him with the repairs of the
walls of his [John's] native city, an undertaking in
which he enriched himself at the expense of the wealthy citizens. . . . Supposing that if he could effect the
ruin of Josephus, he would command Galilee, he directed the rebels under him to pursue their plunders
with greater zeal. He thought that with the rise of
many in the district who desired revolt, he might
either lay an ambush for the general as he came to
its aid, then kill him, or that if he disregarded the
rebels, he might slander him to the inhabitants. He
also circulated far and near a report that Josephus
intended to betray the state to the Romans, and he
resorted to many similar devices designed to ruin the
man. (War II, 21:1-2.)

*In Tarichaea, where Josephus resided, his life was
threatened as that of a traitor; in Tiberias, a city with
a partly prorebellion, partly pro-Roman population,
John tried to undermine Josephus' stand; the general
skillfully escaped an attempted assassination. Later,
John sent messengers to Jerusalem to denounce Josephus as a potential tyrant and to have him recalled.
Josephus had to use arms to ward off the attacks on
his authority and prevent civil strife. (21:3-10; another account is to be found in Josephus' Life.)*

JERUSALEM GETS READY FOR THE WAR

Ceasing from their civil dissensions, the Jews now
directed their attention to preparations against the
Romans. In Jerusalem the [former] high priest
Ananus and those nobles who were not attached to the
interests of the Romans applied themselves to the care
of the walls and the gathering of implements of war.
Missiles and every other kind of weapon were being
forged throughout the city. Multitudes of youths engaged in irregular war exercises, and feverish activity
reigned everywhere. Deep, in the meantime, was the

dejection of the moderate party; and many, foreseeing the approaching disasters, loudly gave voice to their grief. There were omens,[41] too, which to the friends of peace, boded ill, but which those who were aflame for war interpreted favorably. The state of the city before the arrival of the Romans, was that of a place doomed to destruction. It was Ananus' concern, however, to put aside for a while the warlike preparations, to persuade the seditious to adopt a more salutary policy, and to restrain the madness of the so-called zealots; but he was overpowered by their violence. The sequel of our narrative will disclose the fate that befell him. (War II, 22:1.)

Simon, son of Giora, who had distinguished himself at Beth-horon (19:2) and was to play a leading role in the later siege of Jerusalem, raided the country with a band of rebels. He established himself at Masada, awaiting his hour to come. (22:2.)

THE FIRST STAGES OF THE WAR IN GALILEE

VESPASIAN AND TITUS

The defeat of Cestius called for a determined Roman stand. The emperor Nero, then in Achaia, appointed Vespasian, his most experienced general, to deal with the rebellion in Judaea.

When Nero was informed of the disasters in Judaea, he was secretly seized with dismay and alarm, as is natural in such cases; in public however he assumed a haughty and indignant air. He attributed what had occurred to the negligence of his general rather than to the valor of the foe. Bearing the burden of the empire, he thought it fit to treat misfortunes with lofty contempt; he therefore pretended to have a soul superior to any reverse. But his mental perturbation was betrayed by his anxious planning.

As he pondered to whom to entrust the East in its

turbulence, and whose task it should be instantly to chastise the Jewish rebels and to impose a timely check on the surrounding nations, who were catching the contagion, he decided that only [Flavius] Vespasian would be adequate to the emergency and able to support the burden of so vast an enterprise. Vespasian, a man who from youth to age had spent his life in military service, had long ago pacified the West, when it was disturbed by the Germans, and made it subject to the Romans; to his arms, also, Rome owed the acquisition of Britain, a territory hitherto almost unknown. Through this latter conquest, Nero's [step-]father, Claudius, through no exertion of his own, gained the honors of a triumph.

Nero regarded these circumstances as favorable omens. He also realized that Vespasian's years were steadied by experience and that he had as hostages for his fidelity sons whose vigor would make them fit instruments to carry out their father's plans. God also was, perhaps, completely reshaping the [political] structure of all nations. Nero therefore sent him to assume command of the armies in Syria, paying him, because of the urgency of the occasion, many soothing and flattering compliments, such as necessities of this type demand. On his appointment, Vespasian, who had been staying with Nero in Achaia, immediately dispatched from there his son Titus to Alexandria to call up the fifteenth legion. He himself, crossing the Hellespont, proceeded by land to Syria and there concentrated the Roman forces and a large body of auxiliaries from the neighboring kings. (War III, 1:1-3.)

The Jews, inflated by their victory over Cestius, twice attacked the city of Ascalon, but were repulsed by the Roman defenders and suffered great losses. Of their three leaders only one, Niger of Peraea (see War II, 20:4), survived (III, 2:1-3); he had distinguished himself in the battle with Cestius (II, 19:2); later, he was murdered by the Zealots (IV, 6:1).

Vespasian took with him his troops from Antioch, the capital of Syria, which both in size and prosperity ranks indisputably as the third city of the Roman world. There he found Agrippa, with his entire force, awaiting his arrival, and made a rapid march to Ptolemais [Acco]. . . . (War III, 2:4.)

Emissaries from the fortified Galilean city of Sepphoris appeared in Ptolemais and requested Roman protection (War III, 2:4). Sepphoris had previously already asked for and received Roman support (II, 18:11). Vespasian granted them a detachment of six thousand men, led by the tribune Placidus. From Sepphoris the Romans plundered the surrounding country, and by so doing harassed the Jewish commander of Galilee, Josephus (III, 4:1). Before proceeding with his story, Josephus offers a description of Galilee, Samaria, and Judaea (III, 3).

In the meantime Titus, having made the voyage from Achaia to Alexandria more quickly than was usual in the winter season, assumed command of the force for which he had been sent. Proceeding by forced marches, he soon reached Ptolemais. Here he met his father with the two legions under his command, the highly distinguished fifth and tenth, and joined the one he brought, the fifteenth, to them. These were followed by eighteen cohorts. Five more, including a squadron of cavalry, came from Caesarea, and five other squadrons from Syria. Ten of the cohorts had each a thousand infantrymen; and each of the remaining thirteen, six hundred foot and one hundred and twenty horse soldiers. In addition, a considerable number of auxiliaries had been furnished by the kings, Antiochus [IV, of Commagene], Agrippa, and Soaemus [of Emesa], each of whom contributed two thousand foot archers and a thousand horse. The [Nabataean] Arab [king] Malchus [II] sent a thousand cavalry and five thousand infantry, mostly bowmen. The entire army, horse and foot, including the royal contingents, numbered nearly sixty thousand men, exclusive of numerous servants, who because of their military training, should be included in the fighting force. In peacetime constantly engaged in their masters' exercises and in wartime sharing their dangers, they were in fighting skill and prowess, second only to these masters. (War III, 4:2.)

THE ROMAN ARMY: A DESCRIPTION

One cannot but admire the foresight of the Romans in providing themselves with the kind of servants who might prove useful not only in the ordinary offices of life but in war as well. Indeed, if we examine their entire military organization, we shall have proof that they acquired a great empire not as fortune's gift, but by their valor.

For it is not actual war that gives them the first lesson in arms; nor having ceased to use them in times of peace, do they employ their hands only when necessity so requires; but as if they had been born with their weapons, they have no truce with [military] exercises and wait not for emergencies. This training differs in nothing from the actual efforts of combat; every soldier is kept in daily practice and required to expend as much energy as those truly engaged in war. Hence the perfect ease with which they endure the rigors of conflict. No confusion ever breaks their accustomed ranks; no panic upsets; no labor exhausts. It follows, therefore, as a certainty that they invariably conquer those not similarly trained: nor would he err who should style their exercises bloodless conflicts, and their conflicts bloody exercises.

Nor can they fall easy prey to an enemy's sudden attack; at whatever point they may invade a hostile territory, they never engage in battle until they have fortified their camp. This camp is not erected haphazardly or at random, nor do all participate in the work at one and the same time, or in disorderly fashion. If the ground is uneven, it is leveled, and the camp is squared by measurement. And great numbers of carpenters with building tools, follow the army.

The interior of the camp is set apart for tents. Its exterior circumference resembles a wall furnished with equidistant towers; the spans between the towers are occupied by scorpions, catapults, stone-projectors, and other propelling engines, all ready to hurl missiles.

Four gates are constructed, one on each side of the surrounding wall, with level approaches for the easy admission of beasts of burden, and wide enough for a sortie in case of emergency. The camp within is conveniently divided into streets. In the middle are the tents of the officers, and in the center of these that of the commander in chief, which closely resembles a temple. Thus a city seems to have suddenly sprung up —a city with its market place, site for handicraft trades, and seats, as well, for the centurions and division commanders, where, when disputes arise, they adjudicate the camp's differences. Owing to the number and skill of the workmen, the outer wall is raised and everything within it completed more quickly than one would expect; and if the occasion demands it, an outer trench, four cubits in depth and the same in breadth, is dug around the wall.

Thus protected, the Romans occupy the tents in companies, quietly and with decorum. They manage all their other affairs with similar order and precision. The duty of procuring wood, corn, and water, when needed, is imposed on the several companies in turn; nor has any company the option to sup or dine at will, but all take their meals together. A trumpet signals their bedgoing, watch, and rising time; and nothing is done without command.

At the first break of dawn all the soldiers report to their centurions, and the latter to the tribunes, to salute them; together with the tribunes all the superior officers then go to the commander in chief, who as is customary, gives them the day's watchword, and other orders, to relay to their subordinates. They observe the same procedure when they go to battle, conveying themselves promptly wherever required and moving in unbroken ranks whether they attack or retreat.

When the camp is to be broken up, the trumpet gives the signal, and all are on the alert. At that signal they take down their tents and ready everything for their departure. At the second call of the trumpets, which signals equipment-packing time, they in all haste place their gear upon the mules and other beasts of burden, and stand ready to spring forward, as if from a starting post. They then set fire to their camp, not only to prevent its possible use by the enemy but because they can easily re-erect it there. A third call of the trumpets signals departure time, speeding those who may for some reason have been delayed so that none should be missing from the ranks. The herald, standing on the right of the commander, then asks them thrice, in their native tongue, if they are ready for war; almost before the question is asked, they in loud and animated voices, shout as often the reply, "Ready," and inspired with some sort of martial enthusiasm, they simultaneously lift their right hands.

Going forth then, they march quietly and in good order, everyone keeping his own place in the array, as if on the field of battle. The infantry men are protected by breastplates and helmets, and wear swords on both sides; the one on the left is much the longer, for the one on the right does not exceed a span. The picked body of infantry that attends the general bears lances and shields; every other soldier of the phalanx carries a javelin and oblong buckler, a saw and a basket, a mattock and a hatchet, a leather thong, an edged hook, a chain, and provisions for three days, so that the foot soldier differs little from the baggage mules.

The cavalrymen have a long sword on their right

sides, a long lance in their hands, and a shield lying obliquely on the horse's flank. Three or more darts, with broad heads and in size not inferior to spears, are carried by them in a quiver. Like the infantry, all wear helmets and breastplates. Not a single weapon distinguishes those chosen to attend the general from the regular cavalry. The legion picked by lot always leads.

Thus do the Romans march and rest, and such are their several kinds of arms. In battle nothing is done unadvisedly or precipitately; counsel invariably precedes every operation, and actions follow the decisions made. Hence they seldom err; and if they blunder, the mistake is easily rectified.

Moreover, they consider mishaps resulting from prior consultation preferable to success achieved merely through some accident of fortune, for they reason that fortuitous advantages tempt men to negligence, whereas if misfortune befalls, deliberation usefully suggests the exercise of caution against its recurrence. Besides, accidental successes are not to be ascribed to him who attains them; but if, contrary to expectation, disasters occur, it is a consolation that the matter had been duly considered.

By their military exercises the Romans invigorate not only their bodies but their minds as well. Fear, also, is part of their training; their rules mete out capital punishment not only for desertion of a post but also for even slight remissness in duty. Moreover, their officers are even more highly revered than their laws, since by their rewards to the deserving they surmount the imputation of cruelty towards those they punish.

So great is the soldiers' prompt obedience to their officers that while maintaining order in peacetime, in the field the whole army moves as one body: so simple is the construction of their ranks; so easily performed are their evolutions; so quick are their ears to hear orders, their eyes to see signals, and their hands to discharge tasks. Hence all are equally swift in executing orders, and very slow to succumb to suffering. Nor is there any record of their ever having been daunted while in array, either by numbers, stratagems, difficulty of position, or even by fortune, for they always rely more firmly on endurance than on fortune.

Where, therefore, counsel precedes action, and so efficient an army implements that counsel, is it any wonder that on the east, the Euphrates, on the west, the ocean, on the south, the most fertile region of Libya, and on the north, the Danube and the Rhine, are the limits of the empire? It may be said, and justly so, that the possessions are inferior to the men who have acquired them.

I have detailed these particulars not so much to extol the Romans as to console those whom they have vanquished and to deter the disaffected [from revolt]. It may be, too, that those of my readers who are unacquainted with the subject will derive information from this account of the Roman military discipline. I now return to the point from which I digressed. (War III, 5.)

Compare the older description of the Roman army by Polybius, Universal History VI, 19-42.

VESPASIAN SETS OUT TO INVADE GALILEE

Before the appearance of Vespasian on the scene, Placidus tried, unsuccessfully, to capture Josephus' fortress, Jotapata. (War III, 6:1.)

Vespasian himself, intent on invading Galilee, put his army in the marching order Roman usage called for, and marched out of Ptolemias. The light-armed auxiliaries and the archers, he ordered to advance first, to repel any sudden incursions of the enemy and to explore suspicious woods suited to ambuscades. Next came the heavy-armed division of the Romans, foot and horse. These were followed by ten men, drafted out of every hundred, carrying their own baggage and the tools for measuring out a camp. In their rear came the road makers to repair irregularities of the road, level rugged ground, and cut down obstructing woods in order that the troops should not be impeded by obstacles on the route. Behind these, Vespasian arranged his own baggage and that of the officers under his command, protecting it by a large corps of cavalry. He himself followed, attended by a select body of infantry and cavalry and by the spearmen. Next came the cavalry units of the legions, one hundred and twenty horse being attached to each legion. They were followed by the mules carrying the siege engines and the other war machines. Then came the general officers, the prefects of the cohorts, and the tribunes, accompanied by a picked body of troops.

The ensigns encompassing the eagle, which is at the head of every Roman legion, were seen next. The eagle, king and bravest of all birds, seems to them both a symbol of empire and an augury of victory over whomever they attack. These sacred emblems preceded the trumpeters, who were followed by the phalanx, arranged in ranks six abreast and attended by a centurion, who as custom dictated, superintended the order of the march. The infantry was succeeded by the entire retinue of the servants of the respective legions, who led the mules and other beasts of burden that bore the soldiers' baggage. Behind the legions came the crowd of mercenaries, followed for security, by a rear guard composed of light- and heavy-armed infantry and a considerable body of cavalry.

Thus did Vespasian march with his army until he reached the frontiers of Galilee, where he pitched his camp and restrained his soldiers, who were eager for battle. . . .

Vespasian's appearance "caused many to regret their revolt and alarmed all of them." Josephus, who had set up his camp at Garis, in the vicinity of Seppohoris, realized that his forces were insufficiently prepared for facing the Romans and withdrew to Tiberias (War III, 6:3). Vespasian was thus virtually in control of the lowlands of Galilee.

Vespasian reached the city of Gabara, and attacking it when it was destitute of an effective fighting force, took it at the first assault. On entering the town, he indiscriminately massacred both young and old, the Romans, both out of hatred for the nation and in recollection of the affront to Cestius, showing no mercy to any age. The city itself he reduced to ashes, and all the hamlets and small towns in its vicinity shared its fate. Some of these had been totally deserted; the inhabitants of the rest he enslaved.

The arrival of Josephus alarmed the city he had chosen for safety, for the people of Tiberias felt that he would not have fled if he had not utterly despaired of the contest. They were not mistaken about his views; he saw whither the affairs of the Jews would eventually lead them and knew they had but one means of preservation—submission. Yet though he personally expected pardon from the Romans, he would have preferred to suffer a thousand deaths rather than betray his country, and by dishonoring the command entrusted to him, live prosperously among those against whom he had been commissioned to fight. He therefore resolved to write an account of the state of affairs to the men in power at Jerusalem, neither exaggerating the strength of the enemy, lest it result in his being charged with timidity, nor underrating it, lest this inspire them with confidence at a time when they were perhaps inclined to repent. Should they choose to negotiate [he wrote], they should so inform him without delay; or if they decided on hostilities, they should send him a force able to cope with the Romans. Having written to this effect, he immediately forwarded his letter to Jerusalem by courier. (War III, 6:2-7:2.)

It was, of course, too late to change the military plans; negotiations with the Romans were out of the question.

THE BATTLE OF JOTAPATA (67)

JOSEPHUS READY TO DEFEND JOTAPATA

Vespasian was impatient to demolish Jotapata having heard that large numbers of the enemy had fled to that city and that it was their strongest base. He therefore dispatched both horse and foot soldiers to level the road, which being mountainous and rocky, was difficult even for infantry, and quite impractical for cavalry. The work was completed in four days, and a spacious highway opened for the troops. On the fifth day Josephus withdrew from Tiberias, and making his way to Jotapata, revived the dejected spirits of the Jews. The welcome tidings of this change of [Josephus'] whereabouts were communicated to Vespasian by a deserter, who urged him to attack the city, as its capture, if he got Josephus into his power, would seal the fate of all Judaea.

Vespasian considered this intelligence to be most auspicious, attributing to divine providence the fact that the man reputed to be the most sagacious of his opponents should enter a self-chosen prison. Accordingly, he immediately dispatched Placidus with a thousand horse, accompanied by the decurion Aebutius, an officer distinguished both for counsel and action, with orders to invest the city, that Josephus might not secretly escape.

The next day Vespasian followed with his entire force, and marching until evening, reached Jotapata. Leading his army to the north quarter, he encamped on a hill seven furlongs from the city, endeavoring to station himself as fully in view of the enemy as possible, in order to strike them with terror. The Jews were instantly so panic-stricken that none ventured outside the walls.

However, the Romans, having marched all day, were disinclined to engage in an immediate attack. But they surrounded the city with a double row of infantry, and beyond these, a third line of cavalry, in this manner closing every exit. This [encirclement], which cut off all hope of escape, stimulated the Jews to bolder action; for in war nothing is a stronger incentive to valor than necessity. (War III, 7:3-4.)

The first attacks were valiantly repulsed. "The Judaeans were undaunted by the strength of the enemy; the Romans, undeterred by the difficulties they encountered in taking the city" (7:5-6).

Jotapata is almost entirely built upon a precipice. On three sides it is surrounded by ravines so deep that in looking down, the sight fails before it can fathom the bottom. It is accessible only on the north side, where the city is built in a sinuous line on the slope of the mountain. To prevent an enemy from occupying the summit above it, Josephus when fortifying the city, had encompassed that side with a wall. Concealed by the mountains that encircled it, the city was totally invisible until one came upon it. Such was the strong position of Jotapata. (War III, 7:7.)

THE SIEGE

Vespasian, forced to contend with both the nature of the place and the daring valor of its defenders, resolved to prosecute the siege vigorously. Assembling the officers under his command, he held a council to plan the attack. It was resolved to raise a bank against the accessible quarter of the wall, and the entire army was sent out to procure materials. The surrounding mountains were stripped, and vast quantities of timber as well as stones were collected. As protection against the missiles hurled from above, some of the soldiers placed hurdles over the works, and under cover of them, built the banks, little, if at all, impeded by the missiles from the ramparts; others tore up the neighboring hillocks and brought a constant supply of earth; the troops being divided into three sections, no one was idle. From the ramparts, the Jews, in the meantime, cast on the enemy's defenses huge rocks and every kind of missile; though these did not penetrate the hurdles, the crash of their impact was so loud and so terrible that it somewhat impeded the workers.

Vespasian then set up the projectile engines—one hundred and sixty in all—in a semicircle and gave orders to aim at the men stationed on the wall. Simultaneously, the catapults vomited a whizzing storm of lances and the stone-projectors flung rocks the weight of a talent, as well as flames and dense showers of arrows. These missiles rendered inaccessible to the besieged Jews not only the ramparts but also the inner sites of the walls within range of the engines. For the host of Arab archers, the javelin throwers, and the slingers poured forth their volleys simultaneously with the machines.

Though checked in their defense of the ramparts, the Jews did not stay idle. Sallying out in groups, as in guerrilla warfare, they tore down the coverings of the workmen and wounded them when they were thus unprotected; and whenever the latter fell back, they demolished the banks and set fire to the palisades and hurdles. . . . (War III, 7:8-9.)

Josephus directed his men to increase the height of the wall and to erect a number of towers. (7:10.)

Vespasian was exasperated both by the subtlety of this [Josephus'] stratagem and by the boldness of the people of Jotapata. Inspired with fresh confidence by their bulwark, the latter renewed their sallies against the Romans, and in groups, engaged them in daily battles, employing every ruse of guerilla bands, pillaging what came their way, and burning the other works. At long last, Vespasian, restraining his troops from battle, decided to resort to a blockade and starve the city into surrender. He concluded that the besieged either would be compelled by want of provisions to sue for mercy, or obstinately holding out to the last, would perish from famine. Moreover, he expected to find them easier to deal with in battle if he gave them some respite, then attacked them when they were wasted by hunger. He therefore ordered all the various exits from the city to be guarded. (War III, 7:11.)

Josephus rationed the water supply and tricked the Romans into believing the fortress well supplied. Through another stratagem, he brought all necessities into the city (7:12-14). Yet Josephus had no confidence in the survival of the fortress.

Realizing that the city could not long hold out and that his own safety would be endangered if he remained, Josephus conferred with the leading men about means of flight. On perceiving his intention, the people flocked around him and implored him not to abandon them, since they relied on him alone. If he remained, they said, there was still hope of the city's deliverance because everyone would fight for him; and if they were captured, his presence would comfort them. It would therefore be unworthy of him to fly from his foes and desert his friends or to hasten from the city as one leaps from a storm-tossed ship that one had boarded during a calm. His departure would drown the city, for he alone sustained their courage; without him, none would any longer dare to oppose the enemy.

Concealing from them his concern for his own safety, Josephus said that it was for their sake that he contemplated leaving: as long as they were safe, his presence could not be of much help to them, and if they were captured, he would perish with them to no purpose; but if he were freed from the siege, he might be able to bring substantial relief from outside, for he would in all haste assemble the Galilaeans from the district, and by hostilities in another quarter, draw the Romans away from their walls. He failed to see how his staying could, under the present circumstances, be useful to them; it would only stimulate the Romans to press the siege, since his capture was their main objective; whereas, if informed that he had fled, they would relax their efforts against the city.

Despite these arguments the people implored him to stay: "They thought that no misfortune could befall them if Josephus remained with them."

Josephus reasoned that if he decided to stay, that decision would be ascribed to the people's entreaties, but that if he tried to flee, he would be imprisoned. Moreover, compassion for the people's distress completely dissipated his wish to leave them. He therefore resolved to remain. Converting the universal despair of the city into a weapon, he said to the people: "Now is the time to begin to fight, when there is no hope of safety left. It is a brave thing to sacrifice life for glory and through the performance of some noble deed to be remembered by posterity." Having said this, he acted. Sallying forth with the most able men, he dispersed the enemy sentries, and pushing forward to the Roman camp, he tore into shreds the skins that sheltered the men on the banks and he set fire to the works. And for many successive days and nights he carried on the fight indefatigably.

Because they were ashamed to be forced to flee by the Jews, and because even when they repulsed the latter, they were impeded in the pursuit by their heavy armor—and the Jews were able to escape into the city upon execution of whatever action they engaged in, before they could retaliate—the Romans suffered from these sorties. Vespasian therefore directed the troops to shun these attacks and not to engage in battle with men bent on death. "Nothing," he said, "imparts greater vigor than despair; their vehemence will be quenched if deprived of its objective, as fire is without fuel. It is seemly even for Romans to gain their victories safely, since they wage war not out of necessity but to enlarge their dominions." From then on he repulsed the Jews chiefly through the Arab archers, the Syrian slingers, and the stone-throwers. The projectile engines, also, were constantly at work. Greatly distressed by these machines, the Jews would give way; but once within reach of the far-ranging engines, they pressed furiously upon the Romans and fought without sparing soul or body, one group successively relieving another as the latter became exhausted.

When Vespasian considered the time that had been consumed and the sorties of the enemy, he felt that he in turn was besieged. Since the banks were now nearing the ramparts, he decided therefore to bring up the [battering] "ram." This ram is an immense beam, resembling the mast of a ship. Its forefront is armed with a mass of iron, forged in the figure of a ram's head, whence it derives its name. It is suspended by ropes around its middle—like the rod of a balance in scales—from another beam, which is braced on both sides by strong timbers. Drawn back by a number of men and then by their united strength thrust forward again, it batters a wall with its projecting iron. And there is no tower so strong, no wall so thick, that it, though it may resist the initial batteries, can withstand the continued assault. Such was the expedient to which the Roman general resorted in his anxiety to carry the city by storm, because the activity of the Jews had turned the blockade into a harmful measure.

Josephus' men tried to break the impact of the "ram" by letting sacks filled with chaff down the wall; they also set fire to the machines, "throwing the Romans into consternation."

At this crisis a certain Jew appeared worthy of our notice and commemoration. His name was Eleazar, son of Sameas, born at Saab in Galilee. Lifting an enormous stone, he flung it from the wall at the ram with such force that he broke off its head. He then leaped down, picked up the head lying in the midst of the foe, and most fearlessly conveyed it to the wall. A target, in the meantime, for the entire hostile army, and receiving their strokes upon his naked body, he was pierced by five arrows. He disregarded all of them while climbing the battlements, where his great courage was visible to all; then, writhing under his wounds, he fell headlong down with the head of the ram. . . .

Towards evening, the Romans, having repaired the ram, again brought it to bear upon that part of the wall which had already been shaken. On this occasion one of the wall's defenders struck Vespasian with an arrow near the sole of his foot and wounded him slightly, the distance having exhausted the force of the missile. Nevertheless, the incident wrought great confusion among the Romans, for on seeing Vespasian bleed, those close to him were so dismayed that a rumor spread throughout the army that he was wounded. In consternation and terror, multitudes abandoned the siege and crowded around the general. Titus was first on the scene. So great was his concern for his father that the soldiers were as deeply distressed by the anguish of the son as they were out of their affection for the general. However, the father easily dispelled his son's fears and put an end to the turmoil in the army. Superior to his pain, he hastened to show himself to all who were alarmed on his behalf. By so doing he stimulated them to exert more strenuous efforts against the Jews. Each soldier was eager to lead the way to danger, in order to avenge the general, and with shouts of mutual encouragement, all rushed toward the wall.

Determined Roman attacks—during one fearful night—made it clear that the wall could not be defended for any length of time.

Many who fought for Jotapata fell manfully; many

others were wounded. And the morning watch had already arrived, before the wall, assailed without respite, yielded to the engines. But the besieged, protecting their bodies with their armor, raised defenses opposite the breach before the scaling-planks were applied by the Romans. (War III, 7:15-23.)

THE FALL OF THE FORTRESS

Vespasian, having allowed his troops a short rest after the fatigues of the night, assembled them at daybreak for the assault of the city. His plan was to dislodge his opponents from the quarter where the breach had been effected. To accomplish this, he ordered the bravest of the cavalry to dismount and stationed them three-deep opposite the ruins. Completely protected by their armor, they stood, with couched lances, ready to mount the breach the moment the planks were raised. In the rear of these troops, Vespasian marshaled the flower of the infantry. The rest of the horse he extended along the mountainous expanse opposite the wall, to prevent anyone from escaping when the city was taken. Behind these he stationed archers all around, with orders to have their arrows ready to shoot. He gave the same commands to the slingers and to the men at the engines; others he directed to bring ladders and apply them at the unharmed sections of the wall, in order that the defenders of the breaches in the wall be drawn off that defense in an attempt to hinder ascent while the rest of the besieged were overpowered by a storm of missiles and yielded an entry into the city.

Penetrating this design, Josephus placed the aged and weary at the still intact portion of the wall, where they were not likely to be harmed; at the breach, however, he stationed the strongest men, and at the head of them to bear the brunt of the assault, groups of six men, drawn by lot, whose dangers he himself shared. Furthermore, he enjoined them to cover their ears at the shouts of the legions, in order not to be frightened by them; to meet the showers of missiles on bended knees, under cover of their shields, and to fall back a little, until the archers should have emptied their quivers, but as soon as the Romans raised the planks, to dash forward upon them, and to meet the enemy by means of his own preparations; and he enjoined each man to fight for the city not as if it were possible to save it, but as if avenging it as already lost. "Envisage," he said, "the aged, the children, and your wives about to be butchered; summoning beforehand the rage you would feel at these coming calamities, let it loose on those who are to inflict them."

The noncombatants, beholding the enemy, raised a lament "not as if the catastrophe was only imminent, but as if it had already been inflicted upon them."

The trumpets of all the legions now sounded simultaneously, the troops raised a terrifying war cry, and the missiles, flying in unison from all sides, intercepted the light. Remembering his injunctions, Josephus' men covered their ears against the discharges. When the planks were laid, they rushed out across them before those who raised them had set foot on them. Encountering the ascending enemy, they displayed divers feats of strength and valor, endeavoring in this extreme peril to prove themselves no whit inferior to those who, not similarly imperiled, so valiantly opposed them. No one could be pried from the Romans until he either fell dead himself or slew his antagonist.

The Jews grew weary from this unending defense and had not enough men to relieve them, but among the Romans fresh troops succeeded the fatigued, and when one man was beaten down, another instantly took his place. Encouraging each other, side linked to side and protected overhead by their long shields, they formed an impenetrable mass. Their entire phalanx thrusting back the Jews as though it were but one body, they were already mounting the wall.

Josephus ordered scalding oil poured on the at-tackers and boiled fenugreek on the boards of the scaling planks; the Roman soldiers slipped on the fenugreek and fell backward.

Whether retreating or advancing, the Romans could not remain on their feet. Some were thrown on their backs on the scaling planks and were trodden to death; many fell upon the banks and were slain by the Jews, for when the Romans were prostrate, the Jews, freed from close combat, could make use of their missiles. In the evening the general called off the troops who had suffered so severely in the assault; not a few of them had fallen, and still more had been wounded. Of the people of Jotapata six men were killed and over three hundred carried off wounded. . . .

When Vespasian sought to console his troops for these misfortunes, he found that, instead of needing exhortation, they were angry and asked for action. He therefore issued orders to raise the banks still higher and to erect three towers, each fifty feet high and encased in plates of iron. These plates were meant both to firm the towers by their weight and to make them fireproof. Providing the towers with javelin throwers, archers, lighter projectile engines, and the most able-bodied slingers, Vespasian set them on the banks. Screened from sight by their elevated station and the breastworks of the towers, the soldiers discharged their weapons at the men on the wall, whose position they overlooked.

Unable to escape the missiles coming from above or to defend themselves against an enemy they could not see, and realizing that, because of their height, missiles thrown by hand could barely reach the towers and that the iron casing rendered the latter impervious to fire, the Jews abandoned the wall and sallied forth against the assaulters of the breach. In such a manner did the people carry on the battle of Jotapata. Many fell every day; unable to retaliate, they could check the approach of their foes only at the risk of their lives. . . .

Nonetheless, the people of Jotapata still held out manfully, and bore up under their miseries beyond expectation, when, on the forty-seventh day [of the siege], the Roman banks grew higher than the wall. On the same day a deserter informed Vespasian that those still remaining in the city were few and weakened, and that, wasted from perpetual watching and incessant fighting, they would no longer be able to resist a vigorous assault and might if the attempt were made, be taken by ruse, because around the last watch of the night, when they expected some respite from their hardships and when morning slumber is most apt to steal upon people thoroughly weary, the sentinels usually fell asleep. Accordingly, he advised that the city be attacked at that hour.

Vespasian, aware of the Jews' mutual loyalty and of their indifference to suffering, was suspicious of this deserter; especially so, since on a former occasion a captive man of Jotapata withstood all kinds of torture, did not betray a single secret of the besieged though tried by fire, and as he was crucified, smiled at them. However, the likelihood of the report lent credibility to the traitor and led Vespasian to believe that he was perhaps telling the truth. Expecting to suffer no great harm if the report was a fraud, he ordered the man into custody and prepared his army for the capture of the city.

At the hour indicated, the Romans approached the walls in silence. Titus, accompanied by the tribune Domitius Sabinus, who led a few men of the fifteenth legion, was first to mount them. After slaying the sentries, they noiselessly entered the city. The tribune Sextus Calvarius and Placidus, with the troops they commanded, followed. Yet though the citadel was already taken, with the enemy moving in the very heart of the city, and though it was already day, the vanquished were still unconscious of its capture. Exhausted by fatigue, a great many of them had sunk into a deep sleep; in addition, a dense fog, which happened to envelop the city at that time, obscured the vision. Not until the entire Roman army had poured in were they aroused—only to find the miseries that had come upon them. Death supplied the evidence that Jotapata had fallen.

The Romans, remembering their tribulations during the siege, spared none, nor pitied anyone; in one general massacre they thrust the people headlong from the citadel. The difficulties of the site prevented those still able to fight from defending themselves. Pressed in the streets and slipping down the precipice, they were overwhelmed by the tide of war that flowed upon them. This drove even many of Josephus' picked men to suicide. On seeing that they could slay none of the Romans, they anticipated the death that awaited them from hostile hands, and crowding together in the outskirts of the city, killed themselves.

Those guards, however, who had fled at the first discovery of the city's capture, ascended one of the northern towers and for some time defended themselves; but surrounded by a multitude of enemies, they finally ceased their efforts and courageously offered their throats to their assailants. . . .

On that day the Romans slew all who showed themselves; on the ensuing days they searched the hiding places and fell upon those who had fled to vaults and caverns, dealing death to all, whatever their age, except infants and women, of whom twelve hundred were taken captive. Forty thousand were computed to have perished during the city's capture and in previous fighting. Vespasian ordered the city razed and reduced all its fortifications to ashes. So fell Jotapata, in the thirteenth year of the reign of Nero. . . . (War III, 7:24-30; 33-36.)

JOSEPHUS AFTER THE FALL OF JOTAPATA

THE CAPTURE OF JOSEPHUS

The Romans now searched for Josephus, both out of resentment towards him and because their general, believing that his capture would greatly expedite the outcome of the war, was most anxious to apprehend him. They searched among the slain and in the secret recesses of the city as well. But aided by some divine providence, Josephus escaped from the midst of the enemy just as the city was being taken, and jumped into a deep pit. On one side of this pit was a large cavern, invisible to those above. Here he found forty prominent people hidden, with sufficient provisions to sustain them for a considerable length of time.

During the day Josephus stayed hidden from the enemy, who occupied every place in the city, but at night he got up and scrutinized every possible outlet of flight, taking exact note of the sentries. Since, however, every spot was so closely guarded on his account that escape was impractical, he returned to the cavern. For two days he thus eluded pursuit; on the third, when a woman of his group was captured, he was betrayed. Whereupon Vespasian at once sent two tribunes . . . with orders to offer Josephus protection and to exhort him to leave his retreat.

They came and urged their proposition in strong terms, pledging themselves for Josephus' safety. But they did not prevail, for though the manner of those who addressed him was mild, his suspicions were aroused by the likelihood of the penalty he would suffer in retaliation for all his actions. He feared, therefore, that he was being invited to come up solely in order to be punished, until Vespasian sent a third tribune, Nicanor, a man well known to Josephus and his acquaintance in former days.[42]

Nicanor, on his arrival, enlarged upon the innate mildness of the Romans towards vanquished foes. He assured Josephus that his valor had made him an object of admiration, rather than of hatred, to the officers and that the general was anxious to have him brought to him not for punishment—for punishment he could inflict even if Josephus did not come forth— but out of desire to save a brave man. . . .

While Josephus hesitated about accepting Nicanor's proposition, the soldiers, in their rage, rushed forward to set the cavern on fire; but the tribune, anxious to take the Jewish leader alive, restrained them. As Nicanor earnestly pressed his point and Josephus heard the threats of the hostile crowd, he recalled his nightly dreams, wherein God had foretold to him the events about to befall the Jews, as well as those to happen to the Roman emperors. An interpreter of dreams, Josephus possessed the art of deciphering the meaning of the Deity's ambiguous utterances; being a priest and a descendant of priests, he also knew the prophecies of the sacred books. At that moment he was under divine influence, and suddenly recalling the fearful images of his recent dreams, he offered a secret prayer to God: "Since it pleaseth Thee, who hath created the Jewish nation, now to level it with the dust and transfer its fortune to the Romans, and since Thou hast chosen my spirit to announce future events, I willingly surrender to the Romans and choose to live; but Thou art my witness that I go over to them not as a traitor, but as Thy servant."

Having spoken thus, Josephus was about to surrender to Nicanor. But when the Jews who had taken refuge in the cavern with him understood that he was yielding to the solicitations of the Romans, they surrounded him in a body and cried: "Deeply may the laws of our fathers groan and God hide his face in indignation, that God who planted in the Jewish breast a soul that despises death. Is life so dear to you, Josephus, that you can bear to look at the light in a state of slavery? How soon have you forgotten yourself! How great a number have you not persuaded to die for liberty! False, then, was your reputation for manliness and for wisdom if you can hope for safety from those whom you fought so zealously, or consent to accept life at their hands, even were that certain! But though the fortune of the Romans has seduced you into some strange forgetfulness of yourself, we must safeguard our country's honor. We will lend you our right hand and a sword. If you die willingly, you will die as general of the Jews; if unwillingly, as a traitor." As they spoke they began to thrust their swords at him and threatened to slay him if he surrendered to the Romans.

Fearing an attack, and conceiving that it would be a betrayal of God's commands for him to die before he delivered his message, Josephus, in his distress, proceeded to reason with them philosophically.

Here follows a long dissertation on suicide being "alien to the common nature of all creatures and an act of impiety against God, who created us." In this manner Josephus tried to counteract the spirit of self-destruction among his comrades.

These and many similar motives were suggested by Josephus to divert them from suicide. But despair had stopped their ears, for they had for some time dedicated themselves to death, and they were exasperated by Josephus. Condemning him as a coward, they ran at him from all sides with drawn swords, each man ready to smite him. But addressing one by name, acting the general with another, taking a third by the hands, softening a fourth by entreaties he—though in this emergency himself distracted by various passions —succeeded in warding off the blades of all, turning, when hemmed in, from one assailant to another, as does a wild beast. Some there were, also, whose arms were paralyzed by reverence for the general in this, his extreme, distress, and their swords dropped from their grasp; many, in the act of smiting at him, spontaneously let fall their weapons.

Josephus' usual sagacity did not forsake him in this predicament. Trusting in God's providence, he risked his life and said: "Since you are resolved to die, come, let us commit our mutual slaughter to lot, and let him to whom that lot falls first die by the sword of him whose lot comes next. By so doing, all will meet the same fate. Nor will any of us perish by their own right hands. For it would be unjust if after the destruction of the others anyone should repent and save himself."

This proposal seemed to the people to be very just. Having thus far prevailed, Josephus cast the lot. He to whom it fell bared his throat to the one who had the next lot, not doubting that the general would soon share his fate; death, together with Josephus, they deemed sweeter than life. He, however—whether by chance or by the providence of God—was left alone with one other man. Anxious neither to be condemned by the lot, nor if he was the last survivor, to stain his hands with the blood of a fellow countryman, he persuaded the latter to trust him to remain alive together with him. (War III, 8:1-7.)

JOSEPHUS BEFORE VESPASIAN

In this manner Josephus survived both the war with the Romans and that with his friends and was conducted by Nicanor to Vespasian. The Romans crowded from all quarters to see him. . . . Titus in particular was touched by the fortitude with which Josephus bore his misfortunes, and he felt compassion for his youth.[43] Moreover, remembering how recently Josephus had been in battle and seeing him now a captive in the hands of his foes, he was led to reflect on fortune's power, the quick reversal of the tides of war, and the instability of human affairs. He persuaded many

Romans to adopt his views and to commiserate with Josephus; his intercession with his father was chiefly responsible for Josephus' preservation. Nevertheless, Vespasian ordered him to be guarded with unremitting vigilance, planning to send him without delay to Nero.

On hearing this, Josephus intimated that he wished to speak to him in private. Vespasian sent everyone away, except his son Titus and two of his friends, and Josephus addressed him in these words: "You think, Vespasian, that you have taken merely Josephus captive; but I come to you as a messenger of greater tidings. Had I not been sent to you by God, I knew what the law of the Jews prescribes and how it becomes a general to die. You are sending me to Nero? What for? Do you think that those who will succeed Nero, preceding your own accession, will long continue? You, Vespasian, are Caesar and emperor, you and this your son. Bind me, then, still more securely and keep me for yourself. For you, Caesar, are master not only of me, but of sea and land and of the whole human race. And I deserve the punishment of stricter ward if I falsely affirm that what I say comes from God."

When Josephus had said this, Vespasian was at first little inclined to believe him, assuming his words to be but an ingenious ruse to save his life. Gradually however he was led to believe him, for God awakened in him anticipations of power and by other signs foreshowed the scepter. . . .

Vespasian relaxed neither the custody nor the chains of Josephus, though he presented him with raiment and other gifts and continued to treat him with kindness and attention, Titus contributing much to these courtesies. (War III, 8:8-9.)

See also War VI, 5:4. Josephus' prediction of Vespasian's emperorship is paralleled by a prophecy attributed to the great rabbi of Jerusalem, Johanan ben Zakkai, who managed to leave the besieged city and appeared before the Roman general (Gittin 56).

The news of the fall of Jotapata shocked the people of Jerusalem. A rumor spread that Josephus had fallen in the defense of the fortress, and the city mourned the death of the commander. When the facts became known, "they became as vehemently angry with him as formerly they had been loving" (War III, 9:5-6).

The victorious Vespasian gave his soldiers a period of rest in Caesarea (9:1), while he enjoyed the hospitality of king Agrippa at Caesarea Philippi and the festivities in his honor. Tiberias and Tarichaeae, centers of rebellion, were next to be subdued by the Romans, September 67 (9:7-10). Vespasian then besieged the strongly fortified Gamala, on the eastern shore of the Lake of Gennesaret, and took the hotly defended place, November 67. Gischala, in northern Galilee, encouraged to insurrection by the rebel leader John, son of Levi, surrendered to Titus. "Thus was all Galilee taken; but only after it cost the Romans much distress, could it be taken by them." John fled to Jerusalem (IV, 1-2).

THE WAR
WITH ROME:
JERUSALEM

THE MODERATES VERSUS THE FANATICS

JOHN OF GISCHALA IN JERUSALEM
(NOVEMBER 67)

No sooner had John set foot in Jerusalem than its entire population poured forth. Thousands crowded around the several fugitives, eagerly inquiring what misfortunes had befallen outside. But though their hot and still too short breath evidenced their great distress, they talked big in spite of their disasters, claiming that they had not fled from the Romans but came to fight them on safer ground. "It would have been senseless and useless," they said, "recklessly to expose ourselves to danger for Gischala and similar ill-fortified little towns, when we ought to husband our arms and energies for the capital and combine in its defense."

But when they related the fall of Gischala, most men considered their so-called honorable retreat no better than flight. . . . Nevertheless, John . . . went among the people, and by arousing their hopes, persuaded them to go to war. He falsely depicted the Romans as weak, extolled his own power, and ridiculed the ignorance of the inexperienced, asserting that the Romans, even if they had wings, could never surmount Jerusalem's walls. They found it difficult enough [he said] to take the villages of Galilee and had shattered their engines against their walls.

These harangues seduced the majority of the young and incited them to hostilities. But not a man among the prudent and the aged failed to mourn over the prospect of the future, as if the hour of the city's doom had already arrived. Such was the confusion that now prevailed among the citizens. However, discord had broken out in the country even prior to the sedition in Jerusalem. . . . Fierce conflict raged between the advocates of war and the friends of peace. Animosity flared first between families among whom some ancient feud persisted; then those bound by the closest ties broke off contact with each other. Everyone combined with those who held his own views, and these organized themselves into hostile factions. Everywhere, sedition reared its head. By their youth and reckless courage, the revolutionary and the militant overpowered the old and the prudent.

At first the country population addicted themselves separately to pillage; then, banded in groups, the men carried on their depredations throughout the district; so in cruelty and lawless violence they differed in nothing from the Romans; capture by the latter seemed a much lighter fate to the sufferers.

The [Roman] garrisons of the cities, partly out of reluctance to expose themselves, partly out of hatred for the Jewish nation, gave little or no relief to the distressed. Finally, the rebel leaders, satiated with their country-wide pillage, assembled from everywhere, and forming one villainous band, crept into Jerusalem —now a city without a governor, which in accordance with ancient custom, accepted without distinction everyone of Jewish blood, all the more so at this time, since all believed that those who poured in came out of kindness and as confederates. Yet these very men, in addition to the insurrection they raised, were eventually responsible for the destruction of the city, for, being a useless and idle mass, they consumed the supplies that might have long sustained the fighting men, and in addition to the war, were the source of sedition and famine. (War IV, 3:1-3.)

The freedom fighters, led by John of Gischala, won the youth of Jerusalem and pressed for a bold continuation of the war. They agitated against the aristocrats and eminent citizens suspected of a pro-Roman attitude. Among those assassinated by them was Antipas, a relative of Agrippa II. They also appointed a new high priest, one Phanni, son of Samuel, a man not worthy of this office (3:4-8).

Such an outrage was too much for the people. One and all were roused to overthrow this tyranny, for the most eminent of them, Gorion, son of Joseph,[44] and Simon, son of Gamaliel, urged them, in both public addresses to the collective body and private talks with individuals, to chastise at long last these destroyers of liberty and to purge the sanctuary of its bloodstained polluters. Joshua, son of Gamala, and Ananus, son of Ananus, men of highest repute among the [former] high priests, who at their assemblies vehemently upbraided the people's apathy, also incited them against the Zealots, for so they [John's men] called themselves, as though they were zealous in the cause of virtue rather than pre-eminent in the pursuit of evil in its most extravagant forms. (War IV, 3:9.)

Simon, son of Gamaliel, a descendant of Hillel the Elder and leading teacher of the period, is described by Josephus as "a man of great wisdom and judgment, and capable of redressing affairs of state by his prudence when they were in ill posture" (Life, 38). His father, in the Christian tradition, was the teacher of the apostle Paul in Jerusalem (Acts 22:3). Joshua, son of Gamala (Gamaliel), is probably identical with Joshua, son of Gamla, known for his educational reforms in Judaea (Baba Bathra 21a).

THE ADDRESS OF THE FORMER HIGH PRIEST
ANANUS

A people's assembly was convened. Though all were indignant at the seizure of the sanctuary, the rapines, and the murders, none had as yet attempted resistance, imagining, not without reason, that mastering the Zealots would be difficult. Ananus then rose in their midst, and his tear-filled eyes casting frequent glances at the Temple, spoke as follows:

"Gladly would I have died ere I had seen the house of God filled with such abominations and the unapproachable and holy places crowded with the feet of murderers. And yet, clothed with the vestments of the high priesthood and called by that most honored of venerated names, I live, and too fond of life, shrink from a death that would be the glory of my old age. But though I stand alone and, as it were, isolated, I will resign my only life for the sake of God. For to what purpose should I live among a people insensible to calamities, and in whom the will to grapple with present misfortunes has perished? Plundered, you submit; beaten, you are silent; and over the murdered, none dares to groan openly.

"O bitter tyranny! But why do I complain of the tyrants? Have they not been fostered by you and your forbearance? Was it not you who, overlooking their first assemblages, when they were yet few, augmented their numbers by your silence, and by remaining quiet as they were arming, turned their arms against yourselves? You should have repressed their first efforts, when they assailed your kinsmen with invectives; but your negligence incited the wretches to rapine. . . .

"The strongest point in the city has been seized, for henceforth the Temple must be considered a citadel or fortress. But as you are held by a despotism so fortified and behold your enemies over your heads, on what do you deliberate, by what arguments do you calm your minds? Do you await the arrival of the Romans to succor our holy sites? Has the city reached such a degree of misery that even our enemies must pity us? Will you not rise, most enduring of men, and turning upon those that strike you, as does a beast when hurt, take vengeance on those that smite you? Will you not call to mind, each one of you, the afflictions you yourself have suffered, and whet your souls for revenge? Have you lost that most honorable of the passions, the one most indigenous to our nature, the desire for freedom? We are in love with slavery and with the hand that deals it, as though our ancestors had bequeathed us a spirit of submission. Yet many and arduous were the wars they waged for independence. Loath to accept the commands of a conqueror, they bowed neither to the scepter of the Egyptians nor to that of the Medes.

"But what need to speak of our forefathers? We are today engaged in a war against the Romans. I forbear to decide whether that war is advantageous and expedient, or the contrary. But what is its pretext? Is it not freedom? Shall we, then, refuse obedience to the masters of the habitable globe, yet tolerate native tyrants? Truly, though submission to a foreign power may be borne once fortune has doomed us to it, to yield to the wicked of our own country argues an ignoble and voluntary slavery.

"But since I have mentioned the Romans, I will not conceal from you what, as I was speaking, occurred to me and turned my thoughts to them. It is this: that even if we fall beneath their arms—and God forbid that it should be so!—we can be called upon to endure nothing more grievous than what these men [the rebels] have already inflicted on us. . . .

"Who, then, would dread a war from without and with foes who by comparison treat us more leniently than our own countrymen? Verily, if we suit our language to the facts, we may perhaps find in the

Romans, supporters of our laws; and the enemies of these laws to be within our walls. . . .

"It is likely that the majority of you are frightened at their numbers, at their audacity, and at the advantage they have over us in their position. But just as these advantages were occasioned by your negligence, so will they be multiplied by your delay. For their ranks are daily augmented as every evildoer deserts to his like, and having up to now met with no opposition, their daring is the more inflamed. As for their superior position, they will make use of it for engines as well, if we give them time to do so.

"But rest assured that if we attack them, they will, because of qualms of conscience, be lower than we are, and reflection will destroy the advantage they derive from the more elevated site. Perhaps, too, the Deity, whom they have affronted, will turn their missiles back against them, and the impious will perish by their own weapons. Let us but show ourselves to them, and they will come to nothing. And if there should be danger in the attempt, it is honorable to die before the sacred gates and to lay down life, if not on behalf of children and wives, then for the sake of God and for the sanctuary. I will aid you with both my counsel and my hand; nothing on my part that reflection can suggest shall be wanting to protect your safety, nor will you see me spare this body." (War IV, 3:9-10.)

CIVIL STRIFE IN JERUSALEM

With such words did Ananus incite the people against the Zealots. He knew how difficult it would be to subdue them, because of their numbers, vigor, and courage, but above all, because of their consciousness of their deeds. . . . But he preferred whatever suffering might be inflicted upon him to remaining passive while so chaotic a situation prevailed. The people then cried out to be led against those he had denounced, each man ready to confront danger.

But while Ananus was mustering and arraying those fit for service, the Zealots were informed of his enterprise—there being men who acquainted them with everything the people were doing—rushed in great rage from the Temple, in both large and smaller groups, and spared none who happened their way. Ananus hastily assembled the people, who though superior in numbers, were inferior to their opponents in arms and training. But on both sides, ardor compensated for deficiencies. Those from the city, convinced that Jerusalem would be uninhabitable if the rebels were not rooted out, were inspired by a fury more powerful than arms; the Zealots, believing that unless they won the day, no punishment would be too great to be inflicted on them, were moved by a daring no numbers could withstand.

Fighting under the sway of their passions, the opponents at first assailed each other with stones, in the city and in front of the Temple, and maintained a distant combat with javelins; but when either side gave way, the victors used their swords. The slaughter on both sides was great, and many were the wounded. The injured from the people's army were carried by relatives into the houses; but the wounded Zealots retired to the Temple, their blood dripping on the sacred pavement; and it may be said that only their blood polluted the sanctuary.

Up to now the rebels had been successful in all their sallies; but the populace—growing ever more furious, constantly augmented in numbers, and upbraiding those who gave way, while those who pressed on in the rear refused to open a passage to fugitives—turned its entire force against its adversaries. The rebels, no longer able to withstand the shock, gradually withdrew into the Temple; Ananus and his men rushed in with them.

Dismayed at the loss of the outer court, the Zealots fled into the inner one and instantly shut the gates.

Though harassed from above by the missiles of his adversaries, Ananus did not think it proper to assail the sacred doors. He also considered it unlawful, even were it to give him victory, to let the multitude into that court without prior purification. He therefore chose by lot six thousand armed men, whom he stationed as sentinels at the colonnades; others were to relieve them, every man being obligated to stand watch when his turn came. But many of the nobles, permitted to retire by those in command, hired men of the lower classes to mount guard in their stead. (War IV, 3:11-12.)

At this point the Zealots sent messengers to enlist the help of the Idumaeans; twenty thousand men marched to Jerusalem against the party of Ananus. The Zealots secretly managed to open the gates of the city, and aided by their allies, unleashed a reign of terror (3:13-4:1).

THE MURDER OF ANANUS AND JOSHUA

The rage of the Idumaeans still unsated, they turned to the city, pillaging every house and slaying all who came their way. Thinking their time wasted on the populace, they searched for the chief priests, the greater part joining in the pursuit; as soon as they caught these priests, they slew them. Standing over their dead bodies, they reviled Ananus for his benevolence towards the people, and Joshua for his address from the [Jerusalem] wall.

Joshua, son of Gamala, the eldest of the chief priests next to Ananus, had addressed the Idumaeans who increased the reign of terror in Jerusalem. (War IV, 4:3.)

They carried their impiety to such an excess that they cast out the dead bodies unburied, although the Jews are so zealous of the burial of men that they take down those crucified following a sentence and bury them before sunset.[45]

I should not be wrong in saying that the death of Ananus was the beginning of the destruction of the city; and that from the day on which the Jews beheld their high priest, the guardian of their safety, murdered in the midst of Jerusalem, dates the shattering of its walls and the overthrow of the Jewish state.

In every respect Ananus was a man much to be revered. None surpassed him in integrity, and though distinguished by birth, station, and the honors he had acquired, he delighted in placing himself on a level with the humblest. Unbounded in his love of liberty and an admirer of democracy in government, he ever preferred the public welfare to his private interests. Maintenance of peace was his chief objective. He knew that the Romans were invincible and foresaw that unless the Jews conciliated them cleverly, a war would result and the Jews would be destroyed. In a word, had Ananus survived, the Jews would certainly have come to terms with the Romans, for he was powerful in his appeals, successful in influencing the people, and was already gaining control over those who thwarted him. Or had the war continued, the Jews, under such a leader, would have greatly retarded the triumph of the Romans. Associated with him was Joshua [son of Gamala], who though comparatively inferior to him, was superior to others. . . . [Both] were cast out naked and seen to become the food of dogs and wild beasts. . . . (War IV, 5:2.)

"After these were slain, the Zealots and the multitude of Idumaeans fell upon the people"; twelve thousand young men perished (5:4).

THE SLAUGHTER OF ZACHARIAS

The Zealots, now quite weary of simple slaughter, shamelessly set up mock tribunals and courts of justice. Purposing to kill Zacharias, son of Baruch, one of Jerusalem's most eminent citizens, they summoned, in proper form, seventy of the people's leading men to act the role of judges, but without their authority. The Zealots' singular animosity towards Zacharias was occasioned by his extreme hatred of evil and love of liberty. Moreover, since he had ample wealth, they hoped to enjoy the plunder of his property, as well as to get rid of a powerful and dangerous adversary. Accordingly, they accused him of a plot to betray the state to the Romans and of maintaining a treasonable correspondence with Vespasian. . . .

Zacharias, conscious that there was no hope for him of escape, for he had been treacherously summoned not to a trial, but to a prison, did not allow despair of life to deprive him of freedom of speech. Rising from his seat, he ridiculed the likelihood of the accusation and in a few words refuted the charges against him. He then addressed himself to his accusers, enumerated, in order, all their enormities, and deeply lamented the chaotic state of public affairs. The Zealots raised an uproar and with difficulty withheld their swords, though anxious to play out the farce of a tribunal to the end and desiring as well to test the judges— whether disregarding their own peril, they would be mindful of justice. The seventy men, preferring death with the accused to the imputation of being party to his destruction, brought in a verdict of acquittal. On hearing that verdict, a clamor arose among the Zealots, indignant at the judges for not comprehending that their authority had been conferred on them in mere mockery. Two of the boldest of them attacked Zacharias in the center of the Temple and slew him. As he fell, they thus derided him: "Now you have our verdict also, and a more effective acquittal." And forthwith they threw him headlong from the Temple into the ravine below. Then they attacked the judges, and striking them insultingly with the backs of their swords, drove them from the court. They spared their lives for only one reason: that when dispersed throughout the city, they might proclaim to all the servitude to which they [the people] had been reduced.[46] (War IV, 5:4.)

Finally, informed of the true nature of the Zealots, the main body of the Idumaeans departed. The Zealots continued their terrorist activities; they assassinated Gorion, son of Joseph (see War IV, 3:9), "a man of great boldness and freedom of spirit," and the heroic Niger of Peraea (see II, 19:2; III, 2:1). John of Gischala freed himself of his companions in the party leadership and assumed sovereign command in Jerusalem. Well-to-do citizens left the city, eluding the Zealots who guarded every exit. The extremist Sicarii, centered in the fortress Masada, laid waste the environs and the rest of the country. Vespasian, seeing that his enemies were destroying each other, realized that "God was a better general of the Romans than he, for He was surrendering the Judaeans to them without any efforts on their part." He was therefore free to fight the still unconquered sites: Gadara and all of Peraea (March 68), Antipatris (Ras el-Ain, northeast of Jaffa), Lydda, Jamnia and Emmaus, Idumaea and Samaria. In June 68 he reached Jericho (Josephus beautifully describes its region and the Dead Sea). His plan was to encircle Jerusalem on all sides (IV, 5:5-9:1).

THE ISSUE OF THE EMPIRE

THE DEATH OF NERO (JUNE 68)

Vespasian had returned to Caesarea and was preparing to march in full force against Jerusalem itself, when news reached him of Nero's violent death, after a reign of thirteen years and eight days. . . .[47]

Vespasian therefore deferred his expedition against Jerusalem for the present, anxiously waiting to see on whom the empire would devolve after Nero's death. Later, when he learned that Galba was emperor, he would not advance until the latter sent him instructions about the war. He dispatched his son Titus, however, to salute Galba and receive his commands anent the Jews. For the same reason king Agrippa, too, embarked with Titus. But as they were sailing in long galleys around the coasts of Achaea (for it was winter), Galba met a violent death, after a reign of seven months and as many days; Otho succeeded to the throne and assumed the reins of government.[48] Agrippa, not deterred by the change, resolved to proceed to Rome. But Titus, by some divine impulse, took ship from Greece for Syria and hastened to join his father at Caesarea. With the Roman empire in such a state of flux, they were in too great suspense about affairs at large to pursue the invasion of Judaea, deeming it untimely to attack a foreign country while they were filled with apprehensions about their own. (War IV, 9:2.)

The journey of Titus is more fully described in Tacitus' History II, 1-4.

"Another war now broke out in Jerusalem." Simon, son of Giora, another fighter for the freedom of Judaea (see War II, 19:2), who had joined the Sicarii at Masada, rose to rival the leadership of John of Gischala. Simon subdued Idumaea and captured the patriarchal town of Hebron. Invited by the inhabitants of Jerusalem, who wanted to rid themselves of John's tyranny, Simon became lord of the city (April 69). The would-be liberator soon disappointed his supporters; "the remedy proved worse than the disease." Two tyrants fought for the mastery of Jerusalem (IV, 9:3-8, 10-12).

In the meantime, while awaiting the final outcome of the events in Rome, Vespasian had brought under his control all of Palestine, except the fortresses Herodion, Masada, and Machaerus, and except, of course, Jerusalem (IV, 9:9). In January 69, Vitellius was saluted as emperor by his troops; however, the legions in

Egypt, Judaea, and Syria thought of Vespasian as the man whose claim to the empire exceeded that of Vitellius (IV, 10:1-3).

VESPASIAN PROCLAIMED EMPEROR (JULY 69)

After this the soldiers assembled, and encouraging one another, proclaimed Vespasian emperor and exhorted him to rescue the imperiled empire. That general had long been concerned about the state of affairs [in Rome] but did not intend to mount the throne; though aware that his achievements gave him a legitimate claim, he preferred the security of private life to the perils of an exalted station. But when he declined, the officers pressed him still more urgently, and the soldiers, crowding around him with drawn swords, threatened him with death if he refused to live with honor. After forcefully urging him to consider the many reasons that led him to refuse the empire, he, unable to dissuade them, finally yielded to their call.

Mucianus [legate of Syria] and the other generals now urged Vespasian to act as emperor, and the rest of the army demanded to be led against all opponents. Aware that Egypt, because it supplied corn [to Rome], was the most important domain of the empire, he first turned his mind to the affairs of Alexandria. By being master of this corn, he hoped to drive Vitellius from the throne, even were the latter to resist, for the people of Rome would never submit to being starved. He also wanted to join the two legions stationed in Alexandria to the legions already with him and had in mind using that country [Egypt] as defense against the dubious turns of fortune.

Here follows a description of Egypt and the harbor of Alexandria.

There was good reason therefore for Vespasian's anxiety to obtain the government of that country in order to insure the stability of the empire at large. Accordingly, he at once wrote to Tiberius Alexander,[49] governor of Egypt and Alexandria, informing him of the army's zeal, and that forced to accept the burden of the empire, he desired him to be his adherent and ally. After a public reading of the letter, Alexander promptly called on the legions and the people to take the oath of allegiance to Vespasian. The conduct of the latter's command in their vicinity having demonstrated to them his worth, they gladly complied. The concerns relating to the empire now entrusted to his charge, Alexander made all necessary preparations for the emperor's arrival. Swifter than thought, the report spread that Vespasian was emperor in the East. Every city celebrated the good news with festivals and sacrifices. . . . (War IV, 10:4-6.)

JOSEPHUS GIVEN A FREE PARDON

Fortune everywhere attended Vespasian's wishes, and the affairs of state were, in the main, already in his hands. He was therefore led to think that he had not been advanced to the government without divine providence and that some righteous destiny had brought the empire under his power. He recalled the many and varied omens[50] he had everywhere had that foretold the empire, among them the words of Josephus, who had ventured, even in Nero's lifetime, to address him as emperor.[51]

Greatly concerned that this man was still a prisoner, he called Mucianus, as well as the rest of his officers and friends. First he reminded them of Josephus' gallantry and of the great harassment he had caused him at Jotapata. Then he related Josephus' predictions, which at the moment [of their telling] he had suspected to be fabrications motivated by fear, but which time and events had proved to be divine. "It is disgraceful," he said, "that the man who foretold my elevation to the empire, and who was a minister of the voice of God, should still be in the condition of a captive and endure a prisoner's fate." Accordingly, he called for Josephus and ordered him to be freed. Because of this requital to an alien, Vespasian's officers were led to expect glorious things for themselves.

Titus, who was present at this scene, said to his father: "Justice demands that, with the fetters, the disgrace [of having been a prisoner] should also be removed from Josephus; if, instead of loosing, we cut his chain, he will be as one who has never been bound at all." The latter is the customary method of freeing those who have been thrown into irons unjustly. Vespasian approving, a man came forward and severed the chain with an ax. Josephus, having received his freedom as reward for his prediction, was now considered to be a man deserving credence in foretelling future events. (War IV, 10:7.)

Vespasian sent Licinus Mucianus with an army to Italy to help in the overthrow of Vitellius and in establishing order. In Alexandria the new emperor received well-wishing embassies from "all the habitable earth he ruled." He took ship for Rome, entrusting to Titus the continuation of the war in Judaea (IV, 11). Vespasian's reception in Rome is described in VII, 4:1.

THE SIEGE OF JERUSALEM

ELEAZAR, SON OF SIMON, FORMS A THIRD WAR-PARTY

Titus . . . arrived at Caesarea, where he had resolved to organize his forces before the campaign. While he was still in Alexandria, assisting his father in establishing the government that God had recently committed to them, the sedition in Jerusalem had again come to a head and split into three factions, each preying upon the others; a partition that, in cases as evil as this one was, may be called a blessing and an act of retribution. The Zealots' attack on the people, which I consider to have been the first step in the destruction of the city, has already been accurately described [52] both as to its origin and as to the increasing extent of its harm. As for this fresh outbreak, one would not err in saying that it was a sedition engendered within a sedition, and at length, grown mad like a wild beast that for want of other food preys upon its own flesh.

Eleazar, son of Simon,[53] the man who induced the Zealots to separate from the people and to retire into the Temple, pretended to be very angry at John's [of Gischala] daily outrages (for the latter never ceased murdering) ; but the truth was that he could not bear to submit to a tyrant of later standing than himself. Anxious to seize supreme power and to establish his personal tyranny, he seceded from the rest. He . . . [and each of his associates] was followed by a considerable body of Zealots; they seized the inner court of the Temple and ranged their arms over the sacred gates in front of the sanctuary. Possessing an ample supply of provisions, and there being an abundance [in the Temple] of consecrated objects for men who hesitated at no impiety, they were, as far as that was concerned, filled with confidence; their small number, however, made them apprehensive; they therefore stored their arms there and confined themselves to the spot.

But whatever numerical advantage John had over Eleazar was counterbalanced by the inferiority of his position. With the enemy over his head, he could not attack with impunity; at the same time, rage would not let him remain at rest. Though he suffered more from Eleazar and his faction than he inflicted, he would not desist [from assault]. On both sides, therefore, there were continual sallies and clouds of discharged missiles, and the Temple was everywhere defiled with blood.

The tyrant Simon, son of Giora, whom in their distress the people had invited in hope of relief, was

master of the Upper City and a great part of the Lower
City. Now that John and his associates were being
assailed also from above, he attacked them with greater
vigor; he was below them when he attacked, as they
were below those above them. Assaulted at both ends,
John sustained losses as easily as he inflicted them.
Whatever disadvantage he suffered in being stationed
lower than Eleazar was compensated for by the superiority of his position to that of Simon. Accordingly,
he with ease repelled the attack from below with hand
weapons; those who hurled their missiles down from
the Temple he kept in check with his engines.

He had an ample supply of scorpions, catapults, and
ballistas. With these he not only defended himself
against his assailants but killed, as well, many of the
worshippers; for though so mad as to commit every
sort of impiety, these men nevertheless admitted those
who wished to sacrifice, taking care first to search the
native Jews with suspicious vigilance, but receiving
strangers with less apprehension. Yet these worshippers, though on entry deprecating the cruelty [of
Eleazar's men], became at times accidental victims of
the sedition, for the missiles from the engines, carried
by their force to the very altar and sanctuary, lit upon
the priests and worshippers; and many who had hastened from the ends of the earth to a site so famed and
deemed holy by all mankind fell all around it in front
of their sacrifices and sprinkled with their own blood
that altar which was universally venerated among both
Greeks and barbarians. . . . (War V, 1:1-3.)

Josephus laments the sorry conditions in Jerusalem
which "could no longer continue being God's place."
The city had become "the alternate site of devastation
and of battle." In the fury of civil strife vast stores of
grain were destroyed. Thus the various rebel leaders
were "as if designedly, serving the Romans by destroy-
ing what the city had provided against the siege and

severing the sinews of their own strength." The dis-
tressed population "was praying for the arrival of the
Romans." (1:3-5.)

THE ARMY OF TITUS

Titus, having assembled part of his troops, sent orders to the rest to meet him at Jerusalem, and marched out of Caesarea. He had the three legions[54] that under the command of his father, had ravaged Judaea, and the twelfth, which had been defeated under Cestius;[55] this legion, notable for its valor, advanced with greater alacrity in order to revenge the distresses it had suffered. Titus directed the fifth legion to join him by the Emmaus route and the tenth by that of Jericho. He himself moved forward with the rest, attended, in addition, by the contingents, now more numerous than before, from the allied kings and by a considerable force of Syrian auxiliaries.

The detachments drafted by Vespasian from these four legions and sent with Mucianus to Italy were replaced by the two thousand men picked from the forces of Alexandria, and the three thousand guards from the Euphrates that had accompanied Titus. With them was Tiberius Alexander,[56] who because of his loyalty and prudence, was the most valuable of Titus' friends. Formerly governor of Egypt, he was now deemed worthy to have command of the forces, for he had been the first to welcome the new dynasty at its initial ascendancy and had attached himself with signal fidelity to its fortunes when these were still uncertain. Superior in age and experience, he attended Titus as his counselor in the exigencies of the war. (War V, 1:6.)

A few days before the Passover (April 70), the anniversary of Israel's liberation from Egyptian bondage, Titus arrived at the outskirts of Jerusalem. During a first reconnaissance tour, he and his six hundred select horsemen were intercepted by the Jews; Titus saved his life by a display of personal courage. From which "we may learn that both the success of wars and the perils of princes are under divine providence" (2:1-2). In a later part of his War, Josephus relates that while Titus was laying siege to Jerusalem, a large segment of the Germans revolted; the Gauls conspired with them, in the hope of freeing themselves from Roman domination. See also Tacitus' History IV, 12-37, 54-79; V, 14-26. Simultaneously with the Germans, the Scythian people, called Sarmatians, went to war against the Romans (War VII, 4:3).

TITUS AT MOUNT SCOPUS

Joined during the night by the [fifth] legion from Emmaus, Titus moved the next day and advanced to Scopus,[57] as the place is called. From that site the city first became visible and the stately pile of the Temple shone forth; that is why this spot—an elevated plain adjoining the northern quarter of the city—is appropriately called Scopus [the View]. When seven furlongs from the city, Titus ordered a camp to be erected for two of the legions together; the fifth legion he stationed three furlongs in their rear, reasoning, that fatigued by their night march, they needed to be covered in order to erect their entrenchments with less apprehension. They had scarcely begun their operations when the tenth legion arrived. It had advanced through Jericho, where a contingent of soldiers guarded the pass formerly taken by Vespasian.[58] These troops had orders to encamp at a distance of six furlongs from Jerusalem, at the Mount of Olives, which lies east of the city and is separated from it by a deep intervening ravine called Kedron.

Intending to break up from Scopus and encamp nearer to the city, Titus stationed as many picked men, horse and foot, as he deemed sufficient to check the sallies of the enemy and employed the main body of

his army in leveling the intervening ground as far as
the walls. Accordingly, all the fences and hedges with
which the inhabitants had enclosed their gardens and
orchards were demolished, the fruit trees throughout
the intervening space felled, the hollow places and
chasms filled up, and the rocky eminences removed with
iron implements. So was the entire distance from
Scopus to the monuments of Herod . . . reduced to
level ground. (War V, 2:3; 3:2.)

*In the following two chapters Josephus offers a
description of the city of Jerusalem, its walls, its
towers, and Herod's palace; of the Temple mount, the
Temple buildings, and the interior of the sanctuary; of
the priestly office and the high priestly garments; and
of the fortress Antonia adjoining the Temple.*

SIMON, SON OF GIORA, AND JOHN OF GISCHALA, THE DEFENDERS OF JERUSALEM

Jerusalem's entire force of fighting men and insurgents consisted of the following: with Simon were ten
thousand men, exclusive of the Idumaeans;[59] fifty
officers commanded them, with Simon acting as commander in chief; the Idumaeans who had joined them
numbered five thousand and had ten commanders. . . .
John, who had seized the Temple, had six thousand
armed men, commanded by twenty officers. Those
Zealots who had ceased their opposition and had come
over to his side, numbered two thousand four hundred
men, led by Eleazar, their former general, and by
Simon, son of Arinus.

While these factions fought each other, the people
were the prey of both sides, as I have already stated,[60]
and those who would not participate in their wicked
practices were plundered by both. Simon held the Upper City, the [third] great wall as far as Kedron, and
as much of the old wall as, bending eastward from
Siloam, descended to the palace of Monobazus, king
of Adiabene, beyond the Euphrates;[61] he also held the

fountain [Siloam], Acra (which was the Lower City), and the span that reached as far as the palace of queen Helena, mother of Monobazus. John held the Temple and its vicinity, Ophla, and the valley called Kedron. . . . (War V, 6:1.)

While the internal strife between the factions in Jerusalem continued, Titus surveyed the city, gave the soldiers permission to set the suburbs on fire, and ordered banks to be raised against the city (6:2).

However, John, out of fear of Simon, remained in his position, though his men were anxious to meet the enemy outside. But Simon, being closer to the besiegers, did not lie still. He arranged his engines—both those that they [the Jews] had taken from Cestius[62] and those that they obtained when they captured the garrison of Antonia[63]—at proper intervals on the wall. These engines, however, though in their possession, were of little use to them, because the men were so unskilled in working them; only a few, who had been taught their use by deserters, could manipulate them, though inefficiently. They [Simon's men] also hurled stones and shot arrows from the wall at the men raising the banks, and rushing out in companies, engaged them in close combat. The workmen were protected from the darts by hurdles spread over palisades, while their engines defended them against the sallies of the besieged.

The engines of all the legions were admirably constructed, but especially those of the tenth. The dart-shooting engines were more powerful, but the stone-casting ones were larger, so that they not only repelled the sallying parties but knocked down the men on the walls as well. The stones they spewed out were the weight of a talent and had a range of over two furlongs. Their shock was unsustainable, not only to those who stood first in the way but also to those who were stationed far beyond them. The Jews, however, first watched for the coming of the stone, for it could be discerned not only by its whiz, but being white, could be perceived by its brightness. Accordingly, the watch-men on the towers gave warning when the engine was discharged and the stone projected by crying in their native tongue, "The missile is coming." Those, then, who were in its way moved out of it and threw them-selves flat upon the ground; this precaution rendered the stone harmless. But the Romans contrived to pre-vent this by blackening the stone. They were then able to aim successfully, and since the stone could no longer be discerned beforehand, slew many at one blow. Yet the Jews, despite this destructive barrage, did not suffer the Romans to raise their banks undisturbed, but with ingenuity and boldness continued to repel them both night and day.

When the Roman works were completed, the engi-neers measured the distance to the wall with lead and line, which they threw from the banks; exposed to the missiles from above, they could not measure it in any other way. When they found that the battering rams could reach the wall, they brought them up. Titus, set-ting his artillery closer to the wall to prevent the men upon it from repelling the battering rams, ordered them into play. At the tremendous noise that suddenly echoed from three places, the people within raised a cry of alarm. No less was the terror of the rebels.

Seeing the common danger they were in, both parties contrived to combine in defense. The different factions shouted to each other that they had behaved as if wholly in concert with their enemies; they ought in-stead, even if God should not grant them lasting con-cord, to forgo, at least for the present, their mutual enmity and unite in arms against the Romans. Simon therefore permitted the men in the Temple to mount the walls, and John, though he barely trusted Simon, gave them similar permission. Thus both sides forgot their hatred and private quarrels and formed one body. They manned the walls, cast from there a vast number of torches at the machines, and ceaselessly discharged darts at the men who impelled the battering rams. The bolder leaped out in troops, tore to shreds the hurdles covering the machines, attacked their manipulators, and vanquished them, not so much by any skill of theirs as by their daring.

Titus himself ceaselessly sent aid to those hardest pressed; stationing both horsemen and archers on both sides of the engines, he repelled the men who were setting fire to them, drove back those who were hurling missiles from the towers, and set the battering rams to work. But the wall did not yield to their blows, except where the battering ram of the fifteenth legion knocked off the corner of a tower; the wall itself remained intact because it was not in the same immediate danger as the tower, which projected far out and could not easily bring down with it any part of the main wall. (War V, 6:3-4.)

THE BATTLE OF THE WALLS

Titus had given orders for the erection of three towers fifty cubits high, in order that by setting men upon them at every bank, he might from there repel the men on the wall. . . .

Stoutly as the Jews held out against everything else, they suffered great distress from these towers; from them they were shot at not only by the javelin throwers, archers, and slingers but by the lighter engines as well. . . . If, on the other hand, they withdrew beyond the range of the missiles, they could no longer impede the blows of the battering rams, whose ceaseless shocks were gradually taking effect. At long last the wall began to give way before "the Conqueror," as the Jews called the largest engine, because it vanquished everything in its way. They [the defenders] had long been exhausted from passing their nights at a distance from the city, fighting, and watching; moreover, moved by indolence and the fatality that attended all their plans, they thought it superfluous to guard the wall, as two others would still remain. Accordingly, the majority of them slackened in their exertions and retired, and when the Romans mounted the wall at the breach "the Conqueror" had effected, they all abandoned their posts and retreated to the second wall. The men who had scaled the ramparts now opened the gates and admitted the entire army. Having in this manner surmounted the first wall on the fifteenth day [of the siege] . . . the Romans demolished a great part of it. . . .

Titus now transferred his camp to the so-called Camp of the Assyrians. Occupying the entire span between it and the Kedron, but sufficiently distant from the second wall to be out of range of its missiles, he immediately commenced the attack. The Jews, dividing their forces, made a vigorous defense from the wall. John and his faction fought from Antonia, the north colonnade of the Temple, and in front of the tomb of king Alexander [Jannaeus]; Simon's group, intercepting the assault near the tomb of the high priest [and ruler] John [Hyrcanus], manned the intervening space as far as the gate through which water was brought to the tower Hippicus. Frequently dashing out from the gates, they engaged in hand-to-hand fighting. Though, owing to their ignorance of Roman tactics, they were defeated in close combat, when driven back to the wall they had the advantage in their contests from the ramparts. Strength, coupled with skill, encouraged the Romans; a daring spirit, nourished by fear, and their innate fortitude in the face of disaster, emboldened the Jews. They still cherished hope of deliverance, as did the Romans of a speedy conquest. No weariness overcame either side; attacks, fighting from the ramparts, and perpetual sorties in bands wore out the day; nor was any method of warfare left untried. [Though the fighting] began at dawn, night scarcely parted the [antagonists]. Night was a sleepless time on both sides, and more oppressive than the day, one side being in constant dread lest the wall be taken, the other fearing an enemy assault on their camp. Passing the night in arms, both were ready for battle at the first break of day.

Among the Jews each man vied with the others to be first in danger, that by so doing he might recommend himself to his officers. And so great was the reverence and awe they had for Simon in particular, and such the deference paid him by all under his command, that they were ready to a man even to die by their own hand at his command. The Romans, on the other hand, were incited to valor by the habit of victory and by their inexperience of defeat, by repeated campaigns, constant exercises, the vastness of their empire, and above all, by Titus, who was ever and everywhere present; for it seemed a dreadful thing to act the coward when their Prince was with them and fighting at their side, and when he who fought bravely had as witness to his valor the man who would reward it. It was, in fact, already an advantage to be known to the Prince as a gallant soldier. Hence many in their enthusiasm distinguished themselves beyond their natural powers. . . . (War V, 7:1-3.)

Five days after Titus had stormed the first wall, he took the second; but the Jews drove back the Roman band that had pressed inside the wall. After a stubborn fight of four days, the Romans regained possession of the wall and razed it (V, 8). Titus now began to raise banks against both Antonia, defended by John of Gischala, and the Upper City, defended by Simon, son of Giora. Sent by Titus, Josephus attempted to move the defenders of Jerusalem to surrender.

JOSEPHUS' SPEECH

So Josephus circled the wall, endeavoring to find a spot out of range of the missiles that would at the same time, be within hearing distance; and at great length entreated them to spare themselves, the people, their country, and their temple, and not to manifest greater indifference in these matters than did aliens.

The Romans, he said, though they had no part in them, respected the sacred rites and places of their foes and had thus far withheld their hands from them; while those who had been reared among them, who alone would enjoy them were they preserved, were bent on their destruction. Indeed, their firmest walls they saw prostrate, and that alone remaining which was weaker than what has been taken. They knew that the power of the Romans was invincible and that to serve them was no new experience. If, indeed, to wage war for freedom is noble, that should have been done earlier; but having once succumbed, and for so long a period submitted, then to cast off the yoke was the deed not of lovers of liberty but of men madly courting death.

To disdain ignoble masters was perhaps admissible; but not those who ruled the world. For what had escaped the Romans, except perhaps some spot made valueless through heat or cold? Fortune had on all sides been transferred to the Romans, and God, who had bestowed power on all the nations in turn, now rested over Italy. It was an established law, and of the greatest force among brute beasts as well as men, to yield to the stronger, and that dominion should belong to those who are supreme in arms.

Accordingly, their ancestors, who were much superior in mind and body, as well as in resources generally, had yet submitted to the Romans, which they would not have done had they not known that God was with the Romans. As for themselves what did they rely on in holding out, when most of their city was already taken, and when they, though their walls were still intact, were enduring calamities worse than capture? For it did not escape the Romans that famine raged in the city, a famine that was now consuming the people and would soon consume the men in arms as well. For even should the Romans raise the siege and not attack the city sword in hand, a war beyond the strife of arms was besetting them from within and would with each hour gather strength unless the ability were theirs to wield weapons and wage war against famine, or unless they alone among mankind could subdue even the claims of nature.

He added further that it would be well to alter their conduct before their miseries became incurable and to resort to salutary counsels while the opportunity still remained. The Romans would bear no grudge against them for their past deeds if they persisted not in their contumacy, for the Romans were by nature lenient in victory and preferred what was expedient to the gratification of their passions. And how would it advantage them to possess a city devoid of inhabitants and a desert region? For these reasons, Titus, even at this late date, wished to offer them terms. But if he took the city by storm, he would slaughter them to a man, especially if they rejected his offers in this, their direst, distress. That the third wall would be speedily taken, those already fallen gave proof. And even were that bulwark impregnable, the famine would fight for the Romans against them.

As he thus exhorted them, Josephus was by many derided from the wall, railed at by many others, and assailed with missiles by some. On finding his direct advice disregarded, he passed to the history of their nation.

"Miserable men!" he cried. "Are you so unmindful of your own true allies as to wage war against the Romans with weapons and your hands? What other nation have we vanquished by such means? When did God, who created, fail to avenge the Jews if they were wronged? Will you not look back and consider what that place is whence you issue to battle and how mighty an Ally you have outraged? Will you not recall the superhuman exploits of your forefathers and what mighty foes this holy place has in bygone days destroyed for us?

"As for me, I shudder when declaring the works of God to such unworthy ears. Listen, nevertheless, that you may know that you war not only against the Romans but against God Himself.[64] Necoh, king of Egypt, who bore also the name Pharaoh, came with a prodigious army and carried off queen Sarah, the mother of our nation. What did her husband, Abraham, our forefather, do then? Though he had three hundred and eighteen officers, each commanding a countless host, did he take vengeance on this tyrant with the sword? Or did he not rather deem these soldiers as nothing if unaided by God, and lifting pure hands towards this holy site, which you have now polluted, enlist the invincible Supporter on his side? And was not our queen sent back the next morning, unharmed, to her husband, while the Egyptian, revering the site that you have stained with the blood of your countrymen, and terrified by nocturnal visions, fled, bestowing silver and gold upon the Hebrews, beloved of God?

"Shall I pass over in silence or speak of the migration of our fathers to Egypt? Lorded over by, and cowering under, kings of alien birth for four hundred years, did they not, when they might have vindicated their cause with their weapons and their hands, commit themselves to God?

"Who has not heard that Egypt was overrun by every species of wild beast and wasted with every disease; that their land yielded no fruit, the Nile failed; that the ten plagues followed one after the other; and that in consequence, our fathers were sent forth under escort, without bloodshed and without danger, God conducting them as the future guardians of His temple?

"Did not Philistia, and the idol Dagon, groan under the ravage of our holy ark, carried off by the Syrians? Did not the entire nation of those who had removed it rue the deed, until, ulcerated in their loins and their very bowels come down with the food they ate, they, with the hands that stole it, brought it back to the sound of cymbals and timbrels, and with all manner of expiations propitiating the sanctuary? It was God who then led our fathers, because, employing neither hand nor weapon, they committed the issue to His decision.

"When Sennacherib, king of the Assyrians, with all Asia in his train, encamped around this city, was it by human hands he fell? Were not those hands resting from arms and lifted in prayer while an angel of God, in one single night, destroyed that countless host? And did not the Assyrian, when he rose in the morning, find one hundred and eighty-five thousand dead, and with the remanent flee from the Hebrews, who were neither armed nor in pursuit?

"You have heard, moreover, of the captivity in Babylon, where our people passed seventy years in exile and did not shake off the yoke and recover their liberty until Cyrus granted it in gratitude to God. They were accordingly sent forth by him and re-established the temple-worship of their Ally. In short, there is no instance of our ancestors having triumphed by arms or failed of success without them when they committed their cause to God. When they remained within their own borders, they conquered, as seemed good to their Judge; when they took the field, they were invariably defeated.

"Thus, when the king of Babylon laid siege to this city, Zedekiah, our sovereign, having, contrary to the prophetic warnings of Jeremiah, given him battle, was himself taken prisoner and saw the city and the Temple leveled to the ground. Yet, how much more moderate was that prince than your rulers, and his subjects than you! For though Jeremiah proclaimed aloud that they were hateful to God for their transgressions and would be carried away captive if they did not surrender the city, neither the king nor the people put him to death. But you, to pass over what you have done within the city—for I am unable adequately to describe your enormities—heap abuses on me who exhort you to save yourselves and assail me with missiles, exasperated at being reminded of your misdeeds and not brooking even the mention of those crimes that you daily perpetrate.

"Again, when our ancestors went forth in arms against Antiochus, surnamed Epiphanes, who was then besieging the city and who had been guilty of many outrages against the Deity, they were cut to pieces in the battle, the city was plundered by the enemy, and the sanctuary left desolate three years and six months.

"Need I cite still more examples? Who enlisted the Romans against our country? Was it not the impiety of its inhabitants? Whence did our servitude arise? Was it not from a sedition of our forefathers when the madness of Aristobulus [II] and Hyrcanus [II] and their mutual quarrels brought Pompey against the city, and God subjected to the Romans those who were unworthy of liberty? Accordingly, after a siege of three months they surrendered, though they had not sinned against the laws and the sanctuary so grievously as you and though they possessed much greater resources for war.

"And do we not know the fate of Antigonus, the son of Aristobulus [II], in whose reign God again punished the people for their transgressions by the capture of the city when Herod, son of Antipater, brought upon us Sosius, and Sosius the Roman army, by whom they were shut up in siege for six months, until in retribution for their sins they were captured and the city plundered by the enemy?

"Thus it appears that arms have never been granted to our nation; to war is to incur inevitable disaster. For, doubtless, it is the duty of those who inhabit holy ground to commit all to divine disposal, and when they seek to conciliate the Judge on high, to scorn the aid of human hands. But as for you, what have you done that has been blessed by our lawgiver [Moses]? Or what have you left undone that has been condemned by him? How much more impious are you than those who were more speedily subdued! You have disdained no secret sins—thefts, I mean, and treacherous plots against men, and adulteries—while in rapine and murders you vie with each other and cut for yourselves new and strange paths of wickedness. The Temple has become a receptacle for all, and this divine place—which even the Romans from afar revered, forgoing many of their own customs in deference to our law—has been polluted by native hands. And do you after all this expect Him, thus impiously treated, to be your ally? Verily, ye are righteous suppliants, and pure are the hands with which you appeal to your Defender! Did our king lift up such hands in prayer against the king of Assyria [Sennacherib] when in one single night God destroyed that mighty host! And do the Romans commit such wickedness as did the king of Assyria that you may hope for like vengeance upon them? Did not he accept money from our sovereign on condition that he would spare the city, and then come down, in violation of his oaths, to burn the sanctuary? Whereas the Romans ask but the customary tribute that our fathers paid to theirs. Obtaining this, they will neither destroy the city nor touch the holy things. They concede to you everything else—the freedom of your families, the security of your property, and the preservation of the sacred laws. It is madness, then, to expect that God should accord the same treatment to the just as to the unjust.

"But, further, He knows how to inflict immediate vengeance, when necessary. Thus, He broke the Assyrians on the very first night of their encampment. And thus, had He judged our generation worthy of freedom, or the Romans of punishment, He would at once, as He did with the Assyrians, have laid His hand upon them—when Pompey interfered with our nation, when, after him, Sosius came, when Vespasian ravaged Galilee, and lastly, now, when Titus was approaching Jerusalem. Yet Magnus [Pompey] and Sosius, besides sustaining no injury, took the city by assault, while Vespasian went from the war he made against us to become emperor. As for Titus, the very springs that had previously dried up for you more copiously for him. For prior to his arrival, as you know, Siloam and all the springs outside the city had failed, insomuch that water was sold by the *amphora*,[65] while now they flow in such abundance for your enemies as to suffice not only for themselves and their cattle but even for the gardens. This amazing phenomenon you have experienced before, on the occasion of the capture of the city, when the aforementioned king of Babylon advanced with his army and took and burned both city and sanctuary even though, in my opinion, the Jews of the period were not so deeply impious as you. I cannot, therefore, but think that God has withdrawn from the holy places and taken His stand on the side of those against whom you are now in arms.

"Why, since even a good man will flee from a wanton house and abhor its inmates, do you then persuade yourselves that God still remains with you in your evil course—that God who sees all secret things and hears what is buried in silence? Yet what is there buried in silence among you, or what concealed? Nay, what has not been exposed to your foes? For you make ostentatious display of your enormities and daily contend who shall be the worst, making an exhibition of your iniquity as though it were a virtue.

"Nonetheless, a path of safety yet remains, if you will. The Deity is easily reconciled towards those who confess and repent. O iron-hearted men! throw away your weapons; take compassion on your country already on the point of destruction! Turn and behold the beauty of that which you are betraying. What a city!

what a temple! the gifts of how many nations! Against these, would any man guide the flames? Who wishes that these should be no more? And what is more worthy of being preserved than these? Obdurate beings, and more insensible than stone! Even if you look not on these objects with the eyes of natural affection, yet at any rate pity your families, and let each of you have before his eyes children, wife, and parents, ere long to be the victims of famine or of war.

"I am aware that I have a mother, a wife, a family not ignoble, and an ancient and illustrious house involved in the danger; and I may perhaps be thought on their account to tender you this advice. Put them to death, take my blood as the price of your own safety; for I too am ready to die, if upon my death you learn wisdom." (War V, 9:3-4.)

The rebels did not yield, although famine was driving many to despair (10:2-5).

THE ROMANS' PROGRESS

Although the soldiers suffered great distress from the wall, Titus' banks had made great progress. He now sent a detachment of horse to lie in ambush for those who went out into the valleys in quest of food. Some of these were fighting men no longer content with their plunder, but the majority were poorer people, deterred from deserting by fear for their families. . . .

It was the severity of the famine that made them thus bold in going out, and nothing remained for them, if they managed to leave unobserved, but capture by the enemy. When caught, they were . . . prior to death, scourged and tortured by every means, then crucified in front of the walls. Titus pitied their sufferings, five hundred, and occasionally more, being captured each day. Nevertheless, he thought it unsafe to free those taken in arms, while to retain so many in custody would mean placing the guards themselves under ward. His main reason, however, for not forbidding this cruelty was his hope that the Jews might perhaps surrender at the sight [of the crucifictions], out of fear that the same punishment might later be inflicted on them as well. Out of resentment and hatred, the soldiers, for sport, nailed the captives in a variety of different postures. And so great was their number, that there was not room enough for the crosses, nor were there enough crosses for the bodies.

But so far were the seditious from repenting at sight of these sufferings that they seduced the multitude into believing they were inflicted from the very opposite motive. Dragging the deserters' kin to the wall, together with those of the populace who were anxious to accept the security offered them, they showed them the miseries endured by those who sought refuge with the Romans, stating that the seized had been suppliants, not captives. This, until the truth was known, detained in the city many who were eager to desert. Some, notwithstanding, fled immediately, as to certain punishment, deeming death at the hands of their enemies a relief compared to famine. Titus, moreover, ordered the hands of many of the captives to be cut off—in order that they might not be thought deserters and in order that their misfortune should lend credence to their story—then sent them to John and Simon, exhorting them now, at length, to pause and not force him to demolish the city, but through repentance in the last extremity, to preserve their lives, a city so distinguished, and a temple that was uniquely theirs. At the same time he circled the banks, bestirring the workmen, as if intending before long to follow his threats by deeds.

In answer to this message the seditious denounced from the ramparts both Titus and his father, shouting that they despised death, having rightly preferred it to slavery; that as long as breath was left in them they would inflict every possible injury on the Romans; that men who, as he said, were so soon to perish need care little for their city; that the world was a more suitable temple for God than theirs, but that this temple would yet be preserved by Him who dwelt therein; and that having Him for their ally, they derided all threats, which would come to nothing, for the outcome rested only with God. Invectives accompanied these retorts. (War V, 11:1-2.)

After seventeen days' hard work, the Roman banks were completed. But those towards Antonia were destroyed by John of Gischala; those towards the Upper City, by Simon, son of Giora (11:4-6). Now Titus had the whole city surrounded by a wall, in order to prevent the Jews from coming out and to conquer the city by starvation. Many indeed wasted away with famine, and many died as they were burying others. (See also War VI, 3:3-4, and Gittin 56a.) "Deep silence and a kind of deathly night had seized upon the city. . . . The victims died with their eyes fixed upon the Temple." *The Romans now started to erect four new banks against Antonia (War V, 12). Josephus continued making appeals to the rebels to surrender and at one point suffered a wound. Those who did desert the city met with brutal death at the hands of the Romans; Titus tried to restrain the brutality,* "but greed set all punishment at defiance" *(13:3-5).*

THE FALL OF ANTONIA

The Romans meanwhile, though much harassed in gathering timber, completed the banks in twenty-one days, having . . . stripped the entire district around the city a distance of ninety furlongs. Melancholy indeed was the aspect of the country; sites formerly ornamented with trees and gardens were now desolate, with all the timber felled. Nor could a stranger who had seen Judaea as she once was, and the enchanting suburbs of her capital, and now beheld her present desolation, have refrained from tears or suppressed a sigh at the magnitude of the change. The war had obliterated all signs of beauty; and if anyone formerly acquainted with the site were to come suddenly upon it now, he would not recognize it, even if he were at the city itself, but he would, notwithstanding, inquire for it.

To the Romans, as to the Jews, the completion of the banks proved a source of apprehension. The latter feared that if they did not succeed in burning them as they did the others, the city would be captured; the Romans, that they would never take the city if these banks also were destroyed, for there was a scarcity of materials, and the bodies of the soldiers had begun to fail from toil, as did their minds from the repeated disasters. Moreover, the Romans were more discouraged by the city's suffering than were the men within the walls, since its defenders were not at all disheartened by their sore afflictions, while their own hopes were continually crushed, their banks checked by the stratagems of the enemy, their engines by the solidity of the walls, their close combat by the daring of their antagonists. But the greatest discouragement came from finding the Jews' courageous souls to be superior to the numberless miseries they endured from sedition, famine, war, or disasters however great. They considered the vigor of the Jews impregnable, their cheerfulness in distress invincible. For what would not men who were inspired to valor by their disasters endure if Fortune smiled upon them? Because of these considerations, the Romans greatly strengthened the guarding of the banks. (War VI, 1:1-2.)

John and his men, posted at Antonia, assaulted the Roman works, but failed. The Romans then advanced to batter Antonia, which resisted that battering; however, a portion of the wall fell. "The joy of the Romans was quenched at the sight of another wall that John had built inside." Sabinus, a native of Syria, offered

to be first to scale the wall. Having attained his objec-
tive, he slipped and fell headlong to his death (1:3-6).

Two days later, twenty of the guards on outpost
duty at the banks assembled, and inviting the standard-
bearer of the fifth legion to join them, with two horsemen from the lines and a trumpeter, noiselessly advanced through the ruins towards Antonia at the
ninth hour of the night. The sentinels they first encountered, they killed in their sleep; then, having
gained possession of the wall, they ordered the trumpeter to sound. At this, the rest of the guards suddenly
started to their feet and fled before anyone had observed how many had ascended, for panic and the
blare of the trumpet led them to suppose that the
enemy had mounted in great force. On hearing the
signal, Titus immediately ordered the troops to arms,
and with the generals and his detachment of picked
men, was first to mount. The Jews fled to the Temple.
Through the mine John had excavated under their
banks, the Romans, too, advanced into the Temple.

Drawing up in separate divisions, the insurgents of
both factions, John's and Simon's, checked their advance. Considering themselves wholly ruined if the
Romans penetrated the Holy Place, they fought with
the greatest force and vigor. The Romans, at the
same time, viewed this as the beginning of victory. A desperate conflict ensued around the entrances, the Romans pressing forward to take possession of the Temple, the Jews thrusting them back to Antonia. On both
sides missiles and spears were useless. Drawing their
swords, they fought hand to hand. Because the place
of battle was so narrow, the adversaries were so intermixed that it was impossible to distinguish which side
the respective combatants were on. And so loud was
the din that their battle cries fell but confusedly on
the ear.

The slaughter on both sides was great. Trampling

on the fallen, the contending ranks crushed their bodies and their armor. As the fluctuating tide of battle favored first one side, then another, the victors shouted exhortations; the routed lamented. There was no room for flight or pursuit. Confused revolutions and turns succeeded one another, and the armies were intermixed. Necessity compelled the front-rank men to kill or be killed, there being no retreat, for on both sides the rear men pressed those ahead of them forward, leaving no intervening space for the combatants. At long last, after a battle that lasted from the ninth hour of the night until the seventh of the day, the fury of the Jews prevailed over Roman skill, and the entire [enemy] line gave way. The Jews had fought with all their forces combined, and the peril of capture as incentive to valor; but only a partial force of the Roman army engaged in the action, the legions on which they chiefly depended not having reached them yet. Accordingly, they were for the present content with the possession of Antonia.

Titus now ordered his troops to raze the foundations of Antonia and to prepare an easy ascent for his entire force. On the seventeenth of Panemus [Tammuz], having heard that on that day the so-called continual sacrifice had ceased to be offered to God for want of men [to offer it] [66] . . . he directed Josephus to deliver to John the same message he had before. (War VI, 1:7; 2:1.)

In answer to Josephus' solicitation to surrender, John declared that "he could never fear capture, for Jerusalem was God's city." Josephus renewed his appeal; many of the upper class were moved to escape to safety. They, in turn, appealed to the people, whereupon "great numbers fled to the Romans." Titus promised to preserve the Temple if John terminated the conflict; John rejected the proposal. Titus, therefore, "once more proceeded to hostilities" (2:1-6).

THE BATTLE OF THE TEMPLE (AUGUST 70)

The Romans, having "razed the foundation of Antonia, prepared a broad ascent as far as the Temple." The Jews, in turn, attacked the Roman camp on the Mount of Olives. "The Romans evinced military skill, combined with force; the Jews, reckless impetuosity and unbridled fury" (War VI, 2:7-8).

In the meantime, the Jews, suffering greatly from their encounters as the war gradually, yet constantly, moved towards its apex and crept towards the Temple, cut off the limbs already infected, as one does with a mortifying body to arrest the spread of a disease. They set fire to that section of the northwest colonnade which was connected with Antonia, and subsequently destroyed some twenty cubits of it, starting thereby with their own hands the burning of the holy places. Two days later . . . the Romans set fire to the adjoining portico, thus spreading the fire another fifteen cubits. In a similar fashion the Jews destroyed the roof, not ceasing from their labor until the entire communication between themselves and Antonia was destroyed, though it was in their power to stop those who applied the flames. They looked calmly on as the flames caught, and viewed the spreading of the fire as being to their advantage. Thus the conflicts around the Temple grew, and ceaseless were the attacks of sallying parties from both sides. (War VI, 2:9.)

Roman battering rams and siege-engines failed to take effect against "the magnitude and compactness of the stones" of the Temple walls. The Jews vigorously attacked the scaling ladders applied to the porticoes. Titus, "seeing that his forbearance towards the Temple led to injury and slaughter of his own troops, ordered the gates set on fire" (4:1).

The soldiers had already applied the fire to the gates; the melting silver around them quickly carried the flames to the woodwork, whence they continually spread, until they reached the porticoes. At sight of the fire encircling them, the Jews lost all strength of mind and body; so great was their dismay that none attempted to ward off or quench the devouring element, but all stood rooted to the spot as spectators. Yet, though disheartened at what was already consumed, they did not grow wiser about what remained, but as though the sanctuary itself was now in flames, whetted their fury against the Romans. The fire raged throughout the day and the succeeding night, for the Romans could not burn the whole range of porticoes in one operation, but could set fire only to portions of them.

The following morning, Titus, after ordering a division of his troops to quench the flames and make ready a path to the gates for an easier ascent of the legions, convened his generals.

At this war council it was decided to spare the Temple. On the following day attacks and counterattacks continued until the Jews "were overpowered and enclosed in the inner court of the Temple."

Titus . . . decided to attack with his entire force on the following morning around daybreak and to invest the Temple. That edifice God had, indeed, long since destined for the flames; and now, as the years revolved, the day of doom had come, the tenth of the month Lous [Ab], the very day on which the former Temple had been burned by [Nebuchadnezzar] the king of Babylon. But the flames were raised by the Jews themselves and occasioned by them, for when Titus retired, the rebels, after a short breathing spell, again attacked the Romans. A battle ensued between the guards of the sanctuary and the troops who were trying to quench the fire in the inner court. Routing the Jews, the latter penetrated as far as the sanctuary.

At this moment a soldier, neither waiting for orders nor awed by so great a crime, but driven by some supernatural impulse, snatched a brand from the blazing timber, and lifted by a comrade, set fire to a golden window that, on its north side, had an entrance to the chambers surrounding the sanctuary. As the flames ascended, a cry, commensurate with the tragedy, went up from the Jews, who flocked to the rescue, no longer sparing life or husbanding their strength now that that was perishing for the sake of which they had hitherto been so vigilant. (War VI, 4:2-5.)

Jewish tradition has both destructions of the Temple take place on the ninth of Ab (Mishnah Taanith IV, 6, and Taanith 29a). Compare, however, Rabbi Johanan's view: "Had I been alive in that generation, I would have chosen the tenth [as the correct date], because on that day the greater part of the Temple was burned" (Taanith 29a). Concerning the biblical tradition on the destruction of the first Temple, see II Kings 25:8 (the ninth) and Jeremiah 52:12-13 (the tenth).

Titus was reposing in his tent after the action, when someone rushed in with the tidings. Starting up just as he was, he ran to the spot to arrest the flames, followed by all the general officers, who in turn, were accompanied by the astonished legions. The disorderly movement of so large a force created uproar and confusion. Titus, with both voice and hand, signaled to the combatants to quench the fire. But their ears assailed by the louder clamor, they did not hear his shouts, nor distracted as some were by the ardor of battle and others by rage, did they heed his waving. And neither persuasion nor threats could restrain the impetuosity of the legions as they rushed in. Fury guided everyone. Crowding about the entrances, many were trampled by their comrades; and many others, falling amidst the still hot and smoldering ruins of the porticoes, suffered the same miserable fate as the vanquished.

Sulpicius Severus, a fourth-century Christian historian, presumably following a lost account of Tacitus, has

Titus favoring the burning of the Temple (Chronica
II, 30).

As the Romans neared the sanctuary, pretending
not even to hear Titus' orders, they exhorted those who
had preceded them to throw in the torches. The rebels
were now bereft of all power to aid [in quenching the
fire]; carnage and flight reigned everywhere. Most of
the slain were feeble and unarmed people, each butchered where he was caught. Mounds of dead lay around
the altar; a stream of blood flowed down its steps;
down these fell the bodies of those who met their doom
above.

Utterly unable to repress the impetuosity of the
troops, who were wild with fanaticism, and seeing that
the fire was gaining mastery, Titus went inside with
his generals and surveyed the holy site of the sanctuary, and all that it contained—objects far exceeding
its fame abroad and equaling its proud reputation
among ourselves.[67]

*Titus again tried to prevent the spreading of the
conflagration, in order to save the inner court of the
Temple.*

Though Titus had rushed forth to restrain the
soldiers, one of the men who had entered with him
frustrated his intent by thrusting fire, in the dark,
into the hinges of the gate. At the sudden burst of
flames from within, Titus and the generals withdrew,
and no one [any longer] hindered the men outside
from applying their torches. Thus then, was the Temple, in spite of Titus, set on fire.

But deeply as one may mourn the [destruction of
the] most marvelous edifice ever seen or heard of—in
architecture, magnitude, sumptuousness of detail, or
the glory of its holy places—we may, nevertheless,
derive the highest consolation from the reflection that
Fate's inevitability extends as well to structures and
sites as to human beings. And truly remarkable was

the precision of Fate's cycle, for as I have said, it had waited until the very month and very day on which the Temple had previously been burned by the Babylonians. . . . (War VI, 4:6-8.)

WHILE THE TEMPLE WAS IN FLAMES

While the sanctuary was in flames, whatever fell in the victors' way became prey to rapine, and ten thousand of those caught were slain. Pity was shown to no age, nor respect to any rank; children and old men, laity and priests, all perished in one common holocaust. The embrace of war enclosed all ranks, and all were hunted down, those who sued for mercy and those who defended themselves. The flames, borne far and wide, added their roar to the groans of the fallen, and owing to the height of the hill and the size of the burning pile, one would have thought the whole city to be on fire.

Nothing more deafening or more terrifying can be imagined than the din of that moment. The exultant war cry of the Roman legions marching in mass mingled with the screams of the insurgents encircled by fire and sword and with the wailing of the people over their calamities as, cut off from above, they fled in consternation and fell into the hands of the enemy. The multitude within the city joined its cries to the cries of those on the hill, and many who were wasted from famine and whose lips had closed gathered renewed strength for lamentations and cries when they beheld the sanctuary in flames. The city beyond returned the echo, as did the surrounding mountains, deepening the roar.

Yet the sufferings were more terrible still than the confusion. One would have thought that the hill itself on which the sacred edifice stood was seething from its base, for it was everywhere one mass of flame, and that the stream of blood was ampler even than the fire, and the slaughtered more numerous than the slaughterers. The ground was nowhere visible, because of the dead upon it; when in pursuit of fugitives, the soldiers had to climb over mounds of bodies. At length, however, the rebels, having forced back the Romans, with difficulty opened a path into the outer court of the Temple and thence into the city. What remained of the populace took refuge on the outer portico.

Some of the priests at first pulled off from the sanctuary the spikes with their leaden sockets and hurled them at the Romans, but finding all efforts unavailing and the flames already bursting against them, they later retired to the wall, which was eight cubits wide, and there remained. Two eminent men, however—Meirus, son of Belgas, and Josephus, son of Dalaeus—who if so inclined, might have saved their lives by deserting to the Romans or have held out and taken their chance with the rest, plunged into the fire and perished in the flames of the Temple. (War VI, 5:1.)

The Romans set fire also to the buildings around the Temple, the treasure chambers, and the remaining portico of the outer court of the Temple, on which many had taken refuge (5:2).

There were at this period many prophets suborned by the rebel leaders to delude the people by bidding them to await help from God, in order to decrease desertions, and through hope to encourage those who were above fear and restraint. In adversity man readily succumbs to persuasion, and when the deceiver makes him believe that he will be delivered from pressing evils, the sufferer is wholly influenced by hope.

Thus did the impostors and pretended messengers of God beguile at that time the wretched people; while the manifest portents that foreshowed the approaching desolation, the people neither heeded nor believed. As if confounded and bereft of eyes and mind, they disregarded the immediate warnings of God. So was it when a star resembling a sword stood over the city, and a comet lingered an entire year. So also when, prior to the revolt and the disturbances that preceded the war, as the people were assembling for the feast of unleavened bread [March-April] . . . so vivid a light—a light that lasted half an hour—shone round the altar and the sanctuary at the ninth hour of the night that it seemed to be bright day. The inexperienced regarded this as a favorable omen, but the sacred scribes at once pronounced it a prelude to the events that later followed. At the same festival, a cow led by someone to the sacrifice, gave birth to a lamb in the midst of the Temple court. Moreover, the eastern gate of the inner court—a gate of the most massive brass, which, on being shut towards evening, could scarcely be moved by twenty men, and which, fastened with bars shod with iron, had bolts sunk to a great depth in a threshold made entirely of one stone—this gate was observed, around the sixth hour of the night, to open of its own accord.[68] The Temple guards ran to inform the captain, who repairing to the site, scarcely succeeded in shutting that gate. To the ignorant this, too, seemed a most auspicious omen, for God, they thought, had opened to them the gate of blessings. But the learned understood it to mean that the security of the Temple was dissolving of its own accord and that the gate opened for the advantage of the enemy, and interpreted it in their own minds as a portent of impending desolation.

Not many days after the festival, appeared a phenomenon so marvelous as to exceed credibility. What I am about to relate would, I imagine, be deemed mere fable were it not told by eyewitnesses and attended by disasters commensurate with such portents. Throughout the country, before the sun set, chariots were seen in the sky, and armed battalions speeding through the clouds and besieging the cities. And at the feast called Pentecost [Feast of Weeks], the attention of the priests, as at night they entered the inner court of the Temple in the customary discharge of their ministrations, was drawn first, so they related, by a commotion and a clanging noise, then by a voice, as of a multitude, saying "Let us depart hence." . . .

If we reflect on these events, we shall find that God has a care for mankind, foreshowing to His people paths of salvation, and that men perish through their own folly and self-chosen evils. . . .

But what chiefly incited the Jews to the war was an ambiguous oracle, found in their sacred writings, that around this period a man from their country would become ruler of the world. This they construed as referring to one of their own race, and many wise men went astray in its interpretation. In reality, however, the oracle betokened the elevation of Vespasian, he having been proclaimed emperor when on Judaean soil. But it is not possible for men to escape their fate, even when they foresee it. . . . (War VI, 5:2-4.)

Expectations of world leaders to emanate from Judaea are recorded by Tacitus (History *V, 13*) *and Suetonius* (Vespasian *4*).

SURRENDER?

With the sanctuary in flames, the Romans "carried their standards into the Temple court, sacrificed to them, and saluted Titus as imperator" (War VI, 6:1).

The rebel leaders and their partisans, defeated everywhere and so completely surrounded that there was no possible way of escape, sent envoys to request Titus to come to a parley. Desiring out of the kindness of his nature to save the city at all events, and heeding the advice of his friends, who assumed that the rebels had at last been brought to reason, Titus placed himself on the west side of the Temple's outer court. . . . Throngs from both sides crowded around: the Jews, buoyed up by hopes of pardon, near John and Simon; the Romans, waiting to hear the Jews' words, at Titus' side. After charging the soldiers to repress their anger

and withhold their arms and commanding the interpreter to stand at his side, Titus began to speak first,
which was a sign that he was the conqueror.

The speech, in which Titus emphasized Roman hu-
manity in dealing with Judaea, concludes as follows.

"And after all this, most abominable of men, you
now invite me to a parley? What have you left to save
that can be compared with what is lost? Of what deliverance do you deem yourselves worthy after the
ruin of your Temple? Yet even now you stand armed,
and though in the last extremity, do not so much as
assume the guise of suppliants. Wretched men, on
what do you rely? Are not your people dead, your
sanctuary swept away, your city in my power, your
lives in my hands? And still you deem it proof of valor
to struggle with death? But I will not try to emulate
your madness. Throw down your arms, surrender your
persons, and I grant you life, chastising, as does an
indulgent master of a household, the incorrigible and
preserving the rest for myself."

In reply they said that they could not accept a pledge
from him because they had sworn never to do so. They
asked, instead, permission to pass through the enemy
lines with their wives and children, for they would go
into the desert and leave the city to him. Indignant
that men in the position of captives should present
their own terms to him, Titus ordered the following
proclamation to be issued to them: no longer to desert
to him or hope for protection, for he would spare no
one, but would instead fight them with all his might;
they should therefore save themselves as best they
could, since the laws of war would henceforth rule all
his measures.

Orders were then issued to the troops to plunder and
burn the city. On that day, however, nothing was done;
but on the following, fire was set to the residence of
the magistrates, the Acra, the council chamber, and
the site called Ophla. The flames spread as far as the

palace of queen Helena,[69] in the center of the Acra.
The streets, too, were consumed, and so were the
houses filled with the bodies of those who had perished
from famine. (War VI, 6:2-3.)

At the same time the rebel leaders continued to hold
out in the Upper City (7:2-3). Once again the Romans
had to build banks and prepare to attack the wall; but
the rebel opposition had lost its vigor. The leaders tried
to escape through the enemy lines, but were repulsed
and took refuge in underground passages. The cap-
ture of the Upper City (September 70) completed the
Roman conquest (8:1,4,5).

THE TREASURES OF THE SANCTUARY

Around this period, one of the priests, named Jesus,
son of Thebuthi, upon receiving a sworn promise of
security from Titus on condition of his delivering to
him some of the sacred treasures, came out and handed
down from the wall of the sanctuary two candlesticks
similar to those deposited in the sanctuary, as well as
tables, bowls, and cups, all of solid gold and very
heavy. He also delivered the veils, the high priests'
vestments with the precious stones, and many other
objects used in the sacred worship.[70] Moreover, the
keeper of the Temple treasury, whose name was
Phineas, when captured disclosed the tunics and girdles
worn by the priests, with much purple and scarlet
[cloth], which was kept there for making the veils, and
a profusion of cinnamon, cassia, and many other spices,
which used to be mingled and offered daily as incense
to God. Many other treasures were also delivered by
him, and numerous sacred ornaments. As reward he,
though a prisoner of war, was granted the pardon
vouchsafed to voluntary deserters. (War VI, 8:3.)

THE ROMAN VICTORY

On mastering the walls, the Romans planted their
standards on the towers, and with joy and hand clap-

ping raised the song of triumph for their victory. They had found the ending of the war much easier than its beginning. So much so, that when they vanquished the last wall without any bloodshed, they could scarcely believe it, and seeing no one to oppose them, were uncommonly perplexed.

Pouring into the streets swords in hand, they massacred indiscriminately all who fell their way and burned the houses with all who had taken shelter in them. As in the course of their depredations they entered houses in search of plunder, they in many instances found whole families dead and rooms filled with the victims of famine. Shuddering at the sight, they then retired with empty hands. Yet despite their pity for those who had thus perished, they felt no similar compassion for the living. Running everyone who fell their way through, they choked the streets with the dead and deluged the whole city with blood. So great was the flow of that blood that in numerous instances it quenched the flames. Towards evening the slaughter abated, but in the night the fire gained the mastery. Dawn of the eighth day of the month Gorpiaeus [Elul, September] beheld Jerusalem in flames— a city that had suffered in the siege calamities so great that had she from her founding enjoyed as much happiness, she would have been the envy of the world. . . .

Titus, on entering the city, was struck with wonder at its strength, and especially at the towers that the rebel leaders in their madness had abandoned. Indeed, when he saw their solid mass, the size of each stone and the excellence of their masonry, their great breadth and height, "Surely," he exclaimed, "we fought with God on our side, and it was God who brought the Jews down from these bulwarks; for what could human hands or engines avail against these towers?" . . .

Though the number of survivors was still considerable, the soldiers at length grew weary of slaughter. Titus therefore issued orders to kill only men in arms who offered resistance and to make prisoners of the rest. But in addition to those whom they were instructed to kill, the troops slew also the old and the feeble. Men in the flower of youth and fit for service were driven into the Temple and shut up in the women's court. To guard them, Titus appointed one of his freedmen, and commissioned his friend Fronto to decide each one's fate according to his deserts. All the insurgents and rebels who informed against each other, Fronto ordered to be executed. Picking the tallest and handsomest youths, he reserved them for Titus' triumph.

Of the residue, those over seventeen were sent in chains to the works in Egypt, though many of them Titus distributed among the provinces, to be destroyed in the theaters in gladiatorial contests and by wild beasts. Those under seventeen were sold. While Fronto was making his decisions, eleven thousand perished from starvation, owing partly to the hatred of the guards, who denied them food, partly to their refusal to accept it when offered. There was, moreover, an insufficient supply of food for so vast a multitude.

Ninety-seven thousand Jewish prisoners were taken in the war; the number of those who perished in the siege was one million one hundred thousand.

God visited both [rebel leaders] with meet retribution. John, wasted with hunger together with his brethren in the caverns, implored the Romans for that security which he had previously so often disdainfully rejected. Simon, after long struggling with distress, as we shall relate in the sequel,[71] surrendered and was reserved for execution at the triumph. John was condemned to lifelong imprisonment. The Romans set fire to the extreme quarters of the city and razed the walls to their foundation. (War VI, 8:5-9:4.)

So was Jerusalem captured. . . . Taken on five former occasions, it was now for the second time laid waste. Shishak, king of Egypt,[72] and after him Antiochus [Epiphanes],[73] then Pompey,[74] and subsequently Sosius and Herod,[75] all took the city, but, nevertheless, preserved it. Prior to them, however, it had been vanquished and laid waste by [Nebuchadnezzar] the king of Babylon.[76] . . . It was originally built by a prince of the Canaanites, called in the vernacular tongue "Righteous King" [Melchizedek],[77] for he was indeed righteous. Wherefore he was the first to officiate as priest of God, and being first to build a temple, gave the city, till then called Salem, the name of Jerusalem.

The Canaanite inhabitants were expelled by David, king of the Jews,[78] who colonized it with his own people. . . . [But] neither its antiquity, nor its vast wealth, nor the diffusion of its people all over the world, nor the great glory of its religious rites, could stay its ruin. So ended the siege of Jerusalem.[79] . . .

Titus ordered the entire city and the Temple razed to their foundations, sparing only the three highest towers, Phasael, Hippicus, and Mariamne, and that portion of the wall which enclosed the city on the west. The latter was preserved as an encampment for the garrison that was left in charge; the towers, as demonstration to posterity of how splendid and powerful a city had yielded to Roman valor. All the rest of the wall that encompassed the city was so completely leveled to the ground that nothing remained to lead visitors of the site to believe that it had ever been inhabited. So fell Jerusalem, a victim of revolutionary frenzy: a magnificent city, famed throughout the world. (War VI, 10:1; VII, 1:1.)

One of the towers, now called David's Tower, still stands near the Jaffa gate in Jerusalem. A part of the "western wall" of the Temple (the "Wailing Wall") also remains, and has at all times been revered by

Jews as the last remnant of the ancient sanctuary. "The divine Presence shall never depart from the Western Wall" (Exodus Rabbah II, 2).

Titus thanked the victorious army, bestowed rewards on the officers who had distinguished themselves, offered sacrifices of thanksgiving, and held a festive banquet. In Caesarea he deposited the spoils; here, in Caesarea Philippi and in other cities, he held gladiatorial shows and other games. "Many prisoners perished in the contests with wild beasts, by the flames, or in combat with each other. Yet to the Romans, though the prisoners were destroyed in ten thousand ways, it all seemed too light a punishment."

In Alexandria, Titus disbanded the legions, leaving only the tenth (legio X Fretensis) as garrison in Jerusalem (War VII, 1:2-3:1). Judaea became the private property of Vespasian; eight hundred veterans were settled in Emmaus, near Jerusalem. A poll tax of two drachmas was imposed on all Jews (6:6).

AFTER THE
FALL OF JUDAEA

ROME TRIUMPHANT

*Before returning home, Titus visited Berytus (Beirut)
and other Syrian cities and saw the legendary "Sab-
batical river." At Antioch he was petitioned to expel
the Jews from the city; he gave this "very perti-
nent" answer: "How can this be done, since their own
country, to which they would have to retire, has been
destroyed, and no other place would now receive
them?"*

In the course of his journey, Titus came to Jerusalem. Contrasting its mournful desolation with its
ancient glory, and pondering the magnitude of its
present ruin as well as its ancient splendor, he, instead
of boasting, as another would have done, that so great
and fair a city had fallen beneath his arms, deplored
its destruction. Indeed, he often cursed the guilty
authors of the revolt who had brought this chastise-
ment upon the city. It was plain, therefore, that he
did not wish such a disaster to serve as demonstration
of his valor.

Of the vast wealth of the city no small portion still
continued to be found among the ruins. Much of it was
dug up by the Romans, but most—gold and silver and
other highly precious objects that the owners had
stored underground against the doubtful fortunes of

war—was brought to light through information from the captives.

Titus now proceeded on his intended journey to Egypt; crossing the desert as quickly as possible, he reached Alexandria. . . . The leaders of the captives, Simon and John, together with the seven hundred men he had picked as being eminently tall and handsome in body, he ordered to be immediately transported to Italy, wishing to exhibit them at the triumph. . . . (War VII, 5:1-3.)

Titus arrived in Rome about the middle of June 71 and was met by his father "in person." All was set for the triumph.

TRIUMPH IN ROME

Prior announcement having been made of the day appointed for the triumphal pageant of victory, not a single person of [Rome's] immense multitude was left in the city. All issued forth, occuying every spot, those even where it was possible only to stand. They left only as much free space as was needed by those who were to pass in review.

Day had not yet dawned when the entire army marched out in companies and divisions, headed by their commanders, and stationed themselves not at the doors of the upper palace [on the Palatine hill], but near the temple of Isis, for there the emperors had rested that night. As morning broke, Vespasian and Titus came forth, crowned with laurel and clothed in ancestral purple robes, and proceeded to the Octavian Walks, where the Senate, the chief magistrates, and the men of equestrian rank were waiting for their arrival.

A tribunal had been erected in front of the porticoes. Vespasian and Titus ascended this tribunal and seated themselves on the ivory chairs placed there for this purpose. A joyous shout of acclamation burst from the troops, all of whom bore attestations of their valor.

The princes were unarmed, robed in silk, and crowned with laurel. Vespasian, after acknowledging the acclamations, which the soldiers wanted to continue, signaled for silence. When profound and universal quiet prevailed, he rose, covered most of his head with his cloak, and offered the customary prayers. Titus, too, prayed.

After the prayers, Vespasian made a short address to the assemblage, then dismissed the soldiers to the customary repast provided for them by the emperors. He then retired to the gate called Gate of Triumph, so named because all triumphal processions passed through it. Here they first took some refreshment; then, having put on the triumphal robes and sacrificed to the gods whose statues stood by the gate, they commanded the procession to move forward, driving through the theaters, in order to provide the assembled throngs with a better view.

It is impossible to convey any adequate idea of the multitude of the spectacles or of their splendor in whatever sphere one can conceive—works of art, diversity of riches, or nature's rarities. For nearly all the creations of many nations, both marvelous and costly, that the most fortunate of men ever acquired piece by piece—the greatness of the Roman empire exhibited that day in mass. A profusion of silver and gold and ivory, wrought in multitudinous forms, seemed, instead of being carried in a procession, to be flowing, so to speak, like a river.

Here tapestries were borne along, some of the rarest purple, others embroidered by Babylonian art into precise representations of life; here, too, translucent gems, some set in crowns of gold, others fashioned differently. So vast was the display of these that we learned from it how wrong we were in imagining any of them to be rare. Effigies of the gods, remarkable for size and uniquely elaborate workmanship, were also borne in the procession. Nor was a single one of the effigies wrought of any than the most costly materials. Animals of many species were led along, each adorned with appropriate ornaments. A multitude of men, clothed in purple garments interwoven with gold, were in charge of each group of animals. Those destined for the procession wore choice and magnificent ornaments. Nor was anyone in the throng of captives unadorned. The beautiful variety of their garments concealed any unsightliness arising from the wretched condition of their bodies.

But nothing in the pageant excited as much wonder and admiration as the structure of the moving platforms. So great was their size, many of them rising three or four stories, that it alarmed men and led them to distrust the firmness of their support. One was simultaneously delighted and astonished at the splendor of their fabrics. Many were covered with tapestries interwoven with gold, and all were adorned with gold and wrought ivory.

The events of the war were vividly depicted in numerous separate representations. Some showed a happy country devastated; others, whole squadrons of hostile armies slaughtered, fleeing, or led into captivity; still others, walls of extraordinary size demolished by engines, strong fortresses overthrown, the defenses of populous cities completely mastered, and an army pouring inside the walls. They showed also every spot deluged with blood, the hands of those no longer able to resist raised uplifted in supplication, fire cast into temples, houses demolished and their owners buried in the ruins, and after widespread desolation and woe, rivers flowing not over a cultivated country—nor supplying water to man and beast—but through a land still everywhere in flames. Such were the miseries the Jews were destined to endure when they plunged into the war. The art and exquisite workmanship of the displays made men not present at the events believe that they were passing in front of their eyes. The platforms carried the commander of each captured city in the position in which he was taken. A number of ships followed.

The over-all spoils were borne in jumbled mass, but conspicuous above all were the vessels taken from the Temple of Jerusalem—a golden table of [shewbread], many talents in weight; and a candlestick, wrought similarly out of gold but fashioned differently from those in ordinary use among us, for its center branch was fixed upon a pedestal, and small branches shot out from it, giving it the appearance of a trident, and a brass lamp was attached to the top of each of these branches. There were seven of these lamps, betokening the honor in which the Jews held that number. Carried last among the spoils was a copy of the Law of the Jews. The spoils were succeeded by numerous men carrying images of victory, all wrought of ivory and gold. Next came Vespasian in a chariot, followed by Titus and [Titus' brother] Domitian, who, mounted on a horse to be admired, made a splendid appearance.

The triumphal procession terminated at the temple of Jupiter Capitolinus. There it stopped, it being an ancient custom to tarry there until the death of the enemy's general was announced. This general was Simon, son of Giora, who had been led in triumph among the captives. Bound with a rope and scourged by the men who led him, he was dragged to the site overlooking the Forum, where according to Roman law, malefactors condemned to death were executed. At the announcement that Simon was no more, the assemblage responded with a shout of joy, and the princes began the sacrifices. At the conclusion of these offerings, accompanied by the customary prayers, they returned to the palace. Some they entertained at their own feast; for the rest, lavish preparations were made to banquet them at home. For the Roman city kept festival that day in celebration of her victory over her enemies, the termination of her civil dissensions, and the dawning of her hopes of prosperity.

The triumphs over and the Roman empire settled on the securest foundation, Vespasian resolved to erect a temple of Peace. . . . Here he deposited the golden vessels from the temple of the Jews, on which he prided himself. Their Law, however, and the purple veils of the sanctuary he ordered deposited and kept in the palace. (War VII, 5:3-7.)

On the Arch of Titus, erected by the Senate after Titus' death, there is a depiction, in bas-relief, of the Jerusalem spoils. Commemorative Roman coins are inscribed: Judaea devicta, Judaea capta (*vanquished Judaea, captive Judaea*).

THE LAST FORTRESSES

THE SIEGE OF MACHAERUS

Jerusalem was destroyed, but war was not over; the fortresses Herodium, Machaerus, and Masada were still held by the rebels. The new Roman governor of Judaea, Lucilius Bassus, was assigned to capture them. Herodium, to the south of Jerusalem, was speedily vanquished. Now Bassus approached Machaerus, on the southern border of Peraea.

It was imperative that this fortress be destroyed, lest its strength should induce many to revolt, for its natural defenses were uniquely designed to inspire its occupants with great confidence in their security and to retard and alarm its assailants.

Josephus describes the inaccessibility of the fortress, which because of its proximity to Arabia, had been greatly strengthened by Herod.

Having fully reconnoitered the site, Bassus resolved to approach it by filling up the eastern valley. Accordingly, he began his operations, laboring to complete his banks as quickly as possible in order to ease the siege.

The Jews . . . made spirited sorties each day, battling
those who fell their way; though many of them lost
their lives, they slew great numbers of the Romans. . . .

But it was not destined that the conclusion of the
siege should depend on these battles. An accident
forced the Jews to surrender the fortress. There was
among the besieged a youth of great boldness and
vigor, named Eleazar. He had distinguished himself in
the sorties, rousing many to go out and impede the
progress of the banks, and had in the conflicts wrought
fearful havoc among the Romans. . . . On one occasion, after the conclusion of the battle, when both parties had retired, he, not thinking that the enemy would
resume the contest, remained outside the gates con-
versing with the men upon the wall, his attention
wholly engrossed by them. A certain Rufus from the
Roman camp, by birth an Egyptian, spotted the opportunity, dashed suddenly upon him when no one could
have expected it, lifted him, though he was in armor,
and, as the spectators on the wall were stupefied by
astonishment, transferred him to the Roman camp.

The [Roman] general ordered him to be stripped
naked, taken to a site most exposed to the view of on-
lookers from the city, and there scourged. The Jews
were deeply affected by the youth's misfortune. . . .
Bassus ordered a cross to be erected, as if he meant
immediately to crucify Eleazar. On perceiving this, the
men within the fortress were seized with still deeper
anguish, crying that they could not bear to see him
thus destroyed. Moreover, Eleazar beseeched them not
to let him suffer before their eyes this most miserable
death, and now that all others had been subdued, to
contrive their own safety by yielding to the might and
good fortune of the Romans.

The men were greatly moved by what he said, and
since many inside [the fortress] also pleaded for him
—for he was of an eminent and very numerous family

—they, contrary to their custom, yielded to compassion and at once sent a deputation to the Romans to negotiate the surrender of the fortress, requesting safe conduct for their withdrawal and permission to take Eleazar with them. . . . Bassus, feeling bound by his agreement with the men who surrendered the fortress, let them depart and restored Eleazar to them. (War VII, 6:1-4.)

THE SIEGE OF MASADA

Bassus, who died in Judaea, was succeeded as governor by Flavius Silva. The entire country having been subdued, except for a single fortress, he gathered all his forces from their various quarters and marched against it. Masada was the name of the fortress, and Eleazar, a man of influence among the Sicarii who occupied it, held command there. He was a descendant of Judah [of Galilee],[80] who when Quirinius was dispatched as censor to Judaea, induced many Jews, as we have already stated, not to register.[81] It was then that the Sicarii banded together against those who were willing to submit to the Romans. . . .

Josephus continues to criticize the fanaticism of the Sicarii.

The Roman general advanced at the head of his forces against Eleazar and the Sicarii who held possession of Masada. Gaining speedy mastery of the entire district, he stationed garrisons at the most suitable sites. To prevent easy escape by the besieged, he encompassed the fortress with a wall and set guards at various points. He himself encamped on a spot, picked by him as most advantageous for the operations, where the rocks of the fortress adjoined the neighboring mountain. . . . Having completed these arrangements, Silva began the siege, which because of the fortress' strength demanded much skill and strenuous exertion. (War VII, 8:1-2.)

A description of the mighty bastion of Masada, over-

*looking the southwest shore of the Dead Sea, follows.
It had been fortified by Jonathan, brother of Judah the
Maccabee, and perfected under Herod. The Sicarii
found vast stores of corn, wine, oil, and dates deposited
there a century before (8:3-4). The rock of Masada
was high and steep. After overcoming serious difficulties, the Romans built a solid bank for the operation
of the battering ram. The Roman installations were
explored in 1932 by a German expedition; a complete
archaeological survey and exploration was undertaken
by an Israeli expedition in 1955-56.*

Silva built a large battering ram, ordered it ceaselessly to batter the wall, and with some difficulty broke
down part of that wall. The Sicarii, however, had fore-
stalled him by having hastily thrown up another wall
inside, which being soft and yielding and therefore able
to withstand the violence of the blows, was not likely
to meet the same fate from the engines. . . . On seeing this, Silva thought it best to destroy the wall by
fire and ordered the soldiers to hurl on it many flaming
torches. Since it was made chiefly of wood, it soon
caught fire, and owing to the wall's hollowness, was
penetrated all the way through and burst forth in a
volume of flame. At the very start of this fire, a north
wind blowing in the direction of the Romans greatly
alarmed them, since by propelling the fire downward
from above, it drove it directly at them; they were,
therefore, almost in despair for fear their engines
would be burned. But the wind, as if by divine providence, suddenly changed to the south, blew strongly in
the opposite direction, and carried the flames back
against the wall, which was now ablaze throughout its
thickness. The Romans, having thus experienced the
help of God, returned, rejoicing, to their camp. Resolved to attack the enemy the next day, they set their
watch more carefully than usual that night, lest any
of the besieged should secretly escape. (War VII, 8:5.)

But Eleazar did not think of escaping. In a speech,

he reminded his men of their resolve "never to serve
the Romans nor any (master) other than God, who
alone is the true and just lord of mankind," and bid
them to choose freely "a noble death. . . . Let our
wives die before they are ravished and our children
before they have tasted slavery, and after we have
slain them, let us bestow that glorious boon mutually
upon each other and preserve our freedom as a noble
end to our lives." Some of his men were ready to fol-
low Eleazar, others, "of softer mold," were moved by
commiseration for their wives and children and refused
(VII, 8:6-7). Eleazar therefore renewed his proposal
in a second speech. "This speech at the close of the war
forms a sort of counterpart to that of Agrippa before
its outbreak." (II, 16.) (H. St. J. Thackeray.)

ELEAZAR'S SECOND SPEECH

"Truly I was greatly mistaken in thinking that I was
aiding brave men in their struggles for freedom—men
determined to live with honor or to die. But you are,
it seems, no better than the common herd in virtue
or in courage, since you are afraid even of that death
which will deliver you from the direst evils, though you
ought neither to delay nor to wait for a counselor. For
from of old, and from the first dawn of reason, have
our nation's laws and divine revelation, confirmed by
the deeds and noble spirit of our forefathers, continued to teach us that life, not death, is a misfortune
to men.

"For it is death that sets the soul at liberty and
permits it to depart to its proper and pure abode,
where it will be free from every misery. But so long
as it is imprisoned in a mortal body and infected with
its pains, it is, to speak most truly, dead; for asso-
ciation with what is mortal befits not that which is
divine. Great, it is true, is the power of the soul,
even while imprisoned in the body, its sensible instrument, which invisibly, it moves and advances in its

actions beyond the range of mortal nature. But it is not until, freed from that weight which hangs suspended from it and drags it down to earth, the soul has reassumed its proper sphere that it enjoys a blessed strength and a power wholly unrestricted, remaining, as does God Himself, invisible to human eyes.

"For certainly it is not seen when it is in the body. It enters unperceived, and unseen still, withdraws, its own nature one and incorruptible, though a cause of change to the body. Whatever the soul has touched lives and flourishes, whatever it is removed from withers and dies; so much is there in it of immortality."

Here follows a reference to sleep, during which the soul "converses with God because of its relationship to Him," and a discourse on the Indian view of death as the release of the soul from the body. "Should we hold baser notions than the Indians?"

"But even had we from the first been educated in opposite principles and taught that to live is the supreme good and death a calamity, the occasion still is one that calls upon us to bear death cheerfully, since we die by the will of God and out of necessity. For long ago, so it seems, God issued against the entire Jewish nation a common decree—that we were to be deprived of life if we did not use it rightly. Do not ascribe the blame to yourselves, nor the credit to the Romans, that this war with them has involved us all in ruin. It is not their might that has caused these things to pass; a more powerful agent has intervened to give them the semblance of victory."

Here follow examples of persecutions of Jews outside Judaea and not occasioned by the Romans.

"Perhaps, however, it was because they were in a foreign land and unable to offer any opposition to their enemies that these were killed. But had not all those of us who waged war against the Romans in our own country sufficient reason to entertain hopes of certain victory? We had arms, walls, fortresses well nigh impregnable, and a spirit not to be shaken by any perils in the cause of liberty. But these advantages helped us only for a brief season, and only served to buoy us up with hopes, proving in the end to be the source of greater misfortunes; for, as if provided not for the security of those who had prepared them, but for the more glorious triumph of our foes, all has been taken, all has fallen into the hands of our enemies. Those who perished in battle we cannot but count happy, for they died defending, not betraying, liberty. But the multitudes who have been subjected to the Romans—who would not pity them? Who would not make haste to die, ere he suffered the same fate as they? Some have expired upon the rack, some under the torture of fire and from scourges. Some, half-devoured by wild beasts, have after affording derision and merriment to their foes, been preserved alive to furnish these beasts with a second repast. But those men are to be deemed most miserable who, still living, often pray for death, yet cannot obtain it.

"And where is now that great city, the metropolis of the entire Jewish nation, protected by so many walls, secured by so many forts and by the vastness of its towers, that could hardly contain its implements of war and had so many myriads of men to fight for it? What has become of that city of ours which, so it was believed, God himself had founded? Uprooted from its foundations, it has been swept away, and its sole preserved memorial is the camp of its destroyers still planted upon its ruins! Hapless old men are sitting among the ashes of the Temple, and a few women, reserved by our enemies for the basest of injuries.

"Who of us, then, casting these things in his mind, shall bear to see the sun, even could he live unendangered? Who is so much his country's foe, so unmanly, so fond of life, as not to regret that he is still alive? How I would that we had all been dead ere we had seen that holy city overthrown by hostile hands, our holy Temple so profanely uprooted! But since we were beguiled by a not ignoble hope that we might possibly be able to avenge her on her foes, and that hope is now forever vanished, leaving us alone in our distress, let us hasten to die honorably. Let us take pity on ourselves, our children, and our wives while it is still in our power to show them pity. For we were born to die, as were those whom we have begotten; and this even the fortunate cannot escape. But insult and servitude and the right of our wives being led to infamy with their children, these, among men, are not natural or necessary evils, though those who do not prefer death, when death is in their power, must suffer even these because of their cowardice.

"Elated with courage, we revolted against the Romans, and when bidden to assent to an offer of safety, would not listen to them.[82] Who then, if they take us alive, does not anticipate their fury? Wretched will be the young, whose strong bodies can sustain many tortures; wretched, too, the old, whose age cannot endure afflictions! One man will see his wife dragged away by violence, another hear the voice of his child crying to a father whose hands are bound. But ours are still free and grasp the sword. While they are so free, let them do us honorable service. Let us die unenslaved by our foes, and, blessed with freedom, depart, together with our wives and children, from this life. That is what our laws command us to do, what our wives and children implore of us. God Himself has brought this upon us, and the contrary is what the Romans, who fear lest any of us die before they capture us, desire. Instead of giving them their hoped-for pleasure in the possession of our persons, let us hasten, then to leave them in awe at our death and admiration at our fortitude." (War VII, 8:7.)

THE END OF MASADA (MAY 73)

While still anxious to inspire them with courage, Eleazar was cut short by his hearers, who, filled with uncontrollable ardor, were all in haste to commit the deed. . . . Natural passion and love were still alive in every breast, but the belief that what they had resolved to do was best for those dearest to them vanquished everything. They clasped and fondly embraced their wives and took their children in their arms, clinging to them and weeping as they kissed them for the last time. At the same time, and as if executing the deed with the hands of strangers, they carried out what they had resolved to do, deriving consolation in the exigency of slaying them from contemplation of the miseries they would endure if they fell into the hands of their enemies. Nor did anyone waver in the execution of this terrible task; all, in the end, perpetrated the deed upon their closest kin. O wretched victims of necessity, to whom it seemed the lesser evil to slay with their own hands their wives and children!

Unable thereupon, to endure their anguish at the deed they had committed, and deeming it a wrong to the slain to survive them even for a moment, they hurriedly made a heap of all their effects, set it on fire, then chose by lot ten of their number to slay the rest. Stretched at the side of his fallen wife and children, with his arms about them, each then offered his throat to those who were to execute the rueful office. The latter, after slaying all without flinching, adopted [for their own death] the same lot-drawing procedure. The one to whose lot it fell to kill the other nine was, after so doing, to destroy himself on the bodies of his companions. None lacked the courage to equal the others in either execution or suffering. Eventually, the nine bared their throats. The last survivor examined all the bodies to see whether in so widespread a slaughter any perchance were left who still required his hand. On ascertaining that all were dead, he set fire to the palace, then in one collected effort, drove his sword through his body, and fell by the side of his family.

They died believing that not a single soul among them was left alive to be subject to the Romans. But five children, an elderly woman, and still another woman, related to Eleazar and in sagacity and wisdom superior to most of her sex, escaped by hiding in the subterranean aqueducts when the rest were intent on slaughter. Including women and children, nine hundred and sixty perished on this occasion. . . .

The Romans, still expecting opposition, were in arms at daybreak. Having planked bridges from the mounds to the fortress, they advanced to the assault. When they saw no enemy but [only] fearful solitude on every side, flames within, and silence, they were at a loss to conjecture what had happened. In an effort to call forth some of those within, they shouted, as if at the discharge of a missile. On hearing the noise, the women emerged from their retreat and told the Romans what had occurred, one of them describing fully both what was said and how the deed was perpetrated. But the Romans, unable to credit so desperate a measure, did not accept her account. In an attempt to quench the flames, they quickly opened a passage through them and reached the palace. Here they encountered the mounds of the slain. Instead of rejoicing at the death of their foes, they admired the courage of their resolve and the intrepid contempt of death so many had shown by such a deed as this. (War VII, 9:1-2.)

THE REMNANT OF THE SICARII IN EGYPT

Some of the Sicarii succeeded in fleeing to Egypt. Not content with having saved their lives, they re-engaged in revolutionary activities, endeavoring to persuade many who received them as guests to assert their freedom, to esteem the Romans as no better than themselves, and to consider God alone to be their lord. Some of the reputable Jews who opposed their designs, they slew; the rest, they continued to press with exhortations to revolt.

At sight of their madness, the leaders of the council of elders thought it unsafe to overlook their actions any longer. They therefore convened a general assembly of the Jews. There they exposed the madness of the Sicarii, whom they proved to be the source of all their misfortunes. . . . They urged the multitude to ward off the destruction with which these men menaced them, and by surrendering them, to make their apology to the Romans.

Perceiving the magnitude of the danger, the people complied with the proposal and rushed furiously upon the Sicarii in order to seize them. Six hundred were taken on the spot, and all who escaped into Egypt and the Egyptian Thebes were before long arrested and brought back. The fortitude they exhibited on this occasion, and their desperation or firmness of purpose, whichever we may call it, astonished everyone. Though subjected to every bodily torture and pain, devised for the sole end of making them acknowledge Caesar as their lord, not a single man among them complied, nor did anyone waver for even a moment. As though their bodies were insensitive, they submitted to the rack and to the flames, their souls almost rejoicing in them; and all, despite their suffering, kept their resolve. What amazed the spectators most was the courage of the children, no single one of whom could be compelled to call Caesar lord. So completely did the power of endurance master the weakness of their bodies. (War VII, 10:1.)

CONCLUSION

Vespasian, knowing the readiness of the Jews to rebel, ordered the Jewish temple in Leontopolis destroyed; this sanctuary was founded about 163 B.C. by the high priest Onias IV, who was compelled to flee Jerusalem during the early years of the Maccabean uprising. A Jewish rebellion in Cyrene (west of Egypt), incited by the Sicarii and led by one Jonathan, was ruthlessly suppressed by Catullus, the Roman governor in Libya. At the instigation of Catullus, Jonathan falsely accused the historian Josephus, then in Rome, and other Jewish aristocrats of having supported the rebellion. Both Catullus and Jonathan met miserable deaths; Catullus' death "proved an instance of divine providence . . . and is evidence that God punishes wicked men" (War VII, 10:2-11:4.)

Here we shall conclude our history, a history we promised to present with complete accuracy for the enlightenment of those who wish to learn how the Romans conducted this war against the Jews. Its style may my readers judge; but for its truthfulness, I do not hesitate to say, confidently, that throughout the entire narrative truth has been my only aim. (War VII, 11:5.)

NOTES

INTRODUCTION

1. See Elias J. Bickerman, "The Historical Foundations of Postbiblical Judaism." *The Jews*, ed. by L. Finkelstein, Vol. I, New York, 1949.
2. Werner Jaeger, *Paideia: the Ideals of Greek Culture*, Vol. I, New York, 1945, Introduction, *et passim*.
3. H. St. John Thackeray, *Josephus the Man and the Historian*, New York, 1929, p. 56.
4. See Charles N. Cochrane, *Christianity and Classical Culture*, New York, 1957, pp. 134 f.

TEXT

1. See John Strugnell, "Flavius Josephus and the Essenes." *Journal of Biblical Literature*, LXXVI (1958), p. 109.
2. This fact would disqualify a high priest.
3. In 537 B.C. The figure 481 (471 according to War I, 3:1) is incorrect.
4. "Sons of that Onias who built the temple in the district of Heliopolis, which was like that at Jerusalem" (Antt. XIII, 10:4; see XIII, 3:1-3).
5. Comp. the novel by Moshe Shamir, *The King of Flesh and Blood*, New York, 1958.
6. Comp. Antt. XIII, 10:5.
7. See ibid., XIII, 15:4.
8. The text has "fifteen."
9. Actually, Hyrcanus held the office of ethnarch.
10. Synhedrion (called Sanhedrin in rabbinic literature): assembly of 71 scholars acting as supreme court and legislature in Jerusalem.
11. In 47 B.C., during a visit to Antioch, Caesar reorganized the administration of Syria and appointed his relative Sextus Caesar governor.

12. Antt. XV, 1:1 calls Sameas a disciple of Pollio. Some scholars identify Sameas with Shemaiah, a colleague of Abtalion (Pollio?); others with Shammai, the colleague of Hillel.
13. Comp. Antt. XIV, 12:2.
14. Comp. ibid., XIV, 5:2.
15. "Antony had appointed Sosius governor of Syria and ordered him to assist Herod in opposing Antigonus" (War I, 17:2).
16. I.e., a woman and not a man.
17. See note 12.
18. Comp. Antt. XIV, 9:4.
19. Comp. War I, 18:5.
20. A friend of Virgil and Horace.
21. See note 12.
22. See "Herod's Buildings, Foundations, and Endowments."
23. Both Archelaus and Antipas were sons of the Samaritan Malthace.
24. According to Antt. XV, 11:1, in the eighteenth year, i.e., 20 B.C.
25. Upon his liberation from imprisonment.
26. From Latin *sica*, dagger.
27. "An impossible figure" (Thackeray).
28. This sacrifice of lepers (Leviticus 14:4 f.) was meant to be an insulting reference to the charge that the Jews in Egyptian bondage were lepers (Josephus, *Against Apion*).
29. The former procurator of Judaea.
30. Refers to the royal house of Izates, converted to Judaism under Claudius (Antt. XX, 2:3-5).
31. See War I, 7:3.
32. See *Against Apion* II, 6.
33. See War II, 20:1.
34. Comp. Mishnah Taanith IV, 5.
35. See War VII, 8:1.
36. See Antt. XX, 4:1.
37. The hill on the road leading northward from Jerusalem; original site of the Hebrew University.
38. See War II, 13:3.
39. Unidentified.

40. The author of this history. According to his account in *Life* (ch. 7), Josephus (and two other priests) was sent to Galilee merely to pacify the local "brigands and revolutionaries."
41. See War VI, 5:3.
42. See War V, 6:2.
43. Josephus was then thirty years old, four years younger than Titus.
44. Probably identical with Joseph, son of Gorion, mentioned in War II, 20:3.
45. See Deuteronomy 21:22-23 and Sanhedrin 45b. The Jewish law does not recognize crucifixion as a form of capital punishment.
46. The identification of this Zacharias with Zacharias, son of Berechias, mentioned in Matt. 23:35, assumed in bygone days, is no longer maintained.
47. The figure is not exact.
48. On Galba and Otho, see War IV, 9:9.
49. See ibid., II, 11:6.
50. See ibid., III, 8:9.
51. Loc. cit.
52. War IV, 3:2.
53. Ibid., II, 20:3.
54. Ibid., III, 4:2.
55. Ibid., II, 18:9-19:9.
56. See ibid., II, 11:6.
57. Four years before Titus, Cestius Gallus, governor of Syria, had pitched his camp in that region. War II, 19:4. See also note 37.
58. "Vespasian, planning to invest Jerusalem on all sides, set up encampments at Jericho." War IV, 9:1.
59. See War IV, 6:1; on that occasion, however, not all the Idumaeans had withdrawn from Jerusalem.
60. Ibid., V, 1:5.
61. Antt. XX, 2:3-5; 4:1-3.
62. War II, 19:9.
63. Ibid., II, 17:7.
64. Sources for the biblical and later events that follow: Abraham and Sarah, Gen. 12:10-20; Philistia and the idol Dagon, I Sam. 5-6; Sennacherib, II Kings 18:13-19:37; Cyrus, Ezra 1; Zedekiah, II Kings 25:1-7;

Jeremiah, Jer. 27:12-18; Antiochus, I Macc. 1:20-24; Aristobulus II and Hyrcanus II, War I, 6:4-7:7; Sosius, ibid., 17:9; Sennacherib and the Assyrians, II Kings 18:14-16 and 19:35.

65. *Amphora*, about nine gallons.

66. *Tamid*, the daily morning and evening offering of one lamb; Numbers 28:1-8. "On the seventeenth of Tammuz the daily offering was discontinued" (Mishnah Taanith IV, 6). The Hebrew names of the months Josephus replaced by the corresponding Macedonian names.

67. On the talmudic tradition of Titus' visit to the Holy of Holies, see Gittin 56b.

68. Comp. Yoma 39b on the sudden openings of the Temple gates.

69. See War V, 6:1.

70. The spoils of the Temple are shown on a bas-relief on the Arch of Titus in Rome.

71. War VII, 2:2.

72. I Kings 14:25-26.

73. The Temple was plundered in 169 B.C.

74. 63 B.C. See War I, 7:1-5.

75. 37 B.C. See ibid., 17:8-18:2.

76. 587 B.C. II Kings 25:1-7.

77. See Genesis 14:18.

78. II Samuel 5:6-9.

79. The talmudic and midrashic traditions and legends on the destruction of the Temple are recorded, e.g., in Ekhah Rabbati, Ekhah Zutta, Abot de Rabbi Nathan, Gittin 55b-58a, Taanith 28b-30b, Yer. Taanith IV, Yoma 9a-10a.

80. Eleazar, son of Jairus [Yair], a kinsman of Menahem, son of Judah of Galilee (War II, 17:9).

81. Antt. XVIII, 1:1; War II, 8:1.

82. War VI, 6:2.

CHRONOLOGICAL SUMMARY

B.C.	
330	Alexander the Great conquers the Persian empire, including Palestine
3rd c.	Palestine under the rule of the Egyptian Ptolemies
198	Antiochus III of Syria conquers Palestine
166-164	Maccabean rebellion
140	Judaea regains independence under the rule of Simon, the Hasmonaean
140-63	Rule of the Hasmonaeans
2nd-1st c.	The Essenes; Dead Sea (Qumran) Sect
135-104	John Hyrcanus; conquests east of the Jordan; subjection of the Samaritans and the Idumaeans
ca. 125	*The First Book of Maccabees*
104-103	Aristobulus I; conquests in Galilee
103-76	Alexander Jannaeus; conquests east of the Jordan; destruction of Gaza; defeat by the Nabataeans
76-67	Salome Alexandra
67	Civil War between Aristobulus II and Hyrcanus II
67-63	Aristobulus II
63	Pompey captures Jerusalem; strong position of Antipater of Idumaea
63-40	Hyrcanus II, high priest and ethnarch, Roman vassal
55-54	Caesar invades Britain
51-30	Cleopatra VII, last queen of Egypt

49	Caesar crosses the Rubicon Assassination of Aristobulus II by friends of Pompey
48	Pompey killed in Egypt; Herod turns to Caesar
47	Antipater procurator of Judaea; Herod governor of Galilee
44	Assassination of Julius Caesar; Herod turns to Cassius
43	Antipater poisoned by Malchus
42	Cassius defeated at Philippi by Antony; Herod turns to Antony
ca. 40	Hillel comes to Jerusalem
40	Invasion of Palestine by the Parthians; Herod flees to Rome; appointed king of Judaea
40-37	Antigonus, high priest and king
37	Herod and Sosius capture Jerusalem; Herod marries Mariamne; purge of the Synhedrion
37-4	Herod the Great
35	Murder of Aristobulus III, high priest; building of Antonia
34	Execution of Joseph, husband of Herod's sister Salome Cleopatra with Herod in Jerusalem
32	Herod's war with the Nabataean Arabs
31	Earthquake in Palestine Antony's downfall at Actium; Herod turns to Octavian
31 B.C.-A.D. 14	Octavian (Augustus). Augustan age: Virgil, Horace, Ovid, Livy, Strabo
30	Execution of Hyrcanus II; Herod visits Augustus at Rhodes, later, in Egypt Suicide of Antony and Cleopatra
29	Execution of Mariamne
28	Execution of Alexandra
27	Octavian called Augustus Herod rebuilds Samaria (Sebaste)
25	Execution of Costobar and the sons of Babas

ca. 24 Herod builds palace

23 Herod receives Trachonitis, Batanaea, and Auranitis from Augustus

The sons of Mariamne, Alexander and Aristobulus, sent to Rome

22 Building of Caesarea begun

20 Augustus in Syria; presents to Herod territory of Zenodorus

Reconstruction of the Temple begun

ca. 20 Birth of Philo of Alexandria (d. *ca.* A.D. 50)

15 Marcus Agrippa visits Herod in Jerusalem

14 Antipater, son of Herod by Doris, recalled to the court

10 Celebration of the completion of Caesarea

9 Expedition against the Nabataeans

7 Execution of Alexander and Aristobulus; Antipater's power at the court

5 Herod learns of Antipater's hostile schemes

4 Revolt of the people led by Judah and Matthias

Execution of Antipater

Death of Herod

4 B.C.-A.D. 6 Archelaus, ethnarch of Judaea, Samaria, and Idumaea

4 B.C.-A.D. 39 Herod Antipas, tetrarch of Galilee and Peraea

4 B.C.-A.D. 34 Philip, tetrarch of Batanaea, Trachonitis, and Auranitis

A.D.

6 The "enrollment" of Quirinius; Judah the Galilean, rebel leader

6-41 Judaea, Samaria, and Idumaea, a Roman province, governed by procurators

14-37 Tiberius, emperor

26-36 Pontius Pilate, procurator

ca. 30 Crucifixion of Jesus by Pontius Pilate

37-41 Gaius Caligula, emperor

37-44 Agrippa I, king over the territory of Philip; from 41 on, over the former realm of Herod the Great

67 (Spring) Flavius Vespasian arrives in Acco

(Summer) Capture of Jotapata, defended by Josephus; Josephus surrenders to Vespasian

Vespasian conquers Galilee; John of Gischala arrives in Jerusalem; execution of the former war leaders

68 (March) Vespasian's operations in Peraea; later, in western Judaea and Idumaea

(June) Death of Nero; interruption of war operations

69 (June) Vespasian master of all Palestine except Jerusalem and three fortresses

Simon bar Giora, leader of Idumaean rebels, enters Jerusalem

(July) Vespasian acclaimed emperor; Titus in command of the Judaean war

69-79 Vespasian, emperor

70 (April) Titus and four legions lay siege to Jerusalem, defended by John of Gischala and Simon bar Giora

Johanan ben Zakkai of Jerusalem establishes new school in Jabneh

(July) Fall of fortress Antonia; cessation of daily Temple sacrifices (*tamid*); Titus attacks Temple area

(August) The Temple gates burn (9th of Ab)

(September) Romans occupy the Lower City and storm the Upper City

71 Titus and Vespasian celebrate triumph in Rome; execution of Simon bar Giora; Josephus in Rome

73 Some rebels flee to Alexandria; closing of the Onias Temple in Leontopolis (founded *ca.* 163 B.C.)

Masada, last fortress in Judaea, defended by Eleazar, falls

ca. 75-79   *Jewish War*, by Flavius Josephus
    79-81   Titus, emperor
    81-96   Domitian, emperor
    93-94   *Antiquities*, by Flavius Josephus; later, *Life* and *Against Apion*
      100   Agrippa II's kingdom incorporated into the province of Syria

The House of the Hasmonaeans
(all dates are B.C.)

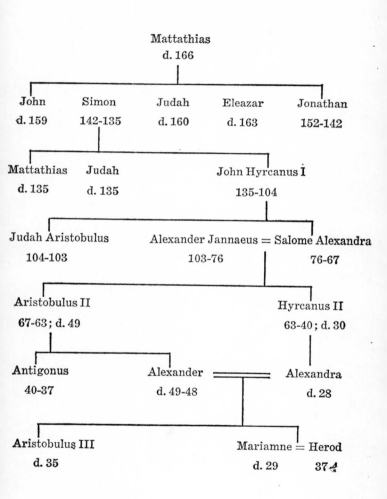

Mattathias
d. 166

John
d. 159

Simon
142-135

Judah
d. 160

Eleazar
d. 163

Jonathan
152-142

Mattathias
d. 135

Judah
d. 135

John Hyrcanus I
135-104

Judah Aristobulus
104-103

Alexander Jannaeus = Salome Alexandra
103-76   76-67

Aristobulus II
67-63 ; d. 49

Hyrcanus II
63-40 ; d. 30

Antigonus
40-37

Alexander
d. 49-48

Alexandra
d. 28

Aristobulus III
d. 35

Mariamne = Herod
d. 29   37 4

The House of Herod .

(m.-married)

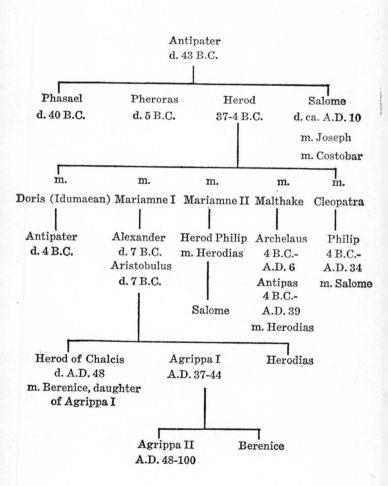

SELECTED BIBLIOGRAPHY

Avi-Yonah, M., Avigad, N. a.o. "The Archaeological Survey of Masada, 1955-1956." *Israel Exploration Journal,* VII (1957), 1.

Baron, Salo W. *A Social and Religious History of the Jews: Ancient Times,* 2 vols. New York, 1952.

Bentwich, Norman. *Josephus.* Philadelphia, 1914.

Bickermann, Elias. *Der Gott der Makkabäer.* Berlin, 1937.

Braun, Martin. "King Herod as Oriental Monarch." *Commentary* XXV (1958), 1.

Burrows, Millar. *The Dead Sea Scrolls.* New York, 1955.

———. *More Light on the Dead Sea Scrolls.* New York, 1958.

Eisler, Robert. *Jesus Basileus ou Basileusas.* Heidelberg, 1929-30.

———. *The Messiah Jesus and John the Baptist.* New York, 1931.

Farmer, William Reuben. *Maccabees, Zealots, and Josephus.* New York, 1956.

Foakes Jackson, F.J. *Josephus and the Jews.* New York, 1930.

Jones, A. H. M. *The Herods of Judaea.* Oxford, 1938.

Laqueur, Richard. *Der jüdische Historiker Flavius Josephus.* Giessen, 1920.

Montgomery, James A. "The Religion of Flavius Josephus." *Jewish Quarterly Review,* XI (1920-21).

Moore, George Foot. *Judaism in the First Centuries of the Christian Era.* 3 vols. Cambridge, Mass., 1927.

Niese, Benedictus. "Josephus." Hastings, *Encyclopedia of Religion and Ethics.* Edinburgh, 1914.

Perowne, Stewart. *The Life and Times of Herod the Great.* London, 1956.

Pfeiffer, Robert H. *History of New Testament Times.* New York, 1949.

Rappaport, Salomo. *Agada und Exegese bei Flavius Josephus.* Wien, 1930.

Reinach, Théodor, ed. *Oeuvres complètes de Josephe.* 6 vols. Paris, 1900-32.

Roth, Cecil. "The Jewish Revolt Against Rome." *Commentary* xxvii (1959), 6.

————. "Simon bar Giora, Ancient Jewish Hero." *Commentary* xxix (1960), 1.

Schlatter, Adolf. *Die Theologie des Judentums nach dem Bericht des Josefus.* Gütersloh, 1932.

Schürer, Emil. *A History of the Jewish People in the Time of Jesus Christ.* 5 vols. Edinburgh, 1886-1890.

Thackeray, H. St. J. *Josephus, the Man and the Historian.* New York, 1929.

————, and Marcus, Ralph. *Josephus with an English Translation.* 7 vols. London and Cambridge, Mass., 1926-43.

Weber, Wilhelm. *Josephus und Vespasian.* Berlin, 1921.

Zeitlin, Solomon. *Josephus on Jesus.* Philadelphia, 1931.

————. *The History of the Second Jewish Commonwealth: Prolegomena.* Philadelphia, 1933.

INDEX